Scholars, p

 ations- ally know_. Nancy Alt- man and Eric K. _fit organiza- tion Social Security Works in 20.. gthen Social Security Coalition, composed of more than 350 of the nation's leading national and state seniors', union, women's, disability, civil rights, netroots, and other organizations. Altman now serves as president and Kingson as board chair of Social Security Works. Both served as staff to the 1982 National Commission on Social Security Reform, the bipartisan commission that forged the consensus leading to the enactment of the 1983 Amendments to the Social Security Act. On the organizing committee of the National Academy of Social Insurance in the mid-1980s, they later served on the academy's founding board of directors. Both also served in 2008 on the advisory committee to President Barack Obama's Social Security Administration transition team.

Altman, a lawyer, is the author of *The Truth About Social Security* and *The Battle for Social Security*, as well as coauthor, with Eric Kingson, of *Social Security Works!* (The New Press, 2015). A member of the faculty of Harvard University's Kennedy School of Government from 1983 to 1989, she also taught courses on private pensions and Social Security at the Harvard Law School. Appointed by Democratic House Leader Nancy Pelosi, Altman is serving a six-year term, which started October 1, 2017, on the Social Security Advisory Board. The seven-person Board is a bipartisan, independent federal government agency established in 1994 to advise the president, Congress, and the commissioner of social security. She also chairs the board of directors of the Pension Rights Center. She lives in Bethesda, Maryland.

Kingson, a professor at Syracuse University's School of Social Work, writes about the politics and economics of aging, generational equity, aging of baby boom cohorts, and caregiving.

Director of the Emerging Issues in Aging Program of The Gerontological Society of America in 1984–85, he also served as senior adviser to the 1994 Bipartisan Commission on Entitlement and Tax Reform, and as member of the 2016 Democratic National Committee's Platform Committee. Among his authored and co-authored books are *Lessons from Joan: Living and Loving with Cancer* (Syracuse Univerity Press 2005) and *Social Security Works!* (The New Press, 2015), co-authored with Nancy Altman. He lives in Manlius, New York.

David Cay Johnston is an investigative journalist and the winner of a 2001 Pulitzer Prize for uncovering loopholes and inequities in the U.S. tax code. He is the president of the 6,000-member Investigative Reporters & Editors and the author of the bestselling trilogy *Perfectly Legal*, *Free Lunch*, and *The Fine Print*. He is the editor of *Divided: The Perils of Our Growing Inequality* (The New Press). He teaches at Syracuse University College of Law.

## ALSO BY NANCY J. ALTMAN

*The Truth About Social Security: The Founders' Words Refute Revisionist History, Zombie Lies, and Common Misunderstandings*

*Social Security Works!*

*The Battle for Social Security: From FDR's Vision to Bush's Gamble*

## ALSO BY ERIC R. KINGSON

*Social Security Works!*

*Lessons from Joan: Living and Loving with Cancer, A Husband's Story*

*The Generational Equity Debate* (ed. with J.B. Williamson and D. Watts-Roy)

*Social Security in the 21st Century* (ed. with J.H. Schulz)

*Social Security and Medicare: A Policy Primer* (with E.D. Berkowitz)

*Ties That Bind: The Interdependence of Generations* (with B.A. Hirshorn and J.M. Cornman)

# SOCIAL SECURITY WORKS FOR EVERYONE!

## PROTECTING AND EXPANDING THE INSURANCE AMERICANS LOVE AND COUNT ON

NANCY J. ALTMAN

**AND**

ERIC R. KINGSON

NEW YORK
LONDON

Requests for permission to reproduce selections from this book should be made through our website: https://thenewpress.com/contact.

Permissions Department, The New Press, 120 Wall Street, 31st floor, New York, NY 10005.
Published in the United States by The New Press, New York, 2021
Distributed by Two Rivers Distribution

LIBRARY OF CONGRESS CATALOGING-IN-PUBLICATION DATA

Names: Altman, Nancy J., 1950- author. | Kingson, Eric R., author.
Title: Social security works for everyone! : protecting and expanding the
  insurance Americans love and count on / Nancy J. Altman and Eric R.
  Kingson.
Description: New York : The New Press, [2021] | Includes bibliographical
  references and index. | Summary: "Presents the case for expanding Social
  Security, explaining why monthly benefits need to be increased, and why
  Americans need national paid family leave, sick leave, and long term
  care protections"-- Provided by publisher.
Identifiers: LCCN 2020041933 | ISBN 9781620976227 (paperback) | ISBN
  9781620976234 (ebook)
Subjects: LCSH: Social security--United States. | Social
  security--Government policy--United States.
Classification: LCC HD7125 .A4467 2021 | DDC 368.4/300973--dc23
LC record available at https://lccn.loc.gov/2020041933

The New Press publishes books that promote and enrich public discussion and understanding of the issues vital to our democracy and to a more equitable world. These books are made possible by the enthusiasm of our readers; the support of a committed group of donors, large and small; the collaboration of our many partners in the independent media and the not-for profit sector; booksellers, who often hand-sell New Press books; librarians; and above all by our authors.

www.thenewpress.com

Book design and composition by Bookbright Media
This book was set in Bembo and Gotham

Printed in the United States of America
10 9 8 7 6 5 4 3 2 1

To the late Robert M. Ball (1914–2008), whose enduring legacy continues to improve the lives of many millions of people every day. Social Security was his calling. For seven decades, he tirelessly devoted his extraordinary intellectual, political, organizational, and personal gifts to advancing Social Security, which he understood to be an instrument of social justice, human dignity, and civility.

# CONTENTS

**Part Five: Where We Go from Here**

# FOREWORD

David Cay Johnston

THIS BOOK IS ABOUT HOW THE MOST SUCCESSFUL AND most popular government program in the history of our republic needs to be—and can be—expanded, improved, and refined for the twenty-first century. It lays bare the distortions and flat-out lies used by those so rich that they have no need for a social safety net, but who selfishly seek to make sure no one else has insurance against poverty in old age or disability during their working years.

Nancy Altman and Eric Kingson are the right people to show us what needs to be done, why it needs to be done, and how to do it. They want to repair the tattered threads of our foundation of economic security, including Medicare and Medicaid, to serve all generations for all time. They know their stuff because they served as staff to the Reagan-era commission that updated Social Security almost four decades ago, back when the American economy was roughly a third of the size it reached before the pandemic. Both have stuck with their study and advocacy ever since.

Social Security was born of the Great Depression, which ravaged the lives of millions of people throughout the 1930s in two stages, with a brief economic upsurge in between. Hardly anyone is still alive who remembers that awful time, when teenage sons and daughters left home so younger siblings would have enough to eat. Farmers and shopkeepers, evicted from their property, existed in Hooverville camps where police and corporate thugs would beat them and burn their few goods for the crime of being penniless.

It was worst of all for people of color, a sad reality that persists to this day.

Such a crisis can happen again, as we should know from the Great Recession in 2007 and the pandemic that began in early 2020. To get an idea of what needs to be done, think for a moment about cars.

Imagine if we could only buy models designed in 1935 and updated once in the 1980s.

Back in 1935, cars had weak mechanical drum brakes, steering columns that impaled drivers in head-on crashes, and windshields that often slashed the throats of drivers and companions alike. Cotton-thread tires lasted maybe eight thousand miles, and engines had to be overhauled or replaced by sixty thousand miles.

Today we enjoy powerful hydraulic disc brakes. Steering columns collapse in crashes while truly safe windshield glass holds back flying objects. Modern tires made with steel cords come with eighty thousand–mile guarantees, while modern car engines may be good for a million miles.

So why is America stuck with a 1935 social program with 1980s updates? We can do better, much better. And we would all benefit from a twenty-first-century foundation of economic security—one that is stronger, that has fewer gaps through which people can fall, and that will make America more humane.

To understand this, it's helpful to know that American old-age income policy used to be based on the model of a three-legged stool: pensions, individual savings, and Social Security.

Stools are sturdy. But in this case, the first two legs have been sawed off for tens of millions of Americans. Traditional defined-benefit pensions that ensure old age income for life are shriveling. Many are severely underfunded because Congress put in place incentives for executives, directors, and state government lawmakers to shortchange workers by not setting aside enough money each year to pay promised benefits. Many union leaders, clueless about the economics of long-term investing, failed to insist on proper funding.

And private savings? At some points in the last forty years the American savings rate was negative. In 2018, the Federal Reserve reported, almost 40 percent of American households could not come up with $400 to cover an emergency expense.

The idea of replacing pensions with individual retirement savings has been a colossal failure for the vast majority of Americans. The giant mutual fund house Vanguard reported that the median 401(k) balance—half had more, half less—was just $22,000 in 2018. Vanguard also revealed that the median income of its 401(k) savers was about $59,000. Only one in four workers made that much in 2018. The median wage that year was less than $33,000— not nearly enough to pay bills and save for old age.

Despite such dismal facts, the enemies of Social Security say we should switch to private savings. Clearly, they haven't a clue. Nor do they appreciate that not everyone has the capacity, discipline, and investment skill to invest profitably. Investing is like fixing broken water pipes, flying a jetliner, or operating on the brain—it requires deep, specialized knowledge. Expecting that just anyone can do everything for themselves is a foolish idea that harms economic growth, as the first modern economist, Adam Smith, taught way back in 1776 in *The Wealth of Nations*. Suggesting everyone save and invest on their own makes as much sense as proposing everyone in cities raise their own food.

Altman and Kingson show that we can do better for all Americans. Significantly, their ideas would benefit not just those who can't save or don't understand investing, but all Americans—including those at the top—by creating a more efficient and robust economy.

Their focus is on the stool's third leg: Social Security and universal health care.

As currently designed, Social Security cannot carry the weight that used to be distributed among three legs. But with the kind of smart redesign advocated in these pages by Altman and Kingson, the lives of tens of millions of retirees, widows, widowers, orphans, and people with disabilities could be improved. The economic and social benefits of expanding Social Security, along with Medicare and Medicaid, would flow through the entire nation.

What stands in the way of a twenty-first-century refurbishment of Social Security, Medicare, and Medicaid is a pack of lies that has been very effectively sold to the American people by billionaires and their well-paid retainers. Not every billionaire is part of this cabal, but hardly any of them have been public advocates for the vast majority, either.

These enemies of Social Security have for decades claimed that the system is unsustainable. They get journalists to write about the next seventy-five years of costs as if the money was all due today, a measure that would be just as scary—and nonsensical—if applied to, say, military spending. They have persuaded many of today's young and middle-aged workers that they will be taxed today for benefits that won't be there when their hair turns gray. And they paint pictures of greedy geezers living it up by taking from younger generations, robbing them of prosperity.

None of this is true. But by consistently applying well-established principles of advertising, especially endless repetition, many Americans have been deceived. It's much easier to scare people and make them fear that they are being ripped off than to explain the truth with its nuances.

Altman and Kingson address the malarkey that older Americans are living the high life on Social Security. Retired workers received an average of $1,517 a month in August 2020. Their survivors averaged just $1,226, and disabled workers, $1,259. And while proposals to raise the normal retirement age may seem benign—as Americans who reach age sixty-five today live six to seven years longer than their peers in 1940—the authors show that raising the retirement age by just two years is the equivalent of paying only eleven months of benefits each year.

Social Security benefits are so modest because the vast majority of Americans are making the same or less money than they did four and five decades ago, thanks to a host of government policies I've spent years revealing in books and columns.

Consider the average income of 90 percent of Americans, measured in 2018 dollars. In 2018 it was $37,328, slightly less than the 1979 average of $37,437. Now let's measure from 1981, the year President Reagan created his Social Security commission. After thirty-seven years, average real income grew so slowly hardly anyone would notice—an average annual increase of just two cents per hour, or $43 per year.

How about comparing the 90 percent to the 1 percent, basically everyone making at least $500,000? In the 1960s and 1970s, the 1 percenters averaged thirteen times more income than the vast majority. That ratio nearly tripled in this century to thirty-six. But even among the 1 percenters, income growth mostly benefited those at the top—the 1 percent of the 1 percent. So how did the vast majority do compared to the best-off Americans, the top 1 percent of the top 1 percent?

For each increased dollar that each taxpayer in the vast majority enjoyed in 2018, each member of the 1 percent of the 1 percent raked in an additional $17,900. Ponder that for a moment: a dollar for you, $17,900 for each of those at the top, another dollar for you, another $17,900 for each of the 1 percent of the 1 percent. Now repeat that until you get $1,596 dollars, and those at the top, $28,600,000 more.

The reasons for this chasm are rooted in government policies that the enemies of Social Security lobbied for, as is their constitutional right. They persuaded Congress to enact laws that savaged unions, weakening the collective influence of working people on what laws and rules Washington adopts. Our so-called campaign-finance reforms made rich donors not just a part of the political fundraising, but pretty much the entire game.

From a peak of 37 percent of private-sector workers in the 1970s, union density by 2020 fell to about 6 percent of private-sector workers. Without unions, workers lost power to negotiate for more pay and benefits, even as corporate profits ballooned. The loss of union influence also hurt tens of millions of nonunion workers whose pay was affected by union contracts at competing firms.

At the same time, rising health-care costs took a growing share of the total compensation of workers, dinging both cash wages and pension plans. Add onto this the expansion of global trade, as more than 56,000 factories closed and production moved to low-wage countries including China, Mexico, and Vietnam. Even many service jobs, like customer service and technical support, have moved to India and the Philippines, thanks to cheap telecommunications.

Altman and Kingson rightly bring to their case improving American health care. Today it is so costly that if we had the French or German systems, we would save each year a sum equal to all the income taxes paid by 99 percent of Americans. Ponder that, too. Universal health care done right is the equivalent of ending income taxes for everyone making less than $500,000 a year. Altman and Kingson would move us in the direction of quality, universal, and less expensive health care with their plan to update our foundation of economic security for the twenty-first-century economy.

Having read their words here and in an earlier book on Social Security, and after my own decades of studying our economy, tax system, and government regulation, I have only one question about what Altman and Kingson propose: what's not to like? Economically, practically, and morally expanding and strengthening Social Security and related economic and health security policies as Altman and Kingson advocate is a clear winner. The only arguments against what this book proposes are ideological.

"Social Security is a unifying force," Altman and Kingson write, "connecting all of us with each other through the values we share. It is also a force for social justice, lifting all of us up, especially those most disadvantaged. Social Security is a solution in the quest for greater economic security, fairness."

Please read their words and tell others what you learn so we can build a more just and vibrant America.

September 2020

PART ONE

# SOCIAL SECURITY IS MORE IMPORTANT THAN EVER

# 1

## SOCIAL SECURITY IS A SOLUTION

*"[The Social Security Act of 1935] represents a cornerstone in a structure which is being built but is by no means complete. . . . It is, in short, a law that will take care of human needs and at the same time provide the United States an economic structure of vastly greater soundness."*

—Franklin Delano Roosevelt, August 14, 1935[1]

Millions of America's working families know that they will never be able to retire with sufficient income. Too many fear that they will have to work until they die. Substantially expanding Social Security's modest but vital benefits will address this crisis.

And Social Security is a solution to so much more. It is a solution to perilous and rising income and wealth inequality where the 400 richest Americans own more than the bottom 150 million of us.[2] It is a solution to the terrible financial squeeze on working families, trying to support their children and aging parents while wages fail to keep pace with costs. And it is a timely reminder that government policies, when guided by the American people's best instincts, can strengthen our national community.

In *Social Security Works for Everyone!*, we propose an All Generations Plan that will address these challenges and more.

Social Security replaces wages in the event of long-term

disability, death, and old age. Like all insurance, it is ideally suited for addressing uncertainty and risks. Though death is a certainty, dying prematurely and leaving young children is what life insurance, including Social Security's life insurance, is all about. While we all hope to live to old age, we don't want to be destitute when we do. Social Security's old-age insurance, providing joint and survivor annuities that last until death, makes sure that we have basic, continuous income that we cannot outlive. And Social Security's disability insurance protects us and our families if we suffer a devastating drop in family income in the event that a serious disability strikes without warning.

Social Security is insurance that is earned, just as paychecks are earned. We proudly claim it as a matter of right. The cost is covered primarily by the premiums from our wages, matched dollar for dollar by our employers. Our work and the insurance contributions (i.e., FICA) we pay are what make Social Security an earned right, not government largesse.

That is what Social Security is in the United States today. The phrase "Social Security" usually is used to refer to Old-Age, Survivors and Disability Insurance (OASDI), although it is sometimes used to include Medicare.

But President Franklin Roosevelt (FDR) and his colleagues who created Social Security had a much more expansive view of what Social Security should be. Three decades after the enactment of Social Security, Arthur J. Altmeyer, the man FDR called "Mr. Social Security," observed:

> The term social security captured the public imagination not only in this country, but throughout the world. In the course of time the term came to be used in other countries in an expansive sense as a synonym for the Good Life. . . . However, gradually the term social security in this country, instead of being used in a more expansive sense, has been used in a more limited sense

to refer only to the Old Age, Survivors, and Disability System. I consider this extremely unfortunate.[3]

Douglas Brown, another architect of the Social Security Act, spoke eloquently of Social Security as an "implied covenant" arising from a deeply embedded sense of mutual responsibility that "rests on the fundamental obligation of the government and citizens of one time and the government and citizens of another time to maintain a contributory social insurance system."[4] Indeed, its financing and functioning are based on mutuality, since how one generation fares in retirement will directly depend upon how the next generation is doing in its working years.

It is time to reclaim these broader understandings of Social Security as economic security of all kinds, a broader ideal, a value to be achieved by a civilized society seeking to provide widespread basic protection against what Franklin D. Roosevelt called "the hazards and vicissitudes of life."[5]

Social Security is a reminder of what our nation can be at its best, and what can be done when we work together to find practical solutions to real problems, to advance the well-being of everyone.

An instrument of civility and democracy, Social Security reflects widely held American values. It stands in sharp contrast to Trumpism, which no matter how described or implemented is oppositional to the very purposes and values that underlie and inform Social Security. It stands in contrast to a toxic political climate where Americans are increasingly divided from each other. It is an important step along the path toward what Martin Luther King called "the beloved community"—where it is understood that "all people [should] share in the wealth of the earth. . . . [where] poverty, hunger and homelessness will not be tolerated because . . . human decency will not allow it, [where] love and trust will triumph over fear and hatred [and] peace with justice will prevail over war and military conflict."[6]

Remarkably successful, today's Social Security provides

widespread protection for workers and their families against lost earnings in retirement or when disability or death strikes. Built to last, Social Security has endured through wars, recessions, stock market crashes, even pandemics—and the continuous barrage of ideological assaults.

*Social Security Works for Everyone!* explains that it is time to expand Social Security and to build on the Social Security vision of economic security for the American people. The richest nation in the world can afford an expanded Social Security. Despite a billionaire-funded effort to undermine Americans' confidence in Social Security, detailed at length in chapter 10, the question whether to expand Social Security, cut it, or radically change it is one of values, not affordability.

## THIS BOOK IS FOR YOU!

Whether you are a member of the Silent Generation or are a Baby Boomer, whether a Gen Xer or a Millennial, this book is for you. In making the case for an All Generations expansion of Social Security, the book shows why doing so is excellent policy, excellent politics, and, most importantly, excellent for all Americans—young and old, people of all races, genders, and ethnicities.

If you are one of the many readers who have heard for decades that Social Security is going bankrupt and won't be there in the future, the idea that Social Security is not going broke—and that a movement to expand it has taken hold—may come as a shock. Armed with misinformation and half-truths, a four-decades-long, well-financed campaign has sought to dismantle Social Security, brick by brick. The campaign has been remarkably successful in undermining confidence in Social Security. In fact, the younger you are, the less confident you are likely to be that Social Security will exist when you are old, but also the more you have to lose if this campaign succeeds.

If you are one of these readers, this is yet another reason why this book is for you. We invite you to leave behind your preconceptions about Social Security and to learn more about it, including what its expansion would mean for families and communities—and for our shared future. Indeed, this book is for all of us, because Social Security reflects the best of American values. Through it, we share our risks and our responsibilities. Through it, we each benefit. In short, Social Security works for everyone.

## LIVING OUR MORAL AND RELIGIOUS VALUES

At its core, Social Security causes us to reflect deeply about the kind of society we, as a people and a nation, want. Social Security gives expression to some of our most fundamental moral values and, if we identify with a religious tradition, to our religious values, irrespective of what religion that may be.

Reflecting mutuality, reciprocity, and interdependence, Social Security is a program that works over the long-term. The program balances individualism with an understanding that individuals thrive in the context of families and communities; that we are all joined as part of the human race and have obligations to each other.[7] And with an understanding of how one generation fares in retirement directly depends upon how the next generation is doing during their working years, and the next at the start of life.

Social Security promotes independence and self-reliance. Americans take pride in earning Social Security benefits. By contributing to a common pot of money, we are able to draw from it, if and when we retire, become disabled, or die leaving dependents. As President Dwight D. Eisenhower explained, when championing the expansion of Social Security:

> Retirement systems, by which individuals contribute to their own security according to their own respective abilities . . . are but a reflection of the American heritage

of sturdy self-reliance which has made our country strong and kept it free; the self-reliance without which we would have had no Pilgrim Fathers, no hardship-defying pioneers, and no eagerness today to push to ever widening horizons in every aspect of our national life.[8]

The expectation and directive to honor our parents is fundamental to virtually every religious and humanistic tradition. By helping to sustain our parents—and others who have shepherded us through life—grandparents, aunts, uncles, teachers, mentors—Social Security implements and institutionalizes the value of caring for those on whose shoulders we stand.

Social Security also embodies ethical principles of respect for the dignity of each person, the dignity of work in the labor force and in the home. Created more than eighty-five years ago in the depths of the Great Depression of the 1930s, this remarkable American institution embodies our best values. These may sound like old-fashioned ideas, but they are just as fundamental today as they were in the 1930s to strengthening our democracy and to advancing strong families, communities, and our nation.

President Franklin Roosevelt understood that governance is nothing other than all of us working together to put our values into action. In a 1934 fireside chat explaining his plan for Social Security, Roosevelt described the program as self-help in which Americans were "to use the agencies of government to assist in the establishment of means to provide sound and adequate protection against the vicissitudes of modern life—in other words, social insurance." [9]

President Roosevelt's secretary of labor, Frances Perkins, also understood this. She spoke of how America "evolved the ethical principle that it was not right or just that an honest and industrious [person] should live and die in misery." "[T]he people are what matter to government," she explained, and "a government should aim to give all the people under its jurisdiction the best possible life."[10]

A practical solution that provides protection to all of us, Social Security reflects the solidarity across generations that is integral to a well-functioning society.

## SOCIAL SECURITY UNITES US

As divided as America seems at this moment in history, Social Security unites us. Politicians and the media decry how polarized our nation's politics are. Electoral maps, depicting red states and blue states, provide a pictorial representation of that polarization. Hot-button topics like abortion and immigration reform are often used by politicians to divide the electorate.

But Americans are overwhelmingly united in our support for Social Security. Poll after poll reveals this. The findings of an online survey of two thousand adults ages twenty-one and over conducted by Matthew Greenwald and Associates in collaboration with the nonpartisan National Academy of Social Insurance found that a large majority of Americans believe that Social Security is more important than ever, do not mind contributing to Social Security because it provides security and stability, and believe that consideration should be given to expanding its benefits (see figure 1.1). [11]

In fact, numerous polls have shown that Americans of all political affiliations—Republicans, Independents, Democrats, self-proclaimed Tea Partiers, union households, and progressives—support our Social Security system by significant majorities. Conservatives and progressives may disagree on most political issues, but not on the importance of Social Security. Those from the Northeast may differ with those from the Deep South about many issues, but both groups support Social Security.[12]

Virtually all demographic groups support Social Security.[13] Majorities of African Americans, Hispanics, European Americans,

## AMERICANS OVERWHELMINGLY AGREE ABOUT SOCIAL SECURITY

### Percent Agreeing with Statements

| Respondent characteristics | Social Security benefits are more important now than ever | I don't/didn't mind paying Social Security taxes because it provides security and stability to millions | We should consider increasing Social Security benefits |
|---|---|---|---|
| Total | 89% | 84% | 75% |
| **Generation** | | | |
| Silent | 93 | 88 | 72 |
| Baby Boomer | 93 | 86 | 76 |
| Generation X | 87 | 85 | 74 |
| Generation Y | 84 | 79 | 74 |
| **Family Income** | | | |
| Less than $30,000 | 89 | 83 | 80 |
| $30,000 to $49,999 | 93 | 90 | 78 |
| $50,000 to $74,999 | 89 | 82 | 70 |
| $75,000 to $99,999 | 87 | 82 | 71 |
| $100,000 or more | 88 | 86 | 67 |
| **Party Affiliation** | | | |
| Republican | 81 | 74 | 62 |
| Democrat | 94 | 91 | 84 |
| Independent | 91 | 86 | 71 |

Data from National Academy of Social Insurance survey, September 2012.

**Source:** Jasmine V. Tucker, Virginia P. Reno, and Thomas N. Bethell, "Strengthening Social Security: What Do Americans Want?," National Academy of Social Insurance, January 2013.

Figure 1.1

and other racial and ethnic groups as well as every age group and gender support Social Security as well. Even younger Americans, many of whom have bought the lie that Social Security won't be there for them, nevertheless support the program for their parents and grandparents and don't want to see it cut.

Not only is our Social Security system popular, but public support for it runs deep. Feelings for Social Security are so strongly held that one highly respected pollster, Celinda Lake, president of Lake Research Partners, says this support is an indication not just of preference but of deeply held values.

This view of the overwhelming majority of the American people should not come as a surprise. The America we know today would not be possible without Social Security. This institution undergirds the economic security of virtually every American, and it puts the American people's best instincts into action.

Whether the American people through our elected officials use Social Security to address challenges to our economic security is a matter of politics and choice. In the chapters that follow, we invite our readers—concerned citizens, the general public, politicians, activists, policy experts, and journalists alike—to consider how much is at stake for you, your family, your neighbors, and our nation. And we invite you to think about what we all can do together to build on this uniquely American institution that those who preceded us left as a legacy to pass forward to those who will follow.

# 2

## ENACTING, DEFENDING, AND EXPANDING SOCIAL SECURITY

THE HISTORY OF SOCIAL SECURITY INCLUDES CHALLENGES as well as hard-earned victories that have expanded benefits and secured Social Security as an institution that is fundamental to the well-being of the American people. The fight for Social Security has been part of a larger struggle over worker security. It is also part of the ongoing struggle between those who view poor Americans, even those who have worked for their entire adult lives, as undeserving versus those who understand that each of us deserves to be treated with dignity, especially when unemployment, health problems, old age, or other circumstances undermine our ability to support ourselves and our families. At base, it is a struggle over the role of government in improving our lives. And it is a struggle about our responsibilities to our families, neighbors, and selves.

At the beginning of the twentieth century, with the growing industrialization and urbanization of the United States, increasing numbers of Americans became dependent on wage income. To ensure a living wage, and to protect those workers in the event of the loss of those wages, a variety of workers' movements arose. These various movements sought minimum wages and maximum hours, workers' compensation for industrial accidents, health insurance, unemployment insurance, disability insurance, survivors or life insurance, occupational safety, an end to child labor, the freedom to unionize, and old-age annuities.

Prior to the Great Depression, most of the efforts took place at the state level. With the onset of the Great Depression and the election of Franklin D. Roosevelt as president in 1932, the leaders of these progressive movements focused more intensely on achieving nationwide legislation at the federal level.

## ENACTING SOCIAL SECURITY

The Social Security Act of 1935 was signed into law on August 14, 1935. In his signing statement, the president was clear that the new law was just a first step, albeit a very significant one, in the march toward economic security—a framework upon which future generations should build.

> We can never insure one hundred percent of the population against one hundred percent of the hazards and vicissitudes of life, but we have tried to frame a law which will give some measure of protection to the average citizen and to his family against the loss of a job and against poverty-ridden old age.[1]

The enactment was not the end of the fight. Social Security became a major issue in the 1936 presidential election. Republican presidential nominee Alf Landon denounced Social Security as "a fraud on the workingman" and "a cruel hoax." He claimed that Social Security's reserves were mere IOUs.[2]

## EXPANDING SOCIAL SECURITY: 1939 TO THE MID-1970S

Despite the attacks, President Roosevelt won reelection in a landslide in 1936 and Social Security proved more and more popular.

The Social Security Amendments of 1939 addressed the economic insecurity when the death of a working parent left children and spouses without a steady income. Surviving wives of deceased workers with young children became eligible to receive benefits, protections that were extended to aged widowers in 1950 and younger widowers with dependent children in 1975.[3] Ever since, parents struggling to maintain their children after the death of a working spouse have had income they can count on.

For the next thirty-five years, Social Security continued to be improved. Our Social Security system was expanded to cover millions of additional workers, including domestic and migrant employment, and new benefits were added. The Social Security Amendments of 1956 established disability insurance protections for workers aged fifty to sixty-four, extended in 1960 to include workers under age fifty. In 1965, the nation added two very significant programs to the architecture of the Social Security Act: the Medicare and Medicaid programs. The Medicare program provides health insurance to nearly all Americans age sixty-five and older, as well as to people with disabilities. Medicaid, targeted to the poor, provides similar medical services and also long-term care services to low-income seniors, families, people with disabilities, and others.

During these same years, benefits were regularly adjusted to keep pace with inflation. Some liberal supporters of Social Security were concerned that, while inflation is ongoing, benefit adjustments tended to occur every other year, just before elections. At the same time, conservatives who supported a more modest Social Security program were concerned that the tendency of politicians was to expand Social Security too much, in these pre-electoral enactments. The two joined forces to support the enactment in 1972 of automatic, annual cost-of-living adjustments.

None of these improvements occurred without opposition. The election of President Dwight Eisenhower in November 1952 brought initial uncertainty in the fight over Social Security. Holding elective office for the first time in his career, Eisenhower had never been forced to take a stand on the issue. But by August of his first year in office, President Eisenhower declared his strong support for Social Security. With this clear, unequivocal support for Social Security expressed by a Republican president, opposition to the basic program became increasingly marginalized. In every generation, though, libertarians and other conservative ideologues, backed by moneyed interests, have been fighting to curtail benefits.

## FINANCING ISSUE DRIVE THE AGENDA: MID-1970s TO 1983

A number of factors in the mid-1970s breathed new life into the cause of those who wanted to undermine and dismantle Social Security.

In 1973, Egypt and Syria attacked Israel. The Organization of Petroleum Exporting Countries (OPEC) announced that its members would ship no oil to the United States or any other country supporting Israel in the war and would quadruple the price of oil worldwide. The prices of everyday goods skyrocketed.[4] Meanwhile, unemployment rates soared, reaching 8.5 percent by 1975,[5] the highest since before World War II.

For the first time in its history, Social Security was projecting deficits.

Although critically important for helping stabilize the incomes of the old, people with disabilities, and surviving family members, the automatic cost-of-living adjustments enacted in 1972 had made the financing of the program more sensitive to economic change. Sluggish wage growth and high unemployment caused Social Security's income to grow more slowly than projected, while at the same time double-digit inflation (more than 10 percent in 1974, 1979, 1980, and 1981) meant the program's payments were higher than had been estimated. For the first time, Social Security started to project a short-range shortfall. Moreover, demographic changes, including declining birth rates, increased life expectancies, and the aging of 76 million Baby Boomers,[6] while well understood and anticipated by experts, nevertheless resulted in long-range shortfalls that had to be addressed at some point. To make matters worse, the long-range shortfall was very large due to a technical flaw introduced in 1972, when the cost-of-living and other automatic adjustments were implemented.[7]

Sensational headlines proclaiming the "impending bankruptcy" of Social Security, together with the declining trust in government as a result of the Watergate scandal during Nixon's presidency, gave opponents of Social Security just the opening they were looking for. Social Security and its projected shortfall presented a perfect target for a conservative infrastructure of think tanks, conservative campus newspapers, and other organized outreach efforts, which was being financed by the very rich. The election of Ronald Reagan as president in 1980 gave added hope to these organized opponents of Social Security. Previously an outspoken critic of Social Security, though, Reagan understood the politics—and the risks—of publicly criticizing Social Security. When called out on his position by President Jimmy Carter in a presidential debate during the 1980 election, Reagan stated, "I, too, am pledged to a Social Security program that will reassure these senior citizens of ours that they are going to continue to get their money."[8]

Reagan remained a hero of the newly invigorated conservative movement, but his statement recognized reality. Social Security was so widely and deeply supported that in the early 1980s, a senior aide to Speaker of the House Tip O'Neill dubbed Social Security "the third rail of politics," a reference to the electrified subway rail that results in instant death when touched.[9]

By April 20, 1983, at a ceremony signing into law the Social Security Amendments of 1983, which eliminated Social Security's short- and long-range projected shortfalls, President Reagan, no longer calling for radical reforms to Social Security, declared:

This bill demonstrates for all time our nation's ironclad commitment to social security. It assures the elderly that America will always keep the promises made in troubled times a half a century ago. It assures those who are still working that they, too, have a pact with the future. From this day forward, they have our pledge that they will get their fair share of benefits when they retire.[10]

## OPPONENTS FIND NEW TACTICS: EARLY 1980s TO 2020

President Ronald Reagan's signature on the 1983 amendments to the Social Security Act was disheartening to opponents of the program.

Unlike the early years when Social Security was just getting started, it had now proven its worth. Built to provide a basic floor of protection, by the mid-1980s it was so exceptionally popular and fundamental to the well-being of the nation's families that it was almost impossible to imagine its absence.

The 1983 legislation was perhaps a wake-up call for opponents. Aware of the powerful support that Social Security generates, they realized that instead of objecting to Social Security on ideological grounds, they needed to undermine public confidence in the future of the program.

Just two months after President Reagan signed the 1983 amendments, a libertarian think tank held a conference on Social Security and then published the resulting papers in its fall volume. A particularly revealing piece was entitled "Achieving Social Security Reform: A 'Leninist' Strategy," which outlined a plan and strategy to dismantle the Social Security system.[11] The plan appears to provide a blueprint for almost exactly what has unfolded over the subsequent thirty years: neutralize the support of older Americans by reassuring them that their benefits will be untouched, undermine the support of younger Americans by convincing them that the program is unsustainable and that they can do better investing on their own, and convince Wall Street to get involved to increase its profits.

Opponents were back on offense again, attacking Social Security, seemingly in an effort to see what might stick. They claimed that Social Security is unfair to the poor because it wastes benefits on those with higher incomes, unfair to the rich because they could do better investing on their own, unfair to African Americans because they have shorter lives on average than whites and so will collect retirement benefits for fewer years, unfair to children because too much is being spent on seniors, and unfair to every other group for whom they could conjure up an ostensibly plausible argument. (All of these claims are refuted in chapter 11.)

In the 1990s, when Social Security began to project a manageable shortfall, decades away, these same forces latched on to the news, proclaiming that Social Security was once again going bankrupt. A wonderful program, some claimed, but badly in need of modernization. In its present form, though, they asserted, it just was not sustainable.

And in 2000, opponents of Social Security saw the election of a president who, unlike Reagan, would seek to radically change Social Security. Once safely elected to a second term, President George W. Bush employed these new tactics and pulled one very old tactic out of mothballs. Just like Alf Landon's 1936 attack, he asserted that Social Security's reserves were nothing more than IOUs—just paper, backed by no "real" assets—and were no guarantee that future benefits would be honored. (This charge too is refuted in chapter 11.)

Following the Leninist strategy to the letter, Bush told those age fifty-five and older that they would get their benefits, but advocated that the program allow young workers to divert some of their Social Security contributions into individual private accounts.

Though his privatization proposal would have ended Social Security as we know it, Bush called Social Security "one of the greatest achievements of the American government," justifying dismantling it as the way to "strengthen and save [it]."[12]

The billionaire campaign has had an impact, though far less than its proponents hoped. Too often, the campaign has been successful in convincing prominent politicians of both political parties that Social Security must be radically changed, or at least scaled back. Too often, the mainstream media have uncritically accepted and advanced a panoply of misconceptions, while largely ignoring the facts.

## EXPANSION PROPONENTS PUSH BACK: 2010 TO PRESENT

The success of the billionaire-funded campaign started to receive pushback from prominent Democrats as they became more and more sensitive to the looming retirement income crisis and the solution that Social Security offers. The 2016 presidential campaign of Senator Bernie Sanders and his full-throated embrace of expansion helped break the spell of the billionaire-funded campaign. By July 2016, four months before the election, expansion became the official position of the Democratic Party. There is much more detail about this in chapters 10 and 12. Suffice it to say, Republicans still spout the billionaires' lie that Social Security is going broke and must be cut; Democrats favor expansion.

To summarize this panoramic history, Social Security was born in partisan division. That division turned to bipartisan support as Americans across the political spectrum grew to value this essential and all-American institution. But then the billionaire-funded campaign created a new bipartisan consensus among the wealthy elites. This time the consensus was not to expand Social Security but to shrink it. Indeed, the last time Congress expanded Social

Security was in 1972—a half century ago. Fortunately, the Democratic establishment has returned to an embrace of the New Deal and Franklin Roosevelt.

The 1930s and the New Deal were transformative. The nation may be in another transformative moment today. The United States is becoming majority-minority, where no one racial or ethnic group will constitute 50 percent or more of the population. Along with that demographic change is a new push for racial justice, along with justice for other historically oppressed groups. The coronavirus pandemic and resulting economic hardships are exposing long-simmering economic insecurities.

Social Security is a unifying force, connecting all of us with each other through the values we share. It is also a force for social justice, lifting all of us up, especially those most disadvantaged. Social Security is a solution in the quest for greater economic security and fairness.

We urge readers of this book—and indeed all who care about the economic security of ourselves, our families, and our nation—to join this fight. The goal of this book is to arm you with the facts so you have informed opinions. That is what chapters 4 through 7 and chapter 12 are about. Chapters 8 and 9 set out our vision for an all generations plan to inspire you to, in the words of the late Senator Robert F. Kennedy, "dream of things that never were and ask, why not?"[13]

To achieve that dream, we must be prepared to fight. Chapters 10, 11, 12, and the concluding chapter 13 make sure those of us fighting to protect and expand Social Security understand who and what we are facing.

The fight may not always be easy, but we have the facts and the overwhelming majority of the American people with us.

# 3

## SOCIAL SECURITY WORKS FOR ALL GENERATIONS

THE IMPORTANCE OF SOCIAL SECURITY CANNOT BE OVER-stated. The most reliable source of retirement income for seniors and working Americans, it is less well known that Social Security is also the primary disability and life insurance protection for the vast majority of Americans, including the nation's children. Each year, 180 million workers make Social Security contributions and 65 million receive earned benefits, totaling $1.1 trillion during 2020.[1]

Whatever age you are now, you, every member of your family, your neighbors, and indeed every American alive today benefits from Social Security. We benefit individually, starting with the first day of life. We benefit together as a result of the kind of country Social Security has helped create.

Perhaps you are a new parent, aware of the promise and vulnerability of the baby you hold in your arms, the financial responsibility to provide, the moral responsibility to nurture. Social Security can't advise you on how to rear your child, but it can, and does, provide the nation's most important life and disability insurance for your family. If working parents of dependent children die or are so seriously disabled that they are unable to work, Social Security is there.

Though premature death or severe disability may seem unimaginable, those tragedies happen all too often. We do not like to think about our mortality or the potential onset of severe disability, but the reality is that a twenty-year-old worker born in 1999 has a more than one in four chance (26 percent, to be precise) of becoming disabled, as well as a 7 percent chance of dying without ever becoming disabled, before reaching age sixty-seven.[2]

If a thirty-year-old worker who is married with two young children and who earns around $35,000 were to die, Social Security would provide the surviving family the equivalent of more than $670,000 in life insurance. If that same thirty-year-old does not die but becomes so seriously and permanently disabled that work is not possible, Social Security would provide benefits equivalent to disability insurance with a face value of more than $700,000.[3]

Or perhaps you are middle-aged, helping your kids through college, and thinking about retirement ten to fifteen years from now. Social Security provides significant retirement security. That same thirty-year-old, married worker, now earning more than $45,000 and retiring at age sixty-five, will earn benefits for the couple equivalent to more than $527,000 in a joint and survivor retirement annuity.[4]

By providing an orderly way for individuals to contribute during working years, in exchange for financial protections against premature death, disability, and old age, Social Security takes some of the tension out of family life and reinforces the independence and dignity of many. Knowing that one's parents have Social Security often frees up the generation in the middle to direct more family resources toward their own children.

Social Security transformed the nation. It eradicated what once was a primary anxiety for the vast majority of Americans: the terror of growing old penniless, dependent, and vulnerable. It provided basic economic protection not previously available to most households. It enabled, as historian Andrew Achenbaum observed, "ordinary workers to take advantage of relatively worry-free time" in their older years, something "that the wealthy took for granted."[5] It ended the complete destitution that often accompanied the death or serious injury of a breadwinner. Again, its importance cannot be overstated.

This chapter briefly explains how Social Security works, the vision on which it is based, and the enormous good it does for everyone. (A more complete description of the details of how Social Security works can be found in appendix A.)

## A PRACTICAL, TIME-TESTED MEANS OF PROTECTING ALL GENERATIONS

Social Security's fundamental structure is thoroughly modern. Just as in 1935, when Social Security was enacted, most Americans today depend on wage-paying jobs to afford the necessities of life. To be economically secure, workers and their families must have insurance against the loss of those wages. To protect against the loss of wages when laid off and unable to find immediate new employment, workers need unemployment insurance. To protect against lost wages due to disability, they need disability insurance. In case they die leaving dependents, they need life insurance for their families. If they are fortunate enough to live to be very old, they need old age annuities that they cannot outlive. Social Security is insurance against the loss of wages in the event of disability, death, or old age. (Unemployment insurance, which is wage insurance in the event of unemployment, was part of the Social Security Act of 1935 but is not generally called Social Security.)

Throughout its history, many have described Social Security as forced savings, but that's not accurate. It is easy to confuse wage insurance in the event of old age on the one hand, and retirement savings accounts on the other, because both are focused on protection in old age—a state virtually all of us hope to reach, and most of us will. However, this similarity obscures fundamental differences.

Retirement savings are, at best, poor substitutes for wage insurance. Most workers in this country find that they have insufficient savings for even short-term needs. But even if workers were willing and able to sacrifice current consumption in order to maintain their standards of living in retirement, they would confront unanswerable questions: How long will they be able to work? What will inflation do to their earnings? How much savings is enough? How much is too little? If too little is saved, one risks destitution if wages are lost. Even if complete destitution is avoided, saving too little may force people to sell their homes, move from their neighborhoods, and cut all expenses drastically.

Workers who, over their working lives, want to save the amount needed to replace their preretirement wages each and every year until their deaths would have the impossible task of trying to predict all sorts of eventualities that actuaries know for groups but that no one can know for themselves. Those worker-savers would have to know in their late teens or twenties, at the start of their working lives, what their wages will be at the time of their retirement, at what age they will retire, whether they will face large unanticipated health-care costs, how inflation and market downturns will affect their savings and whether they will have worked and saved every year until that retirement date, or whether they will have had periods of no wages or even periods of dissaving for more immediate expenses, such as child care, medical costs, and other necessities. They would also have to know their rate of spending in retirement. Extensive medical costs or the need for long-term care can result in the rapid drawdown of savings.

Even more fundamentally, those saving for retirement also have to accurately predict how long they will live, since, if they do not live until retirement, they will not need to save anything for that eventuality. However, if they live to the age of 105, they will need substantially more savings to provide for twenty more years of support than they would have needed if they died, for example, at age eighty-five.

Such uncertainties—impossible to determine for individuals— require an insurance solution, not savings. Wage insurance such as Social Security, where the benefit is explicitly designed to replace wages, is precisely geared to this goal and, in the case of Social Security, provides protection in the event of death or disability before reaching retirement. Wage insurance, not savings, is the most effective way to protect workers and their families when wages are lost as a result of disability, death, or old age. Savings are fine as a supplement—for those who are able to save—but they are not a substitute.

Wage insurance—not simply personal savings and welfare programs, as we elaborate in chapter 11—is needed to prevent economic devastation and mitigate economic hardship. Where welfare programs seek to relieve poverty and require that participants be poor, Social Security prevents extreme financial distress in the first place, in addition to helping to maintain its beneficiaries' standard of living. Built on the principle of universal coverage, it provides a means of pooling risks. In exchange for making relatively modest work-related contributions over many years, this wage insurance provides individuals and their families with basic protection against predictable risks.

## SOCIAL SECURITY'S FINANCING

Social Security insurance contributions or premiums have always been and, under current law, always will be the primary source of money from which Social Security's benefits are paid. It is important to note that these premiums are often called payroll taxes. Of course, one can call all government-mandated payments taxes, but Social Security payments are different from other taxes, because they purchase insurance protection, just as private insurance premiums do. Consequently, this book will not use the phrase "payroll taxes" and instead uses terms such as Social Security contributions or premiums.

Social Security's second, smaller source of revenue is investment income. From the beginning, in any year that Social Security has more income than it needs to cover all benefits and related administrative costs, the surplus is held in trust and invested in interest-bearing treasury bonds, backed by the full faith and credit of the United States: the safest investment on the planet. (If you have heard that the trust funds aren't real and the bonds are worthless IOUs, please read chapters 9 and 11!) In addition to premiums and investment earnings, Social Security has had a third revenue source—income generated every year since 1984 from treating a portion of Social Security benefits as taxable income. (Unlike revenue from the taxation of other income, the revenue that is generated by the taxation of Social Security benefits is dedicated to Social Security and goes into its trust fund accounts, rather than into the general operating fund of the government.)[6]

Social Security is conservatively financed, prudently managed, and closely monitored. Benefits cannot be paid unless Social Security has sufficient revenue to cover not only the cost of those benefits but the cost of administering them as well. In the eighty-five years since its enactment, it has never missed a payment.

## SOCIAL SECURITY'S BENEFITS

Because Social Security is insurance, workers and their families are only eligible for benefits if workers have worked long enough and made sufficient contributions to be insured. In the vast majority of cases, Social Security benefits, whether claimed as the result of death, disability, or old age, rely on the same benefit formula.[7] The formula determines the amount of monthly benefits workers get if they claim their retired worker benefits at their statutorily defined retirement age, also known as a worker's "full retirement age" or "normal retirement age."[8] If workers become disabled or die before retiring, they are generally treated as if they died or became disabled at their full retirement age.[9]

The full retirement age was sixty-five for most of Social Security's history, but as a result of changes enacted in 1983, Social Security's full retirement age has gradually been increasing to age sixty-seven. Workers may claim their retired worker benefits as early as age sixty-two, but their benefits will be permanently reduced for every month receipt begins before their full retirement age. Similarly, workers may claim their retirement benefits after

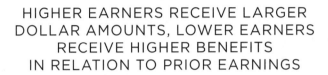

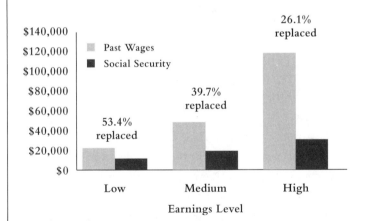

**Note:** "Medium" earners, whose career-average wage-indexed earnings ("Past Wages") were about equal to Social Security's Average Wage Index (AWI: $51,795 for 2018), and who retired at age 65 in 2019, received $23,308 in Social Security benefits in 2019. "Low" earners, whose past indexed wages averages 45 percent of the AWI ($23,308 in 2019), received $12,451. "High" earners, whose past wages were at or above the Social Security contribution cap for each year from age 22 onward ($127,061 for 2019), received $33,134 in Social Security benefits in 2019. (Earnings in excess of the maximum contribution cap are excluded from these calculations.)

**Source:** Michael Clingman, Kyle Burkhalter, and Chris Chaplain, "Replacement Rates for Hypothetical Retired Workers," Actuarial Note 2019.9, Social Security Administration, April 2019.

Figure 3.1

full retirement age, in which case their benefits will be permanently increased for each month they delay receipt up to age seventy.

Social Security's benefit formula is one of its most ingenious and important features. The more you earn and the more you contribute, the higher your benefit will be in absolute dollars. Because those with lifetimes of lower earnings generally have less discretionary income and less opportunity to save, the formula yields benefits that are a larger proportion of their wages for them. Figure 3.1 shows the larger dollar amounts received in 2019 by those with higher earnings, and the larger proportionate amounts received by those with lower earnings.

Social Security also recognizes that even when workers have earned the same wages, those with families generally have less discretionary income than those without dependents. Consequently, based on the same benefit formula, benefits are provided to spouses; divorced spouses, when the marriage lasted at least ten years; dependent children, including adult children who became disabled prior to age twenty-two; and, in some cases, to grandchildren and parents of workers. Figure 3.2 shows how Social Security is not only a program for retirees; it is, more accurately, a family protection plan.

Social Security's wage insurance includes a number of valuable features that are not found in the private sector. For example, private sector annuities and defined benefit pensions reduce the monthly annuity amount of the worker if a spouse is added. In contrast, Social Security's annuities provide add-on benefits for spouses, without reducing by a penny the worker's own benefit. Moreover, if the worker has been divorced after having been married ten years, there are add-on spouse and widow(er) benefits for the divorced spouse, again without reducing the worker's benefit. Very importantly, benefits are annually adjusted to offset the effects of inflation.

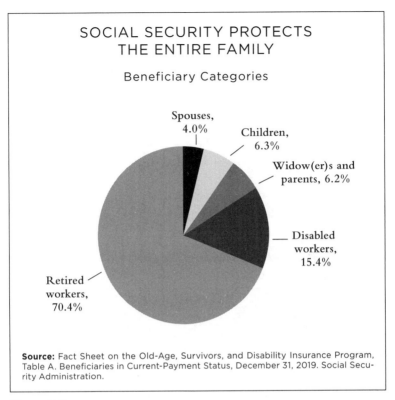

## SOCIAL SECURITY PROTECTS THE ENTIRE FAMILY

### Beneficiary Categories

Spouses, 4.0%

Children, 6.3%

Widow(er)s and parents, 6.2%

Disabled workers, 15.4%

Retired workers, 70.4%

**Source:** Fact Sheet on the Old-Age, Survivors, and Disability Insurance Program, Table A. Beneficiaries in Current-Payment Status, December 31, 2019. Social Security Administration.

Figure 3.2

# EXCEPTIONAL INSURANCE PROTECTIONS FOR AMERICAN FAMILIES

Social Security is not just good insurance; it is the very best insurance available.

First, it is the most secure insurance there is. Current benefits are funded largely from the contributions paid by current workers, with the promise—held together by the taxing power and authority of the federal government—that current workers will themselves receive benefits when they become eligible.

Unlike private insurance companies or employers, the federal government will never go out of business. Moreover, it has the power to tax. Legislative oversight, annual reports by program officials, and reviews by actuaries and independent panels of experts provide an early warning system for financing imbalances that will arise from time to time. These factors along with the self-interest of political leaders and the public to protect promised benefits, guarantee the continuity and financial integrity of Social Security. (As for Social Security going "broke," don't believe it. Read chapters 9 and 11 for discussions of that claim.)

Social Security also offers an advantage over private insurance companies because it delivers its vital protections at the lowest possible cost. This is due to the program's ability to mandate universal coverage and eliminate adverse selection, which is when those who are most at risk purchase the insurance, creating an unusually expensive pool. That results by necessity in more expensive insurance. For example, if everyone who has been diagnosed with a terminal illness buys life insurance when they receive the diagnosis and no young, healthy people buy it, the cost of this life insurance will be much more expensive. Likewise, the risk pool for wage insurance is broadest when all wage earners are covered.

Social Security's efficiency is another advantage over private insurance companies. In fact, it is the most efficient insurance around. Because the federal government is not competing for market share, there are no advertising costs, broker fees, or other marketing costs. Overhead is lower because it is administered by civil servants, not highly paid CEOs, and there is no money taken out for profits. Not surprisingly, Social Security's administrative costs are far lower than private sector insurance and pensions and, remarkably, less than a penny of every Social Security dollar collected is spent on its administration.[10]

Social Security is also the most universal insurance, covering such hard-to-reach workers as household employees, farm workers, other intermittent and seasonal workers, part-time workers, full-time workers working part-time for multiple employers, independent contractors, other self-employed workers, and all employees of small businesses, irrespective of the size. Social Security is also extremely fair in its distribution of benefits, seeking to address the twin concerns of individual fairness and social adequacy.

Today, nearly all workers—94 percent—are covered by Social Security.[11] Social Security is completely portable but imposes few administrative costs on employers. Records are kept accurately and seamlessly by the Social Security Administration (SSA). Wages from all covered employment are automatically recorded by the Social Security Administration and used in the calculation of benefits. No adverse selection is possible, because every covered worker must pay Social Security insurance contributions or premiums as soon as they start to earn wages. This universality and pooling of risks to which we are all exposed is part of the vision that underlies Social Security.

## SOCIAL SECURITY WORKS FOR OUR DIVERSE NATION

This chapter ends where it began. Social Security works for all of us. Today, 180 million working Americans earn Social Security's

### AVERAGE MONTHLY SOCIAL SECURITY BENEFITS, DECEMBER 2019

| | |
|---|---|
| All retired workers | $1,503 |
| Aged couple with both receiving benefits | $2,531 |
| Widowed caregiving parent and two children | $2,907 |
| Aged widow(er) alone | $1,421 |
| All disabled workers | $1,258 |
| Disabled worker, spouse, and one or more children | $2,178 |

**Source:** "Fact Sheet on the Old-Age, Survivors, and Disability Insurance Program," Social Security Administration, December 31, 2019

Figure 3.3

disability, survivor, and retirement protections for themselves and their families.[12] In 2020, Social Security paid $1.1 trillion in benefits to 65 million beneficiaries[13]—nearly one in five Americans (19.5 percent). Figure 3.3 shows the average benefit levels of representative beneficiaries.

With 48 million retired workers, 6 million survivors, and nearly 10 million people with severe disabilities receiving monthly benefits in December 2019, it comes as no surprise that Social Security works for seniors, persons with severe work disabilities, spouses, widows, and widowers. Less well understood:

- **Social Security works for young and middle-aged families:** There is no more secure life and disability insurance available. When unexpected tragedy strikes, these benefits go a long way toward enabling families to maintain their living standards. As today's young and middle-aged workers age, Social Security will be every bit as important to them in old age as it is for their parents and grandparents.
- **Social Security works for children:** Social Security is the nation's largest and, despite its modest benefits, most generous children's program. Its protections are by far the most important life and disability safeguard available to virtually all of the nation's 73 million children under age eighteen.[14] At the end of 2018, 4.1 million dependent children—about 2.9 million under age eighteen, 122,000 eighteen to nineteen year old students, and 1.1 million adults disabled before age twenty-two—receive Social Security checks totaling about $2.7 billion.[15] Another 4.8 million children live in homes where all or part of the household income comes from Social Security.[16] The program lifts 1.1 million children out of poverty.[17] And it is the single most important source of income for the 7.8 million children being raised in a household headed by a grandparent or other older relatives.[18]

- **Social Security works for people of color:** Social Security is very important to people of color, especially African Americans, Hispanics, Native Americans, and Alaska Natives. Having fewer savings and less supplemental pension protection, people of color generally rely on Social Security more heavily than white, non-Hispanic Americans.[19] According to the Commission to Modernize Social Security, people of color do not use Social Security in the same way as whites do, relying more on disability and survivors protections, often due to such disadvantaged circumstances as higher rates of disability and health problems, and holding more physically arduous employment.[20] Because their average income tends to be lower and they tend to have higher rates of unemployment, people of color often benefit more from the way Social Security's benefit formula provides a disproportionately large benefit for low-wage workers and their families. Among beneficiary households with at least one person age sixty-five or older, Social Security provides at least 90 percent of the income for 45 percent of African Americans, 52 percent of Latinos, and 41 percent of Asians.[21] Without Social Security, the poverty rate among African American seniors would nearly triple, from 19 to 51 percent, and the poverty rate among Hispanic American seniors would rise from 17 to 46 percent.[22]
- **Social Security works for women:** The majority (55 percent) of adults receiving Social Security are women. Women, on average, live longer than men and are less likely to have pension income.[23] Consequently, they need to count on a steady stream of income for more years, especially in advanced old age when health expenditures may have depleted their other assets. Without Social Security, the poverty rate among older women would increase from the current 11.1 percent to 41.3 percent.[24]

- **Social Security works for the oldest old:** The reliance on Social Security is even greater as people age and exhaust other sources of support. For beneficiary households with at least one person age eighty or older, nearly three out of four rely on Social Security for half or more of their income. For almost one out of two—42 percent—Social Security constitutes 90 percent or more of their income.[25] For widowed, divorced, or never-married women, and for people of color, the percentages are even higher at those ages.[26]

- **Social Security works for veterans and their families:** In serving those who serve our nation, Social Security pays benefits averaging about $18,000 a year to more than 9.3 million veterans[27]—about four in ten veterans. Nearly all veterans who are not Social Security beneficiaries today will be so in the future. And very importantly, Social Security provides critical frontline protection for family members dependent on those who have served or are serving to protect our nation.[28]

- **Social Security works for same-sex couples and their families:** In the landmark case *Obergefell v. Hodges*, decided in 2015, the Supreme Court ruled that the right of same sex couples to marry is protected by our Constitution. Before then, gender and sexuality diverse persons (referred to hereafter as LGBTQ+ to encompass lesbian, gay, bisexual, transgender, queer/questioning, and others)[29] in committed same-sex relationships were prevented from receiving the same earned spousal, widow(er)s', and family-related benefits for children as everyone else. Social Security, which helps to offset some of the ills of those who have been discriminated against, is especially important to this group.

- **Social Security works for small businesses and local economies:** Social Security beneficiaries tend to spend their benefits immediately on necessities in their local communities. That creates jobs for their fellow Americans. Indeed, these benefits are especially important to the economies of rural communities, which tend to be older and poorer. An AARP report found that every dollar of Social Security benefits generates two dollars in economic output.

The bottom line is that Social Security works for everyone. It works for all ages and all demographic groups. And very importantly, Social Security works because it is a trust based on and reinforcing broadly shared civic and religiously based principles.

For those interested in knowing more about how Social Security works in your state and county, take a look at the fifty state and six related jurisdiction reports (e.g., Puerto Rico, Guam) published each year by Social Security Works, available for download at www.socialsecurityworks.org.

As important as Social Security is today, its importance is likely to be even greater in the future. Part Two of this book will identify a number of challenges facing the nation. An expanded Social Security system is a solution to all of them.

PART TWO

# WHY WE NEED TO EXPAND SOCIAL SECURITY

# 4

## THE PRECARIOUS LIVES OF TODAY'S OLD

THOSE DETERMINED TO CUT SOCIAL SECURITY HAVE GIVEN particularly ugly voice to the outrageous and noxious stereotype that seniors are self-centered retirees, enjoying endless rounds of golf, spending their children's inheritances, and leaving mountains of debt for their grandchildren by fighting cuts to Social Security benefits they don't actually need.

Forty years ago, Baby Boomers, including the authors of this book, were told with great certainty that they wouldn't get their "money's worth" out of Social Security, that it might not even be there for them! That the old of that time were taking more than they had earned or deserved, leaving very little for anyone else. What's more, it was claimed that unjustified spending on the old was undermining investment in the young, especially harmful to children at greatest social and economic risk.

In a 1980 *Forbes* magazine article, Jerry Flint told us that not all elderly persons "are sunk in poverty" (no surprise!) and warned that "growing numbers of the elderly and the lower numbers of workers . . . raised the specter of" an astronomical "Social Security tax of 25% in the next century."[1] (Now that would be a surprise.) In a 1985 article in *Atlantic Monthly,* Phillip Longman, the research director of Americans for Generational Equity (AGE), indicted older generations for spoiling the American Dream by taking too much of everything.[2] In his 1985 book, former Colorado governor Richard Lamm, an AGE board member, asserted that in "the name of compassion for the elderly, we have handcuffed the young, mortgaged their future, and drastically limited their hopes and aspirations."[3] In 1988 Henry Fairlie, then age sixty-four, joined the chorus, writing in the *New Republic* that his cohorts are "Greedy Geezers."[4]

This drumbeat has continued right up to the present day. But there's a big difference: no longer are Baby Boomers the victims of these horrible inequities. Now, receiving or nearing the age of receipt of Social Security benefits, we and today's old are cast as the perpetrators. The only thing that's changed is that we have aged.

These false accusations are apparently timeless. An ongoing narrative designed to put Social Security, Medicare, Medicaid, and other social programs on the "chopping block," it provides convenient but false explanations for the declining fortunes of so many Americans. Never mind stagnant wages, declines in union membership, increased military spending despite the fall of Communism, wasted expenditures of nineteen years of war, slashes to domestic spending, huge tax cuts that benefit the wealthy, and paltry investments in the nation's infrastructure. Ignore the tremendous concentration of wealth, the corrosive effects of campaign contributions, and the inept and morally bereft leadership undermining our democracy. Whatever the problem, it's convenient to focus on the "wasteful and unneeded expenditures" of today's "Greedy Geezers."

Cutting Social Security is indeed, as we discuss in chapter 11, a solution in search of a problem.

Pejorative stereotypes about the old (or any other group) are unacceptable, inaccurate, and undermine civil discourse. Efforts to gain political advantage by stoking division have become all too common, unfortunately. Indeed, an effort to turn Americans against each other has been a staple of those who hate our Social Security system.

The image conveyed by such stereotypes is just plain wrong. Though we can't correct them for all the maligned groups, in this chapter we correct the record with respect to seniors.

We also want to dispatch quickly another fallacious but all too common assertion that most of today's older Americans are on "easy street." As this chapter shows, a very small percentage are; many more are poor or near poor. Some seniors maintain a very modest middle-class lifestyle, often struggling to make ends meet (see figure 4.1). Others, often those employed or retired with significant pension and asset income, may be very comfortable in the moment. But that can change with loss of employment, death of a spouse, costly illness, drops in housing prices, or precipitous declines in stock portfolios. Indeed, over time, the finances of any of us—even those who were well-off at younger ages—can, and often do, change dramatically and for the worse.

This is not to suggest that older Americans, on average, are not doing better today than they were in 1960, when living standards were lower, Social Security benefits were smaller, and Medicare and Medicaid did not exist. Investments in the economy and social programs, along with hard work, have absolutely yielded greater economic security for today's older adults. The poverty rates of persons age sixty-five and older dropped from 35.1 percent in 1959 to 9.7 percent in 2018, according to the official poverty measure. The median income for elderly households—the dollar amount that half of older households are below and half above—rose in 2018 dollars from $24,688 in 1960 to $43,696 in 2018 (in 2018 dollars).[5]

However, contrary to the claims of those who want to cut our Social Security, facts such as these do not mean today's seniors are living high on the hog. Drilling down into these measures shows that only the rare outlier has income that we commonly associate with being rich.

Indeed, as this chapter and the next highlight, retirement insecurity is a growing problem for today's old and, if present trends continue, even more so for generations that follow.

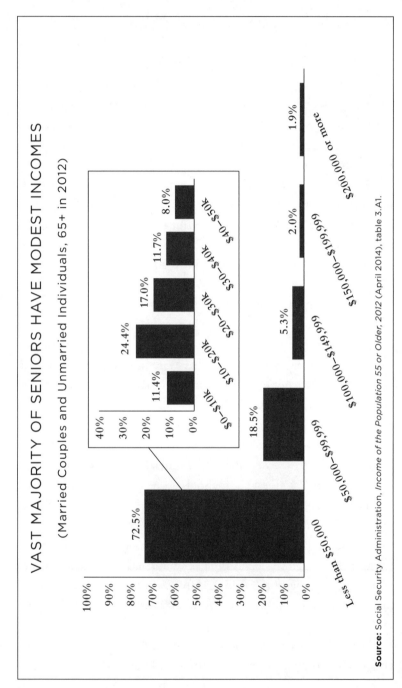

## VAST MAJORITY OF SENIORS HAVE MODEST INCOMES

(Married Couples and Unmarried Individuals, 65+ in 2012)

Less than $50,000 — 72.5%
$50,000–$99,999 — 18.5%
$100,000–$149,999 — 5.3%
$150,000–$199,999 — 2.0%
$200,000 or more — 1.9%

Inset:
$0–$10k — 11.4%
$10–$20k — 24.4%
$20–$30k — 17.0%
$30–$40k — 11.7%
$40–$50k — 8.0%

**Source:** Social Security Administration, *Income of the Population 55 or Older, 2012* (April 2014), table 3.A1.

Figure 4.1

## HOW FARE TODAY'S OLD?

Statistics that describe the economic status of older Americans are important, but not as important as the stories behind the numbers. So, we begin here, and we intersperse throughout the chapter short vignettes that amplify the statistical portraits that follow.

It's important to remember that the best-laid retirement plans can be upended by unexpected health problems and expenses, such as those experienced by Emma and James M. Retiring in 1993 at ages sixty-two and sixty-four, respectively, and in good health, they looked forward to a comfortable retirement.[6] And with good reason. An accountant and a nurse with good work histories, they had accumulated $75,000 in savings and $350,000 in their company-sponsored 401(k) retirement plans; their Columbus, Ohio, home was paid off and their children through college; and they also had Social Security to rely on.

Notwithstanding James's 1997 diagnosis of Parkinson's disease, the first few years were just as anticipated, with travel, civic involvements, friends, and grandparenting. His symptoms were controlled fairly well with medication.

Unfortunately, by 2003, James showed deterioration—slurred speech, memory loss, depression, and difficulty managing personal hygiene. By 2005, taking care of her husband's needs had become too hard for Emma to do alone. She contracted with a home-care agency to provide personal care and chore services three days a week, expanding to seven days, before James entered a nursing home in 2008 as a private pay patient, costing roughly $70,000 a year. Besides James and Emma drawing heavily on their joint resources, the deep recession and drop in housing prices further diminished their resources. When James died in 2013, Emma, then eighty-four, had very little other than her home and Social Security. She worried how she would get by if she needed support one day or if the roof needed to be replaced.

Without warning, hard-earned personal retirement security can be ripped out from under working- and middle-class Americans. Testifying in 2016 before the U.S. Senate Finance Committee on behalf of 270,000 retired Teamsters, spouses, and widows, Rita Lewis tells how the employer pension of her late husband—a decorated Vietnam veteran and semi-tractor trailer driver for forty years—was slashed by 40 percent reducing her husband's pension from roughly $3,350 to $2,000 a month when he was alive, and now her survivor's pension has been cut from $2,000 to $1,500 a month. Faced with less income, she was making plans to sell their home, and she was fearful that she might not be able to provide all the care her father, with stage IV cancer, was likely to need. And plans to help pay for her grandchildren's college were now unrealistic. Not a complainer, she talked about how much harder these cuts are for other retired drivers. Facing a 70 percent cut, from $3,300 to $1,020 a month, Whitlow Wyatt, age seventy-two, and his wife, who had stage IV breast cancer, were drastically downsizing and selling their home. Bob Amsden of Milwaukee, Wisconsin, was told to expect a 55.4 percent benefit reduction, leading him to comment, "The life I spent working for my pension will be for nothing" if these cuts aren't rescinded.[7]

What do all these people and many others have in common? They all worked hard, contributed to family and community, earned a pension, and were looking forward to a comfortable retirement, an expectation dashed due to no fault of their own. Even more dramatic, Neil Friedman's story, as reported in the *Wall Street Journal*, shows that Social Security is important for everyone, even the wealthiest Americans. Ponder how his life changed in an instant.

Neil Friedman, now age eighty-five, saw virtually all of his life savings vanish on the morning of December 11, 2008, when investment adviser Bernie Madoff's Ponzi scheme was revealed. Friedman had invested $4 million with Madoff, including his pension. He never had an inkling that Madoff's investments were fraudulent until the day he learned that the money was gone. He turned to

Social Security to get by, supplemented only by the meager income he earned selling notecards each Sunday at a flea market in Palm City, Florida.[8]

# DEFINING ECONOMIC WELL-BEING IN TERMS OF POVERTY AND NEAR-POVERTY

The economic well-being of older Americans can be measured in a number of ways. One measure involves subsistence: whether or not people have enough income to purchase the bare necessities of life. The Census Bureau's official U.S. poverty index, adjusted annually for inflation, establishes poverty thresholds for households, accounting for such factors as number of people, presence of children, rural/urban location, and age. Counterintuitively, it sets a higher poverty line for adults under age sixty-five than for those over sixty-five—$13,064 for individuals under age sixty-five compared to $12,043 for those over age sixty-five in 2018, $16,815 for couples under age sixty-five, and $15,178 for couples over sixty-five.[9]

Why the difference? The short explanation: the official poverty measure assumes that older people eat less![10]

The incomes of one in ten seniors (9.7 percent), 5.1 million people sixty-five and older, fell below the poverty line in 2018. Another 2.6 million were classified among the "near poor," persons with incomes between 100 percent and 125 percent of the official poverty line. Together, the incomes of one in seven—7.45 million—seniors fell below the near-poor line, 125 percent of poverty. (When you look at Figure 4.2, keep in mind just how low the official poverty line, and even the "near-poor" line, are.)[11]

Responding to criticisms of the official poverty measure, the Census Bureau and the Bureau of Labor Statistics worked with other federal agencies to develop a new, more refined measure,

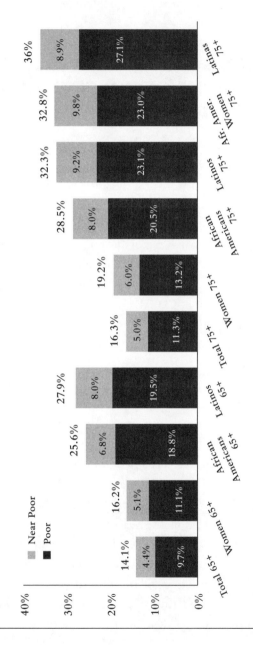

## SENIORS IN POVERTY OR NEAR POVERTY BASED ON OFFICIAL POVERTY MEASURE

(Based on Family Income, 2018)

Legend:
- Near Poor
- Poor

| Category | Total | Near Poor | Poor |
|---|---|---|---|
| Total 65+ | 14.1% | 4.4% | 9.7% |
| Women 65+ | 16.2% | 5.1% | 11.1% |
| African Americans 65+ | 25.6% | 6.8% | 18.8% |
| Latinos 65+ | 27.9% | 8.0% | 19.5% |
| Total 75+ | 16.3% | 5.0% | 11.3% |
| Women 75+ | 19.2% | 6.0% | 13.2% |
| African Americans 75+ | 28.5% | 8.0% | 20.5% |
| Latinos 75+ | 32.3% | 9.2% | 23.1% |
| Afr. Amer. Women 75+ | 32.8% | 9.8% | 23.0% |
| Latinas 75+ | 36% | 8.9% | 27.1% |

**Source:** U.S. Census Bureau, "POV-01. Age and Sex of All People, Family Members and Unrelated Individuals Iterated by Income-to-Poverty Ratio and Race," Current Population Survey (CPS) Annual Social and Economic Supplement, https://www.census.gov/data/tables/time-series/demo/income-poverty/cps-pov/pov-01.html#par_textimage_30 (Accessed 3/2/2020).

Figure 4.2

the Supplemental Poverty Measure (SPM).[12] Unlike the official measure, it counts the value to households of certain in-kind benefits (e.g., food and housing assistance benefits) and nets out selected work-related expenses such as transportation, taxes paid, and child care as well as out-of-pocket medical expenses. It also takes into account geographical differences, as well as home ownership status. Under SPM, poverty rates are higher than under the official poverty measure for most groups, but lower for children and people who are cohabitating. This more refined measure defines 13.6 percent—7.2 million—persons age sixty-five and older as poor.[13]

Even more striking is how many people are at significant economic risk under the Census Bureau's Supplemental Poverty Measure. Defining persons below the SPM as poor and those between 100 percent and 200 percent of this measure as having very modest income, two-fifths (42 percent) of seniors age sixty-five and older—21.4 million seniors—lived in poverty or very modest circumstances in 2017 (Figure 4.3).[14]

The percentage of women in this category of economic vulnerability is even higher. Nearly one out of two—46.5 percent—are poor or economically vulnerable and at risk. For African Americans over age sixty-five, the percentage is higher still—60.3 percent. For Hispanics, the percentage is 65.5 percent.[15]

Another useful measure, the Elder Economic Security Standard Index, evaluates on a county-by-county basis the income seniors need to remain in their homes and meet basic monthly expenses without having to rely on loans, welfare benefits, or gifts from friends or family. The amounts vary by geographical location and for those who own their homes and those who rent. The index suggests that, nationally, one out of two seniors living alone (50 percent) and one out of four couples (23 percent) are unable to pay for basic necessities in 2019.[16]

Despite the stereotype of wealthy seniors, the economic security of even those seniors who do not fall into the various categories of economic vulnerability is far from ensured. Their incomes are

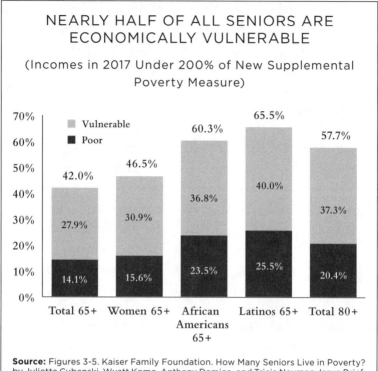

## NEARLY HALF OF ALL SENIORS ARE ECONOMICALLY VULNERABLE

(Incomes in 2017 Under 200% of New Supplemental Poverty Measure)

**Source:** Figures 3-5. Kaiser Family Foundation. How Many Seniors Live in Poverty? by Juliette Cubanski, Wyatt Koma, Anthony Damico, and Tricia Neuman. Issue Brief. November 2018.

Figure 4.3

likely to decline considerably as they advance in age; as they leave work; as inflation bites into their assets; as they draw down savings, which will accelerate if their or a spouse's health declines, if investments falter, or if unexpected financial expenses arise.

## DEFINING ECONOMIC WELL-BEING IN TERMS OF MAINTENANCE OF STANDARD OF LIVING AND WEALTH

Another measure is not whether people can remain out of poverty—quite a low bar—but whether they can maintain their standards of living when wages are lost. Even if not in dire poverty, most people do not want to be forced to alter the way they have been living (e.g., put off necessary repairs or sell their homes). Consequently, financial planners and economists often measure income adequacy of the old based on the idea that the goal of retirement income planning for individuals should be to maintain their standard of living no matter how long they live. They talk about "replacement rates," the percent of preretirement income that needs to be replaced by post-retirement income to maintain one's standard of living—sources such as Social Security, private pensions, and income from assets. Many financial planners and retirement income experts suggest that individuals should aim for between 70 and 85 percent,[17] with higher-income persons having to replace less because they generally, among other things, move into lower tax brackets when they leave work, no longer need to save and, indeed, have savings to draw on, and sometimes have paid off their home mortgages. But, while useful, it is important to keep in mind that replacement rates are a very rough indicator because many factors are at play—for example, how preretirement income is measured, whether households consist of a single individual or married persons, changing financial needs as people age, and the growth in the out-of-pocket costs of health care for retirees.[18]

Social Security, which, as we discuss below, is the main source of income for most seniors, replaces only about 40 percent of average worker's wages if he or she first claims benefits at what Social Security calls the full retirement age (FRA), age sixty-seven for workers born after 1959. The reality, though, is that in 2018 roughly one half—1,640,000 out of 3,082,000—accepted permanently reduced benefits before reaching their full retirement age.[19] One third, 898,000 people, accepted these benefits at age sixty-two, when benefit reductions are largest.[20] Average earning workers who claimed benefits at age sixty-two in 2018, for example, received benefits that replaced only 30.2 percent of their preretirement pay.[21] Moreover, as discussed in chapter 5, these replacement rates have been gradually declining for new generations of retired workers, yet another concern for those reaching old age today, and even more worrisome for future retirees. And many who have accepted reduced benefits over the years had little or no choice due to health and employment circumstances.

In addition to having the means to cover current expenses, it is important to protect against costly contingencies, such as illness, inflation, and longevity. You may not think you will live to age 100 or even older, but consider that, in 2020, an estimated 92,000 Americans are over age 100 and that the Census Bureau estimates there will be 589,000 centenarians in 2060.[22] You may someday be among them!

Another important measure of how older households are faring is wealth. To many it may seem that the old are doing well. The median wealth of older households (including equity in their homes) was $209,300 in 2016.[23] But such reports tell only part of the story. When the value of home equity is excluded, the median wealth is just $64,370—not much of a nest egg.[24]

Older Americans, on average, are doing better today than they were in the past. But, contrary to the claims of those who want to cut our Social Security, the vast majority of today's seniors are not living affluent lives. Indeed, only very few have incomes that we think of as being rich.

## THE IMPORTANCE OF SOCIAL SECURITY

For the large majority of older households, Social Security is the single most important source of income, and its benefits are modest at best.

Among beneficiary households with at least one person age sixty-five or older, almost two thirds receive at least half of their income from Social Security. More than one third receive all, or almost all, from Social Security.[25] That's why, when some politicians call for "little tweaks" in Social Security's level of benefits or argue that they are simply advocating giving a small "haircut" to Social Security benefits, the amounts may sound small to those with higher incomes, but not to those trying to get by primarily on Social Security.

And that is most seniors. One can't overstate the importance of Social Security to their finances. More than 75 percent of the income going to the bottom 60 percent of senior households, those with less than $39,298, came from Social Security in 2014, the last year these data were published by the Social Security Administration. Social Security is also, by far, the most important income source going to the 20 percent of senior households with incomes between $39,298 and $72,129.[26] (See figure 4.4 as an example of how important Social Security is to low income seniors.)

An uptick since the mid-1990s in the labor force participation of seniors, especially those age sixty-five to seventy-five, has increased the importance of earnings, but the benefit of earnings flows mainly to better-off and younger senior households.[27]

It is important to remember, as Emma and James M.'s story exemplifies, that this breakdown is just a snapshot in time, revealing income in a single year. It does not show how the fortunes of the old can change over time—how some start off their older years in very comfortable financial circumstances but later face major difficulties.

Many of those in the top fifth of senior household incomes are still working. They are still receiving a large proportion of their incomes from earnings.[28] Once they leave work, their earnings will disappear, and their incomes are likely to shrink. Over time, many will join the ranks of those senior households with lower annual incomes.

Through good times and bad, Social Security has been, and remains, the most important source of income going to people age sixty-five and over.

As important as Social Security is for virtually all of today's older Americans—and will be in the future—there is still much to be done to achieve the promise of economic security in old age.

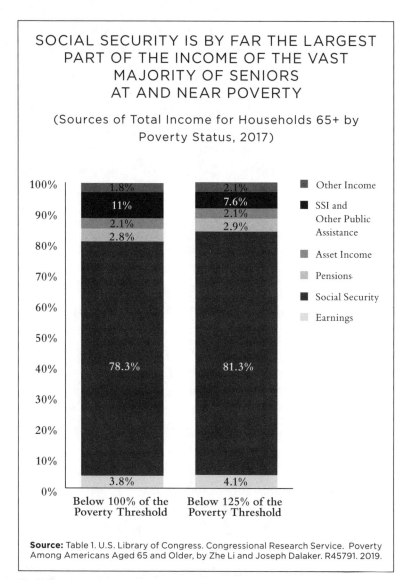

Figure 4.4

Expanding Social Security is important for all of us, but it is especially important for older women, people of color, the LGBTQ+ community, low-wage workers, many early retirees, and the oldest old.

# HEALTH AND LONG-TERM CARE EXPENSES PLACE SENIORS AT RISK

As vital as Social Security is, past policymakers understood that it is necessary, but not sufficient, to insure against loss of earnings in old age. They understood that seniors would remain economically vulnerable as long as they were one serious illness away from bankruptcy. That recognition led to the enactment of Medicare and Medicaid, institutions that have gone a long way in protecting older families.

Medicare has done much to protect the finances of older persons (and persons with severe disabilities) and open up access to hospital-based care, important physician and outpatient services, limited rehabilitation services, and pharmaceutical services.

But Medicare too needs to be expanded. COVID-19 has spotlighted shortcomings throughout our health-care system. Like Social Security, Medicare is a solution. Medicare should be expanded to eliminate out-of-pocket costs and to provide many needed services, including dental, vision, hearing, and most importantly long-term care. Many elders have supplemental Medigap insurance or other forms of insurance that provide some additional protection. Medicaid, in turn, finances hospital and outpatient medical care, long-term care services in nursing homes, and limited long-term care services at home for low-income elders, some who have always had low incomes and others who have expended their resources.

Even so, the economic security of today's elders, even upper-middle-class elders, remains very much at risk because they remain exposed to very significant out-of-pocket health expenses. For example, Medicare beneficiaries—four out of five of whom are sixty-five and over—spent, on average, $5,460 out of pocket in 2016, one third of the average Social Security benefit.[29] Kaiser Family Foundation researchers estimate that median out-of-pocket health-care spending will consume half of individual Social

Security benefits by 2030."[30] Fidelity Investments estimates that a sixty-five-year-old couple retiring in 2019 will, on average, spend $285,000 out of pocket for medical expenses.[31] And this estimate does not include the potential cost of long-term care, which in a nursing home topped $90,000 for a semi-private room and $100,000 for a private room in 2019![32]

Looking at the economy as a whole, the United States spends a huge, unsustainable amount on health care—17.7 percent of gross domestic product (GDP) in 2018 and projected to grow to 19.4 percent in 2027 but with worse health outcomes than other nations that spend far less.[33] Enacting Medicare for All would provide better health care at lower costs. If Medicare for All were structured without premiums, co-pays, or deductibles, as the leading proposals advocate, seniors would be particularly protected. Parenthetically, health-care costs would be lower because profits would be removed and administrative waste caused by numerous private health insurance plans, all with their own details, would be gone. It certainly would make the nation's ability to deal with pandemics much more effective.

## THE RIGHT TO DIGNITY IN OLD AGE

No doubt, today's older Americans are, on average, better off than earlier generations of the old. For a while, as the economy grew, as Social Security, Medicare, and other protections expanded, and as employer-based pension coverage increased it appeared as if a "retirement of leisure" and the further diminution and eventual end of poverty and economic insecurity in old age was on the horizon for the vast majority of Americans. But not so today.

That's why it is time for the nation's leaders to take a sober look at the reality of old age in America and not be seduced by shrill, ignorant claims about so-called greedy geezers. Notwithstanding how critically important Social Security, Medicare, and Medicaid are, seniors remain at risk. And if Social Security is not expanded, tomorrow's seniors are likely to be even more threatened, as we explain in the next chapter.

Such outcomes are unacceptable. No one who has worked hard throughout life and played by the rules should face poverty or fear of financial calamity in old age. That's why it's time to expand Social Security now.

# 5

# THE COMING RETIREMENT INCOME CRISIS

WHILE POLITICIANS AND JOURNALISTS HAVE BEEN DIS-
tracted for years by a faux crisis in Social Security, a very real crisis
has gathered momentum and threatens to undermine the plans and
hopes for a secure retirement of tens of millions of today's workers.

America is facing a looming crisis, writes economist Monique
Morrissey, as generations of workers who mostly participated in do-it-yourself savings plans—or no plan at all—approach
retirement:

> Though a few high-income households have amassed
> small fortunes in tax-favored retirement accounts, such
> as 401(k)s and IRAs, *at least half of working households* are
> expected to see a steep drop in their living standards
> once they retire due to the decline of traditional pen-
> sions, a lack of savings and cuts to Social Security.[1]

The Center for Retirement Research at Boston College (CRR)
has calculated a National Retirement Risk Index for a number of
years. Its most recent analysis found that one out of two working-
age households are at risk of not maintaining their standards of
living in retirement, even if they work until age sixty-five, take
out a reverse mortgage on their homes and annuitize all of their

other assets.[2] CRR found that nearly two thirds of working-age households are at risk when health and long-term care costs are taken into account.[3]

None of this is news to the American people. Numerous polls and surveys over recent years reveal that worry about not having enough money in retirement leads the list of Americans' top financial concerns. A Gallup poll, for example, reported that nearly six out of ten Americans—58 percent—were very or moderately concerned about "Not having enough money in retirement." That topped six other financial challenges, including "Not having enough money to pay for your children's college" and "Not being able to pay your rent, mortgage or other housing costs," and tied with "Not being able to pay medical costs in the event of a serious illness or accident."[4]

Concern about the nation's developing retirement crisis crosses party lines. In a 2019 poll, 80 percent of Democrats, 75 percent of independents, and 75 percent of Republicans agree that the nation is facing a retirement income crisis.[5] As these polls show, too many Americans have already discovered the hard way that the American Dream of maintaining one's standard of living in retirement after a lifetime of work—something that was never a reality for millions of workers—is endangered for nearly all but the wealthiest among us.[6]

Younger workers have even more reason to be concerned. Currently a temporary worker, Karen O'Quinn, age forty-six, explains: "I worked for corporate America for many years and after being laid off, I had to re-create myself. I, like millions of people in this country, have no retirement and no savings for retirement. I do not know how I am going to make it."[7] Small business owner Brian Edwards, age thirty-nine, says, "I have a 401(k), but now that I am self-employed nothing else is getting put into it. It is basically sitting there."[8]

Childbirth educator Alana Rose, age twenty-nine, explains that her "business is not profitable enough to pay all [her] bills and save for retirement." David Muse, a fifty-three-year-old audio technician, warns, "You work until you either fall apart, your health totally crumbles, or you die." And C. William Jones, a retired executive, age seventy-nine, worries that his "kids and grandchildren are really going to have a difficult time, because as of right now, I don't know what kind of pension they can depend upon."[9]

These are but a few examples of Americans caught in the crosshairs of the nation's growing retirement income crisis. As we explain in this chapter, the crisis is most acute for those in their mid-forties, fifties, and early sixties—those nearing retirement age—whose prospects for a secure retirement have been greatly diminished by already-enacted cuts to Social Security, the declining availability of occupational pensions, the inadequacy of 401(k)s and other retirement savings vehicles, and the stagnation of wages.

Depending on how things play out, the crisis is likely to affect those just entering the workforce as much as, or even more than, today's older workers.[10] The younger you are, the more you may be at risk. Many young people are starting their work lives with mountains of student debt. Those who are part of the gig economy and treated, improperly in many cases, as independent contractors, lack the protections accorded wage workers. They have no minimum wage, inadequate as it is. Gig work has been analogized to work life at the start of the last century. Long hours, little to no protection.[11]

## THE RISE AND FALL OF RETIREMENT SECURITY

The fifty years following the enactment of the Social Security Act of 1935 ushered in what some, a bit too effusively, called the golden age of retirement in America. Economic growth, rising wages, improving standards of living, Social Security, Medicare, Medicaid, home ownership, senior housing, congregate meals, Meals on Wheels, other federally funded social services, and employer-sponsored pensions meant that growing numbers of Americans could count on at least a modicum of economic security in old age. Many were free to choose to continue or discontinue work, pursue new interests, recreate, give to family and community, and live with their children or by themselves. Not that aging in America was without problems, particularly for disadvantaged and low-income workers Yet from 1935 until near the end of the century, things appeared to be moving in the right direction.

Although not a reality for everyone, the promise of the 1950s and 1960s was that Social Security would provide a foundation upon which workers could build a secure retirement and then enjoy a period of leisure after a life of hard work.

Unfortunately, fewer and fewer workers today feel confident in that ability. While no one thinks that a return to poorhouses and the mass insecurity in old age that preceded Social Security is around the corner, working-age Americans are increasingly worried about their ability to maintain their standards of living in retirement.

Today's patchwork retirement income system is sometimes described metaphorically as a three-legged stool, with those legs representing Social Security, private pensions, and savings. The system, if it can be called that, is in many ways a historical accident—certainly not a carefully considered, rational policy response to the quest for secure, adequate, universal retirement income for the nation's workers.

Shortly after Social Security was enacted in 1935 and then expanded in 1939, the United States entered World War II. During the war, no further expansions of Social Security were enacted. Moreover, because Congress failed to raise Social Security benefit levels even to keep pace with inflation, Social Security benefits eroded in value substantially during this period. Not only was about half the workforce not covered by Social Security but the benefits became less and less adequate for those who were covered.

At the same time, because of raging inflation, the federal government imposed controls on prices and wages as part of its war effort.

Importantly, deferred wages were exempt from the controls. Private pensions became a convenient vehicle to escape government controls, reap tax benefits, and compete for labor at a time when it was very scarce due to the demands of war. Unions aggressively bargained for private pensions as substitutes for current compensation. Thus, the combination of wage controls, high corporate tax rates, union pressure, high individual income taxes, and the tight labor market propelled employers to create and expand private pension plans.

## WHAT THREE-LEGGED STOOL?

These were the conditions under which the three-legged stool metaphor was born. In 1949, an executive with the Metropolitan Life Insurance Company used the three-legged stool metaphor in a speech, and it caught on.[12] The executive, of course, had a professional stake in selling private sector annuities that supplemented Social Security.

The image was descriptive for the time. Because Social Security benefits had not been increased for a decade and there was no guarantee that Congress would act in the near future, the minimal Social Security benefits would have to be supplemented to have any hope of beneficiaries receiving adequate retirement income.

But the three-legged stool metaphor was never accurate, because the legs were never equal. Even for the half of the workforce fortunate to have employer-provided pensions, Social Security was generally the most important and secure source of retirement income. A more apt picture of the patchwork of retirement income would have been a pyramid, as in figure 5.1.

But recent events and trends render even the more accurate pyramid image irrelevant. Indeed, Peter Brady, an economist with the Investment Company Institute, suggests that, "instead of a stool," most Americans "have a pogo stick: Social Security" with which to negotiate their retirement years. This goes a long way in explaining why working Americans are increasingly fearful.[13] Although Social

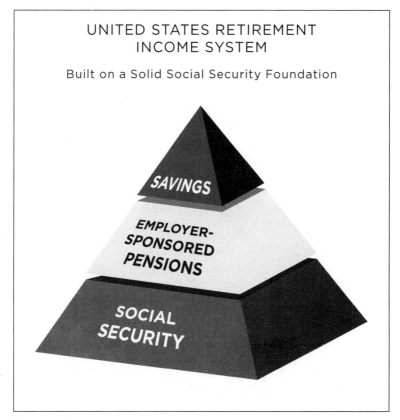

**UNITED STATES RETIREMENT INCOME SYSTEM**

Built on a Solid Social Security Foundation

SAVINGS

EMPLOYER-SPONSORED PENSIONS

SOCIAL SECURITY

Figure 5.1

Security is much more stable than a pogo stick, the three-decade-long, billionaire-funded campaign to undermine confidence in the program, discussed in detail in chapter 11, may make the receipt of benefits feel less secure than it is. Moreover, the benefits by themselves are inadequate and will be less so in the future.

## SOCIAL SECURITY'S BENEFITS HAVE ALREADY BEEN CUT

Not widely recognized, the Social Security foundation is gradually weakening. Social Security benefits have been chipped away and will be roughly 24 percent lower for workers born after 1959.[14]

Here's why.

As discussed in chapter 10, Congress in 1983 passed legislation that included significant reductions in benefits. Very importantly, the 1983 legislation raised Social Security's full retirement age from age sixty-five to sixty-seven, a change that is still being phased in.[15] The 1983 amendments set full retirement age at sixty-six for those born in 1943 through 1954. It is now gradually increasing to age sixty-seven, and will only be fully phased in for those born after 1959. As previously explained, it's sixty-seven for those turning age sixty-two in 2022.

For those not thoroughly immersed in how Social Security benefits are calculated, increasing Social Security's "full" retirement age sounds like just a small, reasonable adjustment for changes in life expectancy. But, as we will see in chapter 11, this is not accurate. Because of the way that Social Security benefits are calculated, raising the full retirement age by one year is mathematically indistinguishable from about a 6.5 percent cut in retirement benefits, whether one retires at age sixty-two, sixty-seven, seventy, or any age in between. Raising the statutorily defined retirement age sounds like it should mean that if you work longer, you will eventually get what you would have gotten. But you will never catch up, because you will always get less than you would have without the change.

The 1983 enactment, which gradually phases in a two-year increase in the full retirement age from age sixty-five to age sixty-seven, has already lowered benefits. When fully phased in, the change will cut the benefits of those born in 1960 or later by around 13 percent. In addition to increasing the full retirement age, the 1983 legislation delayed the annual automatic cost-of-living adjustment by six months, from June to January. Again, it's a bit complicated to understand without knowing the details of benefit calculations, but this delay translates into a 1.4 percent cut for everyone, now and in the future.[16] Finally, decisions made in 1983 and 1993 to treat a growing portion of Social Security benefits as taxable income effectively will have lowered benefits (i.e., net after-tax benefit income) by 9.5 percent in about thirty-five years.

The result of all these cuts together is that Social Security—by far the most important retirement asset that most working Americans have—is now on a trajectory to replace less and less preretirement earnings. But even so, it remains the most widespread, effective, secure, and significant source of retirement income for today's workers and those who will follow. This is why it is so important for Social Security's retirement protections to be expanded, especially because, as the discussion that follows shows, the prospects for relief from other quarters are slim to none.

## TRADITIONAL PRIVATE-SECTOR PENSIONS ARE DISAPPEARING

Traditional private-sector pensions, also called defined benefit plans, have been disappearing at a rapid rate. Structured to pay employees a pension that generally reflects the number of years worked and average earnings, defined benefit plans stand in contrast to defined contribution plans, to which workers, and sometimes employers, make regular, specified (i.e., defined) contributions to a retirement savings plan—but without any guarantee regarding the amount of savings or the monthly benefits that can be derived from those savings, if annuitized. The advantage of defined benefit plans for employees is that their employer generally funds it (or most of it) and bears the financial risk of investments and other funding decisions. While employees still carry some risk (e.g., company bankruptcy, unscrupulous raiding of plans, loss of coverage when transferring jobs), anticipated pension income is far more predictable and does not fluctuate with stock market returns.

Even at their height, employer-sponsored defined benefit plans had serious shortcomings. They never covered more than about half the workforce. They have never been portable—that is, able to be carried from job to job. That presents a number of significant disadvantages. Primary among them is their inadequacy for mobile workers, who might be entitled to benefits based only on the low pay earned at the start of their careers. In addition, private sector defined pension plans, which promise annuities not payable for decades, are inherently insecure. The plan may have insufficient funds when the time for payment arrives, and the employer sponsoring the plan may no longer be around. (While job mobility has declined over the last few decades and, not surprisingly, is highest among younger workers,[17] nevertheless, millions of workers start and leave their employment every month. In May 2020, for example, 6.5 million workers were hired and 4.1 million left their employment; in December 2019, those numbers were 5.7 million and 5.4 million, respectively.)[18]

The Employee Retirement Income Security Act of 1974 (ERISA) sought to improve the security of private sector defined benefit plans by mandating that they be funded in advance and meet minimum standards, including that they be insured by the Pension Benefit Guaranty Corporation. As regulation of traditional private pensions increased, as accounting rules changed regarding how pension liabilities are to be reported, and as unions and manufacturing declined, employers have increasingly terminated, frozen, or closed their plans to new employees. Today, those plans are nearing extinction in the private sector. Where in 1979, nearly four out of ten private sector workers participated in these plans, in 2018, just one out of six do so (17 percent).[19]

## PUBLIC PENSIONS ARE UNDER ATTACK

The large majority of state and local government employees—83 percent in 2018—and nearly all federal workers still participate in defined benefit plans, but their pensions are under sustained, ideological attack.[20] If successful, this attack will have caused a destructive race to the bottom.

Utilizing a divide-and-conquer strategy, those seeking to dismantle public employee unions and benefits play workers against each other by seeking to turn some workers, labeled "taxpayers," against other workers, labeled "public employees," though, of course, public employees are taxpayers, too.

While some state and local pensions need to be financially buttressed, the attack on public employee defined benefit plans is fueled and driven by ideology and anti-union animus. An Economic Policy Institute report reveals that the "champions of anti-union legislation often portrayed themselves as the defenders of non-union workers—whom they characterized as hardworking private-sector taxpayers being forced to pick up the tab for public employees' lavish pay and pensions."[21] Why should public employees receive "plush pension benefits," they argue, when so many taxpayers do not? Never mind that these benefits were negotiated and earned, that many have forgone more lucrative private sector jobs for public service, and that some are in harm's way every day. Never mind that many state and local budget deficits have been driven in large part by imprudent tax cuts. Instead of dealing with the real budgetary challenges, it is easier for politicians to scapegoat public employees—the first responders, teachers, sanitation and public health workers, community and state college employees, prison personnel, social and mental health service providers, and other civil servants.

## 401(K) RETIREMENT SAVINGS PLANS AND OTHER SAVINGS CANNOT DO THE JOB

Social Security benefits are being cut by about one-quarter, public pensions are under attack, and private employer–provided traditional pension plans are disappearing. When replaced at all, employers are generally substituting tax-favored 401(k) or similar retirement savings vehicles.

Consider too that unlike defined benefit pensions, 401(k) and related retirement plans are savings accounts and not insurance. Consequently, employees bear the risk of sometimes volatile declines in the value of their savings, before and during retirement. Financial management fees and poor investment decisions can undermine growth of these assets. Employers often do not contribute to them at all. And, unlike defined benefit plans and Social Security, individuals can tap these savings, often without penalty, to fund educational, home-buying, and health-care expenses—all potentially good uses of household wealth but detrimental to accumulating meaningful retirement savings. They are portable from job to job, good for mobile workers, but are no substitute for Social Security.

As discussed in more detail in chapter 9, this system works very well for the super-rich. For example, during his run for the presidency in 2012, Mitt Romney disclosed that his individual retirement account (IRA), a 401(k)-type vehicle for those who do not have employer plans, had an account balance of between $20.7 million and $101.6 million.[22] In 2015, the combined retirement savings of the top 100 CEO totaled $4.7 billion, equivalent to that of 116 million Americans. The assets of these CEOs were sufficient "to provide them with $250,000 per month for the rest of their lives[!]"[23]

Contrast this with the reality that in 2018 more than 100 million persons—59.3 percent of persons of working age—did not have any retirement account assets, e.g., Individual Retirement Arrangements (IRAs) or employer-based 401(k)s or 403(b)s.[24] Among those who do, the median value of their savings is just $40,000. Even for persons on the cusp of their retirement years, those aged fifty-five to sixty-four, the median account balance is just $88,000, well below what most workers would need to maintain their standards of living in retirement.[25]

The retirement prospects of working Americans are further diminished by rising student debt; loans taken by parents to help their children through college; continuing high levels of unemployment; little wage growth, except at the top; and credit card debt. Moreover, growing wealth and income inequality, combined with the near-collapse of the economy in 2007 to 2009 triggered by the sub prime mortgage crisis and again in 2020, this time precipitated by the COVID-19 pandemic, also feed into the retirement income crisis. Making matters much worse, current out-of-pocket expenditures for medical and long-term care costs pose major risks for all but the richest retirees, now and in the future, as discussed in chapter 4.

## HARDWORKING AMERICANS OF ALL AGES AT RISK

By virtually all measures, the harsh reality is that the majority of today's workforce—probably the large majority—are heading toward increasingly difficult and, in some cases, financially disastrous retirements.

The National Retirement Risk Index (NRRI), developed by the Center for Retirement Research at Boston College, reveals a large rise in the proportion of households with workers under age sixty-five on the road to a financially insecure retirement. In 1983, 31 percent were assessed as being at risk of not being able to maintain their standard of living in old age, rising to 44 percent in 2007 and 53 percent in 2010, with modest improvement to 50 percent in 2016 (see figure 5.2).[26] The NRRI's estimate takes into account the various changes in the U.S. pension and Social Security systems, assumes that everyone works until age sixty-five, and assumes that housing and other wealth are annuitized.

The outlook is even more dismal when anticipated health and long-term care expenditures are counted. The Center for Retirement Research estimated that in 2006 and 2007, just before the Great Recession, 44 percent of working-age households would be at risk of downward social mobility in retirement. But here's the

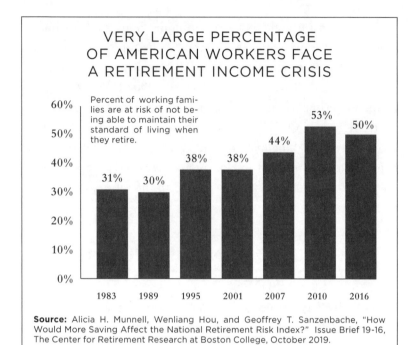

VERY LARGE PERCENTAGE
OF AMERICAN WORKERS FACE
A RETIREMENT INCOME CRISIS

**Source:** Alicia H. Munnell, Wenliang Hou, and Geoffrey T. Sanzenbache, "How Would More Saving Affect the National Retirement Risk Index?" Issue Brief 19-16, The Center for Retirement Research at Boston College, October 2019.

Figure 5.2

scariest part: this percentage rose to 61 percent when health-care costs were included.[27] And to 64 percent when long-term care costs were counted—an additional 21 percentage points.[28] The aggregate risks were estimated to be somewhat greater for Gen Xers than Baby Boomers. Still more frightening, consider that the CRR's post-recession at-risk estimate jumped up from 44 percent in 2006 and 2007 to 50 percent in 2016.[29] If health and long-term care expenses are counted, likely seven out of ten working households today would be at risk.[30] And this analysis is based on conservative assumptions that everyone will work until at least age sixty-five and takes out reverse mortgages on their homes!

Other analyses tell roughly the same story. The Employee Benefit Research Institute (EBRI) produces a Retirement Readiness Rating that measures whether households will have enough resources to pay for "basic" retirement expenses—defined as "aggregate minimum retirement expenditures" and out-of-pocket health and long-term care costs. Using this more restrictive definition, EBRI estimates in 2019 that 40.6 percent of "households where the head of the household is between 35 and 64, inclusive, are projected to run short of money in retirement."[31]

While virtually every demographic group is at risk, some are more so—including African Americans, Latinos, Native Americans, single women, people with disabilities or in poor health, the unemployed, those in the LGBTQ+ community, and low-wage workers.

With Social Security retirement benefits declining and with retirement savings schemes falling short for the vast majority of Americans, some are suggesting that working longer, much longer, is the solution to the retirement income crisis.

While there's nothing wrong with working to seventy, eighty, ninety, or even one hundred if you want to and are able, beware of political, corporate, and opinion leaders—even academics—who are selling "brave new world" visions of longer work lives and retirement age benefit cuts as a solution to the retirement crisis. Often unwilling to step outside their privileged social and economic position, they are blissfully unaware, or just do not care, that their "solution" would do great harm to many of those whose life experiences are very different from theirs. They may live in the same city as Joanne Femino Jacobsen, age sixty-three, but they either do not see her or do not care how different her story is from theirs.

I have worked in some form or fashion since I was 15. I saved money, supported my sons, and planned for my retirement. Yet when I reached what should have been my retirement age, the promise that I would receive health and pension benefits for the rest of my life was broken, and so were my hopes of retiring comfortably in Florida. Like many Baby Boomers battered by the

Recession, I am still in the work force and will probably remain on the job for the foreseeable future. The older people like me you see working at places like WalMart and Home Depot—a lot of us are not doing this because we're bored with retirement; we're doing it to survive.[32]

Even with the uptick in work among today's older workers, as noted in chapter 3, the majority claim permanently reduced Social Security benefits before reaching the full retirement age.[33] The problem here is that many people accepting permanently reduced Social Security benefits in their early sixties do so because they have little or no alternative. An estimated 20 to 30 percent of workers in their sixties have work-limiting health conditions.[34] Consistent with this estimate, an Urban Institute researcher found that among employed persons ages fifty-one to fifty-five who said they did not experience work-limiting health conditions in 1992, 35 percent "developed an impairment or health problem by age 65 that limited the type or amount of work they could do."[35] Further, 45 percent of today's older workers ages sixty-two to sixty-nine experience physically demanding or otherwise difficult work conditions,[36] one in four twenty-year-olds will likely be disabled before age sixty-seven,[37] and one in five older Americans provides care to a family member that often compromises their ability to work.[38]

And this says nothing about employment discrimination, which though illegal still occurs. Older workers generally spend longer periods unemployed, and those who find new jobs often experience significant cuts in salary.[39] Appleton, Wisconsin, resident Tonya Adams's story illustrates problems older job seekers run into.[40] She lost her job in 2009 at age sixty-two. She told the *Wall Street Journal* that with experience as a freelance art director for advertising agencies and as a sales associate, "I never would have dreamed that I could not find a job, that I was unemployable." Unfortunately, like millions of other Americans—particularly older job seekers who can be the victims of age discrimination—she was still without work three years later. As a result, Adams was forced to claim Social Security benefits early, resulting in smaller Social Security checks for the rest of her life. The $1,280 provided by Social Security is not enough for Adams to cover all of her bills. To help bridge the gap, she utilizes food stamps and help from her elderly parents.

Not everyone can work into their sixties; not everyone wants to work into their seventies. Moreover, scheduled increases in the full retirement age to sixty-seven will harm many, and additional increases would harm even more, especially those with health problems or who have worked for low and modest wages. And many working Americans of all income classes look forward to—and by the time they are in their sixties will have earned—the right to more choice in how they use their time: to give care, work longer, study, be with grandchildren, give back to their family and communities, or to just plain play.

Providing greater opportunity for Americans to work longer is desirable, as long as the possibility of such work is not used to justify cuts in Social Security's modest benefits, and not used to impose difficult and unfair expectations on older workers. Enforcement of age discrimination laws, flexible retirement, part-time work, retraining opportunities, second and third careers, small-business entrepreneurship, community service, and the like all have a place in our aging society. But the broad experiences of the American people need to be respected. While working longer may be a viable option for some, it is not for all. And even if many Americans worked longer, the crisis would not disappear. Expanding Social Security remains the single most effective, and the only widespread, solution to the retirement income crisis. And it addresses other serious problems, as the next two chapters explain.

# 6

## THE DEBT OWED
## TO THOSE WHO CARE

*"We can view the Elder Boom as an opportunity to respond from the basis of something that all of us across the political spectrum hold dear: our right to live with dignity, independence, and self-determination. From that place, we can work together to reorganize society so that in all phases of life we can count on love, connection, and care. What could feel like the beginning of an epic national crisis in care can in fact be one of our greatest opportunities for positive, transformative change at every level."*

Ai-jen Poo, author of *The Age of Dignity*[1]

Care—*normal* and *extraordinary*—given by family and friends is the stuff of everyday life in America. It's what well-functioning, and even not-so-well-functioning, families do best. In its absence, children fail to thrive, community bonds fray, and generations—within families and society—cannot progress.

Imagine that you have just given birth to your first child. Most likely everything went well. But there is no guarantee. Your child, for example, could be among the one in five (18.8 percent)—nearly 14 million in 2017—children and youth under age eighteen with special health-care needs.[2] A severely disabling accident or illness could strike. No matter what, you'll do what you must because you could not do otherwise. You are just made that way. But the time, angst, and financial costs will be great, possibly so much so that there is little left over for other life activities.

Another thought experiment. Your children are grown and doing well, but your mother, your father, your spouse, partner, or maybe a sibling just had a stroke and lost the ability to function without expensive in-home help. Again, as the estimated 40 million adults—16.6 percent—who provided unpaid care to adults in 2015 did, you'll do what you must, perhaps providing demanding personal care for many years.[3]

Across the political and cultural spectrum, politicians and other opinion leaders talk about the importance of the family, often praising those who give freely of themselves to care for others; those providing normal, everyday care to children; and those providing extraordinary unpaid care to family and friends with serious illnesses or disabilities. But even before COVID-19 turned up the pressure, public deeds generally fell short of words. There are few supports that help share the burdens—emotional, physical, and financial—carried by family and friends giving care, more often than not women. As a result:

- Too many parents of young children have no choice but to juggle work in the home, paid employment, child care, children's schedules, and the rest of life
- Parents caring for children with serious disabilities are often overwhelmed providing special physical care, supporting their child, accessing special services, and caring for their other children.
- Older parents who have cared many years for their now-adult developmentally disabled children often fear what will happen to their children once they themselves have died.
- The incomes of persons providing significant, ongoing care to functionally disabled or very ill family and friends are far lower than they should be.

- The health of very old caregivers is put at risk because of the absence of respite and other supports.
- And the pay and respect given to care workers—persons employed by functionally disabled persons, families, home-care agencies, group homes, nursing homes, and behavioral health organizations—rarely match their responsibilities and personal investment.

## THE NATION RELIES ON FAMILY CAREGIVERS

Family and friends regularly provide both normal and extraordinary care. Normal care is generally what is given to and what supports children every day as they grow into adulthood—time, meals, love, discipline, child care when parents need to work, and the like. It is also what is given to family members who are temporarily ill, to grandchildren needing a little supervision when a parent cannot be home, to adult children as they struggle with life choices, and to older relatives needing a little company. With the Census Bureau estimating 73.4 million children (22.4 percent of the U.S. population) under age eighteen in 2018, it is not surprising that the vast majority of normal care flows from parents and other adults downward to children.[4]

Estimates of how many people give extraordinary care vary, but the number is large. The Pew Research Center reports that 36 percent of all adults provide unpaid care to an adult needing assistance with normal activities of life. Eight percent provide care to children with significant health problems or disabilities.[5] A 2015 study by the National Alliance for Caregiving in collaboration with AARP estimates that 43.5 million people provided unpaid care to functionally disabled children or adults in the course of 2015.[6] Roughly 1 in 4 of these people "provide care for 41 hours or more each week (23 percent) and 3 in 10 provide between 9 and 40 hours of care (31 percent)."[7]

Families, as a *Washington Post* article[8] highlights, are the heart and soul of the long-term services and support system (LTSS), with millions of caregivers echoing the type of sentiment expressed by Barbara Tucker Parker. She and her husband opened their home to care for her eighty-seven-year-old mother, Dorothy Tucker, whose dementia, brought on by a stroke, made independent living impossible. While her mother could still put on her own clothes when Barbara set them out, she had lost the ability to read, to converse, to remember. What's been lost is "horrifyingly sad," Barbara told the reporter, and the constant care requirements are stressful, but there's nothing else that she could do. Besides, as she said, "It's work, but there's also a lot of fun." "[I]t's my job . . . she's my mother." "Who's going to take care of her better than me? Nobody."[9]

Parents and other family members participate in the care of our nation's wounded warriors, such as Sergeant Cory Remsburg, who received a long standing ovation when President Obama recognized him during the 2014 State of the Union address. Suffering devastating injuries from a 2009 roadside bomb in Afghanistan, slowly, and with numerous surgeries, resilience, and the continuing help of his parents, he fought back, regaining speech and ability to walk. His parents commuted for two years to be with him at a veterans' hospital in Tampa, his mother eventually leaving employment to help with his ongoing physical therapy. Still needing 24/7 assistance, he moved to his family home in 2013 and then moved nearby to a specially equipped house with full-time support.[10]

Some estimates drill down to more specific types of extraordinary care. The Alzheimer's Association estimates that "16.2 million family and other unpaid caregivers provided an estimated 18.5 billion hours of care to people with Alzheimer's and other dementias."[11] A U.S. Department of Health and Human Services report identifies nearly one in four U.S. households (23 percent) as caring for one or more children with special needs; that's 11.2 million children, some of whom (27.1 percent) are greatly limited in their activities, while others (34.4 percent), despite having one or more special needs, can do everything other children do.[12] Many young and middle-aged parents invest countless hours and other resources as they care for, advocate for, and love their children with special needs. They are often the backbone of their children's care team, as highlighted by the following story, written by a mother named Keisha whose son, Ibrahim, was diagnosed with autism at age two and a half.

> My heart sunk. . . . I became a little depressed and unsure of myself as a mother, many questions raced through my head: what will become of him, what kind of life [will he] have, how will people treat him, etc.? My husband and I [discussed]. . . . how we could best help Ibrahim throughout his journey. I started looking for information about autism on the Internet since his doctor and daycare had no real information to share. . . . I had to find the strength to advocate for him to ensure his access to the resources he needs. As . . . I help my son along this journey, I hope to help others by raising awareness in my community while steering parents away from cultural biases and the stigma associated with having a special needs child.[13]

We often think of extraordinary care as flowing, as in the story of Keisha and Ibrahim, from parents to their young children, but sometimes it's the other way around. For example, the National Alliance for Caregiving reports that 1.3 to 1.4 million children, ages eight to eighteen, take on significant caregiving responsibilities, often providing assistance with daily activities for functionally disabled grandparents, parents, siblings, and others.[14]

Similarly, grandparents and other relatives often step in to care for young children when parents are not able. Nearly 7.9 million children under age eighteen live in "grandfamilies," households headed by a grandparent or other relatives, sometimes with a parent present. One third, 2.65 million children, are being reared without a parent present.[15] There are grandparents like Melanie, age sixty, who is rearing four grandchildren, ages nine, ten, eleven, and fourteen, the oldest of whom has Asperger's. Their resources are very limited, but the family gets by. She reports:

> I am raising these kids on state assistance, food stamps and death benefits from the 14-yr-old's father. There is absolutely nothing extra to do anything for the kids except things that are free. . . . My health (arthritis & fibromyalgia) has definitely been affected . . . Mom comes to visit every two weeks, so it's like having 5 kids when she comes. She had been head injured in a car accident when she was young, so is cognitively and emotionally impaired. . . . [I]t is really hard at this age to be taking on the responsibility of these 4 kids, but I love them to pieces and wouldn't trade the experience for anything.[16]

The large majority of people needing long-term services and support live in the community, usually in their own or a family member's home. A small proportion live in residential communities that provide a range of supportive services. Others are in institutions such as nursing homes. A patchwork of informal and formal supports and services—private and public—provide assistance in people's homes. These include chore and personal care services (e.g., bathing), homemaker, home health, visiting nurse, and other medical and social services. But as the stories related above illustrate, families are the backbone of this system, providing everything from financial management to very personal care, from household chores to monitoring medications, from caring for their loved ones in their homes to supporting them in assisted living, nursing homes, and other residential settings.

# A FINANCIALLY VALUABLE NATIONAL RESOURCE

Taken together, informal care and support, normal and extraordinary, represent a huge contribution to the economy and society, not to mention to the well-being of many people.

The future of our economy and communities depends on how well we rear, invest, and educate our children, the next generation of workers, parents, and taxpayers. More than any other institution, the family is responsible for these critical tasks. The federal government estimates that the typical middle-class family will spend $233,610 in 2015 dollars rearing a child born in 2015 to age eighteen, about $254,000 in 2020 dollars.[17] Of course, many continue to provide much financial support to their young adult children—for education, housing, and the like.

Arguably far more valuable for children is parents' investment of time. Ironically, as MacArthur Fellow Nancy Folbre notes, the nation's most significant domestic investment—the care and time given to children—goes uncounted in the most important measure of productive output in the course of a year, the gross domestic product.[18] That time simply is not factored in. If it were, our GDP would be much larger. For example, the U.S. Department of Commerce's Bureau of Economic Analysis estimated unpaid work at home to be $4.5 trillion in 2017.[19]

Caregivers are demonstrably the most valuable economic component of the nation's long-term services and support system (LTSS), serving 12 million people who needed such services in 2013, 5 million of them under age sixty-five.[20] AARP's Public Policy Institute estimates that the economic value of informal care to all adults, ages eighteen and older, was $470 billion in 2017.[21] Focusing exclusively on elders needing long-term and community services and supports, the Congressional Budget Office estimates that the economic value of informal unpaid care of family and friends amounted to $234 billion in 2011, considerably more than the $192 billion cost of community services and residential (e.g., nursing home) care.[22] In turn, the Alzheimer's Association estimates the value of 18.5 billion hours of unpaid caregiving to 5.8 million persons with Alzheimer's and other dementias at nearly $234 billion in 2018.[23] And by keeping children out of foster care, "households headed by grandparents or other relatives . . . [save] U.S. taxpayers more than $4 billion dollars each year."[24]

Individuals and cohorts are often positioned at one point in their development to primarily receive care, but over the course of their lives they are expected to, and nearly always do, provide care to others. There's an ebb and flow of resources to individuals and cohorts over time. Viewed over time, the young child being cared for now often becomes the adult child who cares for a functionally disabled parent. The strong and the healthy who are giving care may later become the people who need care. Human society requires this reciprocity and interdependence, and shifting flows of giving and receiving.[25]

In terms of normal caregiving, there's been considerable convergence over the past fifty years in involvement of fathers and mothers—married and unmarried—in normal child-rearing and housework activities. But, no surprise, women generally still do the lioness's share. Including hours spent on unpaid work (housework and child care) and paid work (jobs), mothers with children in their homes devoted 83 percent of their time to unpaid work in the home in 1965 compared to 59 percent in 2011. Fathers devoted 14 percent of their time to unpaid work in the home in 1965 compared to 31 percent of their time in 2011.[26]

Based on findings from their 2020 survey, the National Alliance for Caregiving and AARP estimate that nearly one in five adults, 53 million people, provided unpaid care to functionally disabled children and adults in the previous twelve months. Caregiving "occurs among all generations, racial/ethnic groups, income or educational levels, family types, gender identities, and sexual orientations."[27]

A few more statistics about those providing care: Six in ten have been employed outside the home at some point during the previous twelve months, more than half full time.[28] On average, they spend about twenty-four hours a week giving care and have been doing so for four years.[29] Almost half of those caring for functionally disabled relatives perform medical tasks, including wound care and administering medications.[30] Low-income families of children with special health-care needs experience the greatest time demands, with 20 percent of poor families spending eleven hours or more each week providing care to their child compared to 6 percent of the families with incomes in excess of 400 percent of poverty.[31]

The home is the primary setting for long-term services and supports to adults. A 2017 survey based on a representative sample of persons forty and over drives this point home. Three out of four (76 percent) persons who reported that they receive care indicated that their care was provided in their own homes. The majority (56 percent) of those reporting that they give care do so "outside their own homes."[32]

## THE COSTS OF CARING

As the saying goes, "No good deed goes unpunished." Unpaid caregiving is no exception.

The provision of unpaid informal care—normal and extraordinary—is costly to caregivers. There are the obvious financial costs: housing, health care, education, and recreation. Emotional costs may arise from having to be available 24/7, from tensions within the family, and sometimes from constant worry. There are opportunity costs. "Time devoted to the care of children," economist Nancy Folbre reminds us, "must be withdrawn from other activities, such as housework, paid work, sleep, and leisure."[33] The same applies for those giving informal care to family and friends with significant functional disabilities. Such opportunity costs, generally far less visible, are borne disproportionately by women—even as the benefits of their unremunerated labor protect families and potentially substitute for what might otherwise be costly public expenditures.

There are also significant personal and emotional costs. For example, one AARP study suggests that 40 to 70 percent of those giving care to older adults exhibit symptoms of depression, a fourth to half showing signs of major depression.[34] Another study finds 17 percent of caregivers believe their health was worsened by caregiving.[35]

Because more than half (58 percent) of all unpaid caregivers are employed, they, women especially, have had to become masters at balancing their work, caregiving, and other family roles. It is no surprise, then, that seven out of ten caregivers (69 percent) report adjusting their work—reducing hours, taking time off, starting early or leaving late, or stopping work altogether.[36]

Giving care has its rewards, but financial security is not one of them, for women or men. A MetLife study based on a sample representative of 10 million daughters and sons over age fifty caring for parents in 2008 presents stunning information about the aggregate loss in wage and retirement benefits.

> Total wage, Social Security, and private pension losses due to caregiving could range from $283,716 for men to $324,044 for women, or $303,880 on average for a typical caregiver. When this $303,880 amount is multiplied by the 9.7 million people age 50+ caring for their parents, the amount lost is $2,947,636,000,000, or nearly $3 trillion. [37]

For many, caregiving can be thought of as a lifelong career. Women especially often provide multiple sequences of care, beginning with their young children, then aging parents, perhaps followed by grandchildren and a very old functionally disabled spouse, sibling, or friend. Although participating in the labor force at very high numbers, women are more likely than men to reduce or leave work at various points in the course of their lives caring for others.

Social Security benefits are based on a formula that essentially averages earnings over a worker's life. Because women generally have lower wages and are also more likely than men to adjust their work lives to the demands of children, home, and older relatives needing care, they tend to have more years of very low or no earnings, greatly reducing their potential Social Security benefits. (It is important to note that Social Security provides spousal benefits that compensate some unpaid family caregivers who are married or divorced after ten years of marriage.)

Other financial burdens further diminish the security of caregivers and bolster the case for policies that ameliorate losses to unpaid caregivers. In estimating the loss in reduced earnings accruing to unpaid caregivers of elderly persons, one study estimates cumulative losses of $67 billion in 2013, averaging $5,250 for each caregiver. Moreover, accounting for population changes, the opportunity costs will likely increase to $132–$147 billion by 2050.[38] Out-of-pocket expenditures also erode financial security. A 2016 AARP national study estimates that "caregivers spent, on average, nearly $7,000 on caregiving expenses that included home modifications, paid care at home, and transportation."[39]

Adding to the pressures on families and caregivers, the United States provides very limited support for those needing to leave work to care for newly born or newly adopted children, for those leaving to care for children or adults needing extended support due to illness or functional disability, and for those needing time off to recover from their own health problems. The Family and Medical Leave Act of 1993 was a step in the right direction. It mandates that employers with fifty or more employees, as well as some smaller employers, provide up to twelve weeks of unpaid leave for eligible workers. Some employers, eight states, and the District of Columbia—California, Connecticut, District of Columbia, New Jersey, New York, Massachusetts, Oregon, Rhode Island, and Washington—either provide direct financial support or mandate employers to do so for persons needing such leave.[40]

Even with those important developments, we have utterly failed as a nation to adequately recognize and respond to the costs—financial and personal—incurred by those who care. Unlike almost every other industrial democracy, the United States federal government does not provide any protections against loss of income for those who must take leave. Among the thirty-four industrial democracies making up the Organisation for Economic Co-operation and Development (OECD), paid maternity leave averages about eighteen weeks; our federal government stands alone, providing none.[41] Responding to the value of family leave, both to the economy and to society, we advocate in chapter 8 for expanding Social Security to provide insurance against wages lost by such leave, and we also propose a benefit at the birth or adoption of a child.

The United States also lags with respect to the public support for long-term care (LTC) health and social services for persons needing support for their activities of daily living over an extended period of time. Social insurance and other public LTC expenditures range from 3.7 percent of GDP in the Netherlands to 0.2 percent in Estonia and Hungary, averaging about 1.7 percent. The United States public LTC expenditure represents just 0.5 percent of GDP.[42] Similarly, out of thirty-seven OECD nations, the United States invests less, just 0.4 percent of GDP, in early childhood education and care than all but two, Iceland and Turkey.[43]

It is well past time to join the rest of the industrialized world and support caregivers in the way that their invaluable work deserves. No matter how reciprocal or heartfelt, providing unpaid care to a family member is often exceptionally taxing. Currently, public policies provide limited support for child care. Public long-term support and services are fragmented and often very limited—some funded by Medicaid, others through other government and private providers.

Politicians sometimes express concern that there is danger in doing too much for caregivers; that caregivers may take advantage of supportive public policy to shift more of the burden of care to the public sector. However, the larger risk is that far too little is being done to support the caregiving of family and friends.

## THE INFORMAL CARE CRISIS IS HERE AND GROWING

It's no secret that the number of Americans age sixty-five and older is projected to increase, from roughly 56 million in 2020 to 81 million in 2040, and to 95 million in 2060, when the youngest Baby Boomers will be ninety-six years old. As a percent of the total population, persons ages sixty-five and older will increase rapidly from 17 percent in 2020 to 22 percent in 2040, and then level off at 23 percent in 2060.[44] Less well known, the fastest growing age group is the very old, the one most at risk of needing informal and formal long-term support and services. Persons age eighty-five and older are projected to increase from roughly 7 million in 2020 to 14 million in 2040, and to 19 million by 2060, including 600,000 centenarians.[45]

The pool of potential informal caregivers is shrinking, largely because of the drop-off in birth rates following the large numbers of Baby Boomers born from 1946 through 1964. Assuming for the moment that people aged forty-five to sixty-four are the only people in the pool of potential caregivers for people eighty and over, AARP reports that where there were seven potential caregivers in 2010 for each person over age eighty, this ratio will drop to four to one in 2030 and to less than three to one in 2050.[46] Of course, there are many caregivers of all ages, and in today's world, persons in their late sixties and seventies often find themselves caring for parents and others. And there are many other aspects of life in the twenty-first century that constrain the potential size of the caregiver pool—for example, employment pressures and geographic mobility. Without question, the availability of informal caregivers will almost certainly shrink relative to growing demand.

## AND THERE'S A GROWING DIRECT CARE WORKER CRISIS

The nation also faces a growing crisis in the direct care workforce—the home-care, home health, personal care, and nurses' aides who provide long-term services and supports in people's homes, group homes, nursing homes, and other settings. Their work provides critical support for the health, dignity, and optimal independence of persons with significant disabilities and illnesses. Nine in ten formal care providers are women. Nearly six in ten are people of color. One in four are immigrants.[47]

The wages and incomes of direct care workers are low. In 2016, America's 2.1 million home-care workers earned a median wage of $11.03 an hour and a median annual income of $15,100. That same year, 600,000 nursing assistants in nursing homes received a median wage of $12.84 an hour and a median annual income of $21,200.[48]

Such low earnings pale in comparison to direct care workers' responsibilities. Some of their services—such as assisting with dressing, feeding, and bathing—must be performed properly to avoid injury or even death to care recipients (e.g., falls and choking). Depending on training, these essential caregivers may also help with clinical tasks such as administering medications and taking blood pressures that, if done incorrectly, can cause serious adverse outcomes for those in their care. Even tasks of less immediate consequence, however, are very important, such as accompanying people to medical appointments, housekeeping, running errands, and driving them to meet friends.[49]

Research demonstrates that in the face of occupational

challenges—which include difficult working conditions, social stigma, limited opportunity for advancement, poor treatment by management, and heavy physical and emotional demands—direct care workers often attach deep meaning to their jobs. For example, one study of certified nursing assistants (CNAs) in nursing homes found that:

> CNAs articulated the meaning of their work as representing "good work" or "God's work," in developing "closeness to residents," and in "caring for those who cannot care for themselves" . . . CNAs' assertions of the value of themselves and their work helped CNAs to reconstitute their identities in the face of negative and demeaning interactions and messages. At the same time, these assertions of meaning, which depended upon providing good care to residents regardless of financial reward or management respect and support, made CNAs, like caregivers in other sectors, vulnerable to exploitation.[50]

Attaching deep meaning to their work is often insufficient to overcome direct care workers' low pay, adverse work conditions, and social stigma. The result is high turnover rates and worker shortages—problems that will only intensify as the demand for direct care workers, especially for home-care workers, grows rapidly. The Bureau of Labor Statistics (BLS) projects a 28 percent increase in the number of care worker positions, from 4,460,580 in 2018 to 5,781679 in 2028. BLS also projects that high employee turnover during this period will result in 6,863,000 vacancies for employers to fill. As a result of this growth in positions and employee turnover, BLS projects 8,184,100 direct care worker job openings from 2018 to 2028.[51] The "direct care workforce will grow more than registered nurses and fast food workers *combined*, which are ranked second and third for net job growth" by the BLS from 2016 to 2026.[52]

Who will fill these jobs? What changes need to be made to attract and keep experienced and caring workers? It should be noted that, given that one in four direct care workers are immigrants, Donald Trump's anti-immigrant rhetoric and policies are already exacerbating the growing crisis, at least in the short term.

Plainly, the growing need for and shortage of caregivers demand bold action to harness, sustain, and appropriately reward these most human and critical services we provide for each other.

## CONCLUSION

For too long, the financial and emotional pressures of the care family and friends give to each other have been viewed primarily as a private matter, what sociologist C. Wright Mills called "private troubles"—a problem that is not recognized as requiring a public response.[53] Normal risks, experienced over life by every family and every person, are still not yet fully recognized as requiring greater public response. As families experience more constraints on their time, as the health-care system shifts more costs and expectations onto caregivers, and as the nation ages, the pressures on families and informal caregivers will expand, and the expectation and demand for strengthening the family through support of its caregivers will grow.

We believe Social Security is the right vehicle, effective and time-tested, to play a key part in addressing the nation's emerging caregiving crisis. As chapter 8 highlights, Social Security should be expanded to provide financial supports for working families in ways that other nations do, allowing all of us, collectively through our Social Security system, to recognize, support, and reward those who provide care—family, friends, and direct care workers—to the young, the old, and those in between.

# 7

# THE NEW GILDED AGE

*"Between 1990 and 2020, the U.S. billionaire class has seen its net worth increase over 1,130 percent. Meanwhile, U.S. median household net worth between 1989 and 2016 grew by a mere 5.37 percent. Billionaire wealth has grown 210 times faster than median wealth."*

—Institute for Policy Studies, *Billionaire Bonanza 2020: Wealth Windfalls, Tumbling Taxes, and Pandemic Profiteers*[1]

Galloping inequality makes Social Security expansion more important than ever.

Economic inequality is reaching levels last seen in the United States just before the Great Depression of the 1930s[2] and, before that, during the Gilded Age at the end of the nineteenth century. Greater and greater proportions of income and wealth are now captured by the top 1 percent, and especially the top 0.1 percent of American households.[3] Consider:

- Today, the combined wealth of three people—Jeff Bezos, Bill Gates, and Warren Buffett—exceeds the wealth of 160 million Americans![4]
- Three families—the Waltons, Kochs, and Mars—have

combined fortunes of $349 billion in 2018. Those families' combined wealth is more than four million times the median wealth of all of American families.[5] Their combined wealth increased by nearly 6,000 percent from 1982 to 2018, while the wealth of the median household actually declined by 3 percent.[6]

- During the COVID-19 crisis, just from January 1, 2020, to April 10 2020, thirty-four billionaires increased their wealth by more than $1 billion each, with Amazon founder Jeff Bezos and novelist Mackenzie Bezos leading the way as their combined wealth increased by $33 billion by April 15![7]

- Average CEO compensation in 2018 for the 350 largest publicly traded companies was $17.2 million, roughly 287 times more than those companies' average employee's compensation. In stark contrast, the average CEO to average employee compensation was a 20-to-1 ratio in 1965. Today's ratio of 287-to-1 is 4.8 times greater than the 58-to-1 ratio it was in 1989.[8]

It is not simply that the rich are getting richer. It is that the rich are getting richer while almost everyone else is treading water or even losing ground. From 1948 to 1979, two thirds of aggregate income growth in the United States went to the bottom 90 percent. In sharp contrast to the earlier period, virtually all aggregate income growth from 1979 to 2012 has gone to the top 10 percent, roughly two thirds to the top 1 percent! While the post-tax income of all adults ages twenty and older grew by 61 percent from 1946 to 2014, it grew by 113 percent for the top 10 percent, 194 percent for the top 1 percent, and an astounding 616 percent for the top 0.001 percent![9] And from 1993 through 2018, the top 1 percent captured half (48 percent) of the total economic growth of real family incomes.[10]

As dramatic as these large disparities in the distribution of income are, the distribution of wealth is even more striking. In 2016, the top 1 percent held 39 percent of all the financial wealth in the United States and the bottom 90 percent held just 23 percent (figure 7.1).[11] More starkly, Federal Reserve Board economists reported that the share of wealth held by the top 10 percent increased from 60 percent in 1989 to 70 percent in 2018, while the bottom 50 percent's share of total wealth fell during this period from 4 percent to 1 percent.[12]

But what does this have to do with Social Security? Everything. Enacted in the face of the last disastrous period of income and wealth inequality, Social Security helped to build the middle class and make our economy and society more economically equal and just. Today, those same economic and political forces responsible for the nation's current inequality crisis threaten our Social Security system. The growing inequality has resulted in signifi-

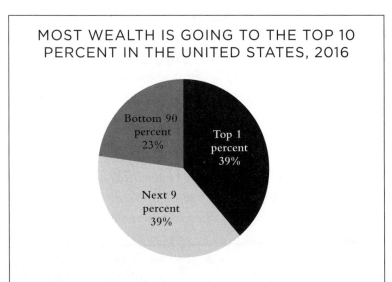

## MOST WEALTH IS GOING TO THE TOP 10 PERCENT IN THE UNITED STATES, 2016

Bottom 90 percent 23%

Top 1 percent 39%

Next 9 percent 39%

**Source:** Stone, Chad, Danilo Trisi, Arloc Sherman, and Emily Horton (December 11, 2018), A Guide to Statistics on Historical Trends in Income Inequality (Center on Budget and Policy Priorities, Washington, D.C.), https://www.cbpp.org/research/poverty-and-inequality/a-guide-to-statistics-on-historical-trends-in-income-inequality#_ftn35.

Figure 7.1

cant reductions in Social Security revenues. The concentration of political power that has naturally followed the concentration of income and wealth has caused the elites among us to claim a false crisis in order to undermine our earned Social Security benefits. At the same time, though, the widening gap between the rich and everyone else strengthens the political and economic argument for expanding benefits. This chapter pulls the curtain away so all of us can see what is going on.

## DÉJÀ VU ALL OVER AGAIN

Today's enormous concentration of income and wealth didn't just happen by accident, or on its own. Nor is it a brand-new phenomenon. The concentration of income and wealth and the economic and political power it generates in the hands of relatively few have all happened before. Mark Twain termed the late nineteenth century the Gilded Age, when on the surface the times looked golden, but where venality, exploitation, and hardship lurked just below. It also happened during the Roaring Twenties, a time of excess memorialized by F. Scott Fitzgerald's *The Great Gatsby*. Both of these periods ended with economic breakdowns—the Panic of 1893 and the Great Depression of the 1930s—with businesses collapsing, banks closing, and widespread unemployment and poverty.

During both periods a vicious cycle took hold. Income and wealth inequality allowed those at the top to exert oversized political influence; their influence was used to enact policies, control the judiciary, and take other steps that gave the wealthiest even more income and wealth. Those who benefited most from the upward redistribution of wealth—and the political power that is a by-product of that wealth—often justified their privileged positions with claims of Social Darwinism; the wealthiest, in their eyes, were the fittest. For example, John D. Rockefeller—who captained Standard Oil so that, by the 1880s, it controlled the delivery of 90 percent of the nation's oil—justified monopolistic practices, telling students at Brown University in 1904: "The growth of large business is merely a survival of the fittest. . . . [T]he American Beauty rose can be produced in splendor and fragrance which brings cheer to its beholder only by sacrificing the early buds which grow up around it. This is not an evil tendency in business. It is merely the working out of the law of nature and the law of God."[13]

These early Masters of the Universe, as the novelist Tom Wolfe labeled their spiritual descendants in his 1987 novel *Bonfire of the Vanities*, deified laissez-faire capitalism and "free" markets—though governments, of course, have always been involved in commerce and markets. Governments—federal, state, and local—build public roads that assist in getting goods to market, establish courts that adjudicate contract disputes, fund police and fire services to protect property, and play countless other roles.

Notwithstanding the reality, those titans of industry justified their business practices and the accumulation of great wealth as well as their disregard for the inequities and casualties of the system they profited from by claiming they were self-made and the font of economic progress. Seemingly without regard for human and moral consequences, many argued that there was nothing the federal government should do when the Great Depression threw one third of workers out of work.

President Herbert Hoover's secretary of the treasury, Andrew Mellon, an industrialist, banker, and one of the richest men in the country, advised, "Liquidate labor, liquidate stocks, liquidate the farmers, liquidate real estate. . . . It will purge the rottenness out of the system. . . . People will work harder, live a more moral life. Values will be adjusted, and enterprising people will pick up from less competent people."[14]

## LESSONS FROM THE GREAT DEPRESSION AND THE NEW DEAL

The excesses of the Gilded Age and the Roaring Twenties were followed by periods of social reforms: the Progressive Era and the

New Deal. Concerned with excessive speculation, bank panics, monopoly control of key industries, and unfair labor practices, laws were written during both periods to regulate banking, commerce, and working conditions.

The Progressive Era witnessed successful movements to enact state workers' compensation laws and advance public health as well as an unsuccessful push to enact government-provided health insurance. A number of states enacted minimum wage and maximum hour laws, only to have the Supreme Court rule the statutes unconstitutional on the grounds that they interfered with the right of employers and workers to enter into contracts freely.[15] Concerned with political corruption and the undemocratic concentration of wealth and political power, progressives successfully advanced constitutional amendments giving Congress the power to directly levy progressive income taxes (Sixteenth Amendment), requiring that U.S. senators be elected by popular vote and not by state legislatures (Seventeenth Amendment), and empowering women to vote (Nineteenth Amendment).

The New Deal built on this legacy. The National Labor Relations Act of 1935 brought more balance to the worker-employer playing field, establishing ground rules enabling private sector employees to join unions and requiring employers to bargain collectively with their employees' representatives. The Fair Labor Standards Act of 1938 restricted child labor and established a minimum wage, maximum hours, and overtime pay rules for covered workers. The Social Security Act of 1935 established unemployment insurance and what today we call Social Security.

These and other New Deal enactments laid the foundation for our modern economy. They added more protections to the nation's markets and economic enterprises. They gave increased power to workers in an effort to allow them to bargain with their employers on more equal footing, thereby underwriting their economic security and dignity. They provided, in the form of Social Security and unemployment insurance, government-run mandatory wage insurance for workers. They supported state and local child welfare, vocational rehabilitation, and public health services. And they established an ongoing federal role in responding to the financial needs of poor families with children, poor elderly, poor blind people, and, in time, poor people with disabilities more generally.

The large industrial expansion during World War II, together with these New Deal innovations and, later, the G.I. Bill of Rights and the growing size and influence of unions, sparked the twenty-five-year postwar economic expansion. Economic growth resulted in more opportunities for leisure (vacation, retirement, and education), higher standards of living, and strengthened health and employee pension protections, especially for unionized workers in both the private and public sectors. Not without its challenges, most significantly racial oppression, gender inequality, the enforced closeting of those in the LGBTQ community, and the continuing threat of nuclear war, the American Dream was in reach of many and the "rules of the game" were clear for middle-class families: you worked hard and played by the rules. Others did, too. You could get ahead; if not you yourself, then your children.

The shared prosperity of much of the 1950s, 1960s, and early 1970s built a strong, robust middle class. Family incomes grew; home ownership became widespread. Unionized workers could, increasingly, count on defined pension benefits to supplement their Social Security benefits in retirement. Enactments of Medicare and Medicaid and expansions of Social Security provided growing protections against financial risks to workers and families, greater economic security, and the sense of personal security that one could weather difficult financial times if and when they struck. The highest marginal tax rates were thirty to fifty percentage points higher than today—ranging between 70 percent and 92 percent from 1946 to 1980, compared to 37 percent today.[16]

Though many Americans were strongly isolationist in the 1930s, the vast majority emerged from World War II believing that America's involvement in that war was right and just. The construction of the interstate highway system was again seen as government working for the benefit of all. And regular expansions of Social Security during the 1950s and 1960s were enacted by wide margins with broad bipartisan support.

Notwithstanding some strong political differences, these were not years in which most politicians sought to pull apart the understandings that emerged during the 1930s and 1940s. Writing to one of his brothers in 1956, President Dwight D. Eisenhower, a moderately conservative Republican, remarked on the strength of these understandings: "Should any political party attempt to abolish social security, unemployment insurance and eliminate labor laws and farm programs you would not hear of that party again in our political history. There is a tiny splinter group, of course, that believes you can do these things . . . Their number is negligible and they are stupid."[17]

## GOVERNMENT'S NEW ROLE IN THE UPWARD REDISTRIBUTION OF WEALTH

The first rumblings of tectonic changes to come could be heard by the 1960s. The consensus supporting government action was fraying. Tensions generated by just demands for civil rights, women's rights, and gay rights; an unpopular war; assassinations that shook the nation; urban riots; a president and vice-president resigning from office in disgrace; and an economy simultaneously experiencing high unemployment and high inflation all contributed to unrest and a questioning of whether government played a positive or negative role in its citizens' lives.

This shift was felt powerfully with the election of Ronald Reagan. On January 20, 1981, in his first inaugural address, the newly elected Reagan asserted that "government is not the solution to our problem; government is the problem."[18] With that simple declaration, the so-called Reagan Revolution began, setting in motion an upward redistribution of income and wealth. Transforming his words into actions, his administration pursued policies that tilted power in favor of the most advantaged among us.

# HELPING THE RICH BY DRASTICALLY CUTTING THEIR TAXES

Since government is the problem, according to Reagan, "starving the beast" became a major strategic goal.[19] The beast, of course, is federal spending, primarily social spending. What feeds this spending are revenues. So "starving it" means choking off its revenues through tax cuts and by running deficits to create political pressure for cutting social benefits and programs. The playbook—tax cuts mainly benefiting the most well-off and defense spending increases—did indeed usher in large federal deficits. This is the same playbook in use today.

The anti-tax approach gained steam in 1984, when Democratic presidential nominee Walter Mondale lost in a landslide, after asserting, in his speech accepting his party's nomination, that raising taxes was inevitable.[20] It gained even more steam when Vice President George H.W. Bush emphatically declared, in his Republican presidential nomination acceptance speech in 1988, "Read my lips: No new taxes."[21] When Bush signed a budget compromise as president, which did include tax increases, Democratic presidential candidate Bill Clinton pointed out the flip-flop in several ads, and Bush lost, many pundits attributing the cause to the breach of his pledge.

The 1990s were a predictably strong economic time, because the Baby Boom generation was at its most productive, peak-earning years. The Social Security Amendments of 1983 resulted in Social Security building up large reserves in anticipation of the coming retirement of Baby Boomers. President Bill Clinton resisted pressure to cut taxes, and indeed produced a small surplus by adding Social Security's growing surplus to the smaller general fund surplus. It was projected to grow over the subsequent ten years to $5.6 trillion.[22] (As discussed in the next section, Clinton did exacerbate inequality by repealing Aid to Families with Dependent Children, enacted as part of the Social Security Act of 1935.)

But President George W. Bush secured two rounds of new tax cuts, again primarily benefiting the well-off. And responding to attacks on 9/11, President Bush called for, and Congress supported, large increases in military spending, which along with tax cuts turned projected surpluses into large budget deficits.

Not to be outdone, President Trump, with the support of Republican majorities in the House of Representatives and the Senate, followed suit. The Congressional Budget Office estimates that the Tax Cuts and Jobs Act (TCJA), signed into law in December 2017, will add $1 trillion to $2 trillion to the federal debt over the ten years following its enactment.[23]

To see the decline in tax rates for the wealthy during this period, see figure 9.3. in chapter 9. To see a discussion of Republican hypocrisy over the federal debt, see chapter 12.

More recently, in proposing a $4.8 trillion budget with a $966 billion deficit for fiscal year 2021 as preview of what is to come if he is reelected, President Trump's 2021 budget proposal would extend the 2017 tax cuts, initially scheduled to terminate in 2025, through 2035, at a cost of $1 trillion. Using the pandemic as an excuse, Trump repeatedly called for cutting Social Security's dedicated revenue in response. Cutting FICA is not well targeted and inefficient, with the wealthiest realizing the largest cuts to their premium contributions. It has the advantage, though, of looking like a middle-class tax cut that eventually will undermine Social Security.[24]

In addition to straightforward cuts in income tax rates and FICA, more hidden tax breaks in the form of tax deductions and credits for the fossil fuel industry and other special interests have also been part of the strategy. These so-called tax expenditures cost the government trillions of dollars each year but are largely invisible. All of those tax cuts have had their predictable result. In 2010, the top 0.1 percent of earners—those making more than $3 million—received the benefit of the bulk of the Bush tax cuts. Their average tax cut of around $520,000 is more than 450 times larger than the one enjoyed by the average middle-class family. Indeed, more than half of these tax benefits went to those earning more than $170,000.[25]

The 2017 Trump-GOP tax cuts also shower the richest 1 percent in 2020 with $78 billion in reduced taxes—roughly the same as the aggregate cut as for the bottom 80 percent. That translates into average cuts of $49,950 for the top 1 percent and just $60 for the bottom 20 percent. And corporations saw their tax liabilities slashed so much that ninety-one did not pay a penny on their 2018 earnings—including Amazon, Halliburton, Eli Lily, Netflix, and Prudential Financial.[26]

The impact of the Trump tax cut will be even more skewed in a few years. In 2027, a whopping 83 percent of the tax breaks from that legislation will go to the top 1 percent! In contrast, the bottom 95 percent will see little tax benefit at all.[27]

## HELPING THE RICH BY CUTTING DOMESTIC AND INCREASING MILITARY SPENDING

In addition to starving the beast by cutting taxes, the Reagan administration sought to cut spending—but not all spending. By the time Reagan left office, military spending had been increased by a whopping 43 percent over what it had been at the height of the Vietnam War.

A favorite target for cuts was means-tested welfare. Often drawing on pernicious gender and racial stereotypes, such as the so-called Welfare Queen, Reagan routinely vilified those who were dependent on those programs, implying that they were undeserving and lazy or, worse, outright crooks.[28]

Other domestic spending was cut as well. In 1981, Congress repealed Social Security benefits for children ages eighteen to twenty-two in college or vocational school whose parent had lost wages as the result of death, disability, or old age, and cut the program in other ways. Further cuts were enacted in 1983.

Reagan's successors did little to change the overall narrative that government is the problem, nor the shift from domestic to military spending. Indeed, it was Democrat Bill Clinton who signed legislation in 1996 ending Aid to Families with Dependent Children, which had been enacted as part of the Social Security Act of 1935, substituting the much less adequate Temporary Assistance for Needy Families. Poor children would no longer have a right to a federally supported welfare benefit. And president George W. Bush dramatically increased military spending in the wake of the 9/11 terrorist attacks.

Under Donald Trump, domestic spending has gone down even more. Indeed, the military budget has grown enormously every year of the Trump presidency while domestic spending has declined.[29]

Social welfare spending helps middle- and lower-income Americans; military spending primarily benefits the defense industry. For the most part, those who serve or have served our nation so honorably in uniform have not been the beneficiaries of this new military spending. Instead, they and their families have been harmed by domestic spending cuts.

## HELPING THE RICH AND HURTING EVERYONE ELSE BY PRIVATIZING GOVERNMENT FUNCTIONS

The deification of the market system and the vilification of government have led conservative activists to call for, and in many cases successfully advance, policies that shift risks onto the poor, working, and middle classes while redistributing wealth upward through the privatization of government functions and jobs.[30] Echoes of this animus to the traditional use of government to help citizens do what cannot be done alone were on full display as President

Trump used the platform of the 2020 State of the Union Address to advocate for charter schools as the solution to supposedly "failing government schools."[31]

Even in as essential a part of government as national defense, privatization has happened, enriching corporations to the detriment of most Americans and our values. This privatization is perhaps most visibly and starkly epitomized by Halliburton and all the other private contractors employed to help with the Iraq and Afghanistan wars.[32]

Given the privatization in an enterprise as important and life-threatening as war, it should not be a surprise that conservatives would seek to dismantle Social Security by privatizing the goal of achieving retirement security, despite Social Security's proven superiority to all private-sector counterparts. While President George W. Bush's effort to privatize Social Security was defeated, a number of well-meaning but misguided politicians still seek what some call the back-door privatization of Social Security.[33] They work to expand private retirement savings vehicles, while leaving open the possibility of cutting Social Security—accomplishing in two steps essentially what President Bush sought to accomplish in one.[34]

Although unsuccessful in privatizing Social Security, President Bush was successful in partially privatizing Medicare. He signed the 2003 Medicare Modernization Act, which added prescription drug benefits to Medicare and moved incrementally in the direction of privatizing Medicare.[35] The drug benefit opened up new markets for insurance companies. The law also created greater opportunity for beneficiaries to select a private plan, Medicare Advantage, as an alternative to the traditional public Medicare plan, providing, as enacted, significantly larger per capita reimbursement for those covered by private plans.[36]

The privatization of government functions enriches some corporations often while costing taxpayers.[37] It has resulted in the upward redistribution of wealth indirectly, as well as by trading good paying public sector jobs, protected by strong unions, for

generally nonunionized jobs with fewer protections and less security.[38] Cutting or, more radically, privatizing Social Security would,
like other efforts to shift functions from the public sector to the
private, benefit powerful interests while drastically reducing the
economic security of America's families and intensifying the dan-
gerously skewed distribution of income and wealth.

## HELPING CORPORATIONS AND HURTING TYPICAL AMERICANS BY FAILING TO PROTECT WORKERS WHO ORGANIZE

Privatizing government functions sometimes serves, intended or
not, to redistribute wealth upward by weakening unions.

Early on in 1981, Reagan signaled his disregard for the role
unions played in building a strong middle class. Firing 13,000
striking air traffic controllers, he destroyed their union and, with
anti-union appointments to agencies created to protect workers,
including the National Labor Relations Board and the Department
of Labor, he sent a message that union-busting would be tolerated
and even actively encouraged.[39]

These attacks are with us still—and they have had their impact.

In 1983, 21.6 percent of workers were members of unions.
Today, it is only 10.3 percent, 14.6 million workers, half of whom
work in the public sector. Only 6.2 percent of today's private sector workers are unionized.[40] Moreover, the attack against unions
has been relentless, replete with legal efforts; regulatory efforts;
appointment of anti-union ideologues to important federal agencies, including the U.S. Department of Labor; and an ongoing
stream of anti-union rhetoric.

Having weakened unions representing private sector workers,
anti-union conservatives have placed a target on public unions, as
well. And they are succeeding.[41] This anti-union effort has, if anything, accelerated under Donald Trump's administration.[42]

The fight against unions has indirect but serious consequences for Social Security. Union support for Social Security has been essential in both protecting it from cuts and successfully pushing for its expansion.

## HELPING THE RICH AND HURTING EVERYONE ELSE BY DEREGULATING

The attacks on unions were just one aspect of weakening worker protections and promoting the upward redistribution of income and wealth. Eroding the federal minimum wage was another. Using 2018 dollars, the real value of the federal minimum wage declined from a peak of $11.55 per hour in 1968 to $10.03 in 1979 and to $7.25 in November 2018.[43] (The federal minimum wage did not increase by even a penny during the Reagan presidency. It last increased in 2009 to $7.25 per hour in non–inflation adjusted dollars (nominal dollars).[44] The failure to increase the minimum wage not only affected workers' income but also robbed Social Security of revenue, since its premiums are assessed against wages.[45]

These policies were part of a larger redistribution of wealth upward through the reduction of so-called anti-business regulations. The focus on deregulation started with presidents Richard Nixon and Jimmy Carter, but it accelerated under Reagan. Economist Paul Krugman blames Reagan's deregulation of the savings and loan industry—enabling banks to make risky investments with government-backed funds—for turning the savings and loan collapse of the 1980s and 1990s into "an utter catastrophe" and paving the way for the Great Recession.[46] These deregulation policies continued under Reagan's successors. Perhaps most visibly, in 1999, the New Deal's Glass-Steagall legislation, which had protected us against irresponsible action by banks, was repealed, another important cause of the Great Recession.

The response to the banking crisis and the 2007 to 2009 Great Recession it sparked was necessarily swift. To stabilize the economy, the banks defined as "too big to fail" were bailed out by the public through the Troubled Assets Relief Program. But not so for the many middle-class workers and families straining under the press of declining housing prices, foreclosures, job loss, and credit card and student debt.

The economic lessons of the past were largely ignored: that active and large federal government investments are needed to jump-start a depressed economy, not laissez-faire economics and budget balancing; and that to help citizens help themselves, large-scale government action is needed, not callous disregard and domestic budget cuts when many jobs are being lost and homes foreclosed.

## THE HIGH COST OF INEQUALITY

The result of these policies—which all flow from the idea that government harms us rather than helps us and evens the playing field—has led to the startling rising income and wealth inequality that the nation continues to experience because the game is rigged for the very rich and against everyone else.

Where the 1950s and 1960s were a time when the middle class swelled, the current one is a time of a disappearing middle class. When once a single paycheck could support a family, now it generally takes two.[47] When once young adults could emerge from college with manageable debt and bright prospects, now they are often greeted with enormous debt and, all too frequently, few job opportunities.[48] And the trajectory of student debt is upward, increasing from $253 billion in 2003 to $1.6 trillion in 2020.[49]

And these conditions have a serious and corrosive impact on our society. Rising inequality and declining upward mobility harm our economy.[50] They also harm our stability and cohesion as a nation. And, perhaps most seriously, those twin conditions harm our very democracy.

The vast majority of today's federal politicians depend on large donors from the business world. Ignoring the lessons of the past, some people with extraordinary economic power (e.g., the Koch brothers and the late Peter G. Peterson, discussed in chapter 10) have been bending the nation's politics, democracy, and economy in ways that redirect enormous amounts of income, wealth, and political power to the most well-off.

## EXPANDING SOCIAL SECURITY REDUCES INEQUALITY

The income inequality of recent decades has undermined Social Security's revenue stream substantially. Congress did not anticipate that wage growth over the last four decades would go primarily to higher-income workers, a reality responsible for more than one quarter of the program's projected long-term shortfall (which is discussed at length in chapter 9).[51]

Nor did Congress anticipate growing wage inequality's unexpected consequence for Social Security benefits. Because benefits are based on earnings—relatively flat and for some declining—American workers are earning lower Social Security benefits than they would have earned if wage growth had been distributed more evenly across income groups (as they were from roughly 1950 to 1979).[52]

Because Social Security and those earning its benefits have been hurt by income inequality, an expanded Social Security is a solution, helping to lessen that very inequality. Funding these expanded benefits by requiring the wealthiest among us to contribute more is a further solution to that income and wealth inequality.

Expanding benefit protections is not a panacea, but it is a critical start for addressing the problems facing those receiving today's modest Social Security benefits. Nor is it a panacea for the nation's unacceptable level of inequality. But it is an important step in moving the nation in the right direction.

The preceding four chapters have explained why Social Security should be expanded. The next two chapters explain how.

PART THREE

# THE SOLUTION

# 8

# EXPAND SOCIAL SECURITY FOR ALL GENERATIONS

IT IS LONG PAST TIME TO EXPAND SOCIAL SECURITY. AN expanded Social Security system is a solution to the income insufficiency of today's seniors; the retirement income crisis confronting today's middle-aged and young workers; inadequate recognition and public support for caregiving; and increased inequality, now hollowing out the middle class. It is a solution or partial solution to those challenges and others.

This chapter and the next present our plan, the Social Security Works for All Generations Plan—a comprehensive package of benefit and revenue changes that expands Social Security's protections in important ways. Our plan is but one among a number of excellent plans. A growing number of U.S. senators, members of the House of Representatives, academics, and leading organizations have put forward and support Social Security plans that expand benefits, with no cuts, and restore Social Security to long-range actuarial balance.

In this chapter and the next, we discuss the various elements of our plan, as well as other possible expansions included in some of the other plans. The next chapter explains why and how the richest nation in the world[1] can pay for these benefit improvements and how doing so can slow the rapid growth of income inequality and offset some of the damage it causes to Social Security's financing.

At the end of chapter 9, we provide a summary of our plan. Greater detail about all of the proposals in the two chapters, including a chart showing costs and revenues of the All Generations Plan, can be found in appendix B. A chart summarizing other major expansion plans that have been put forward at the time of this writing can be found in appendix C.

## INCREASING THE ECONOMIC SECURITY OF CURRENT AND FUTURE SENIORS

As we discuss in chapters 1 and 2, prior to the enactment of Social Security, the large majority of workers were unable to retire with enough income to live with independence and dignity. Social Security changed that. But, as chapters 4 and 5 explain, we may be returning to a time when out burdening their children will lack the financial resources to do so. As chapter 4 discusses, the majority of today's seniors are at significant economic risk—some living in or close to poverty, and many others just one economic shock away from trouble meeting basic needs. And, as chapter 5 makes clear, tomorrow's seniors are likely to be in worse financial shape.

Social Security currently provides a strong foundation, but its benefits are far from adequate by themselves. Indeed, they are modest by virtually any measure, averaging just $1,517 a month in August 2020 ($18,204 annually). They do not come close to replacing a large enough percentage of wages to allow workers to maintain their standards of living once wages are gone. Moreover, these already minimal replacement rates will be lower in the future, as the result of the already enacted cuts, now being phased in, described in chapter 5.

In light of Social Security's near universality, efficiency, fairness in its benefit distribution, portability from job to job, and security, the obvious solution to the nation's looming retirement income crisis is to increase Social Security's modest benefits. Recognizing the retirement income crisis, a number of policymakers have proposed additional savings vehicles and incentives to save. Some have proposed building on tax-favored IRAs and 401(k)s. But savings will not be effective for the vast majority of workers; what will unquestionably be effective is insurance, in the form of time-tested Social Security, as chapter 3 explains.

Increasing Social Security's benefits can be done simply and quickly, with no start-up costs, no additional regulation, and virtually no additional administrative costs. Importantly, benefit improvements will, over time, be conveyed to all generations in the family and those to come. In fact, younger generations will reap greater benefits from proposed expansions than today's old. That's because, in raising the benefits of current beneficiaries, we would also raise the benefits of those who will receive them in the future, and because today's old will receive this benefit improvement for fewer years than tomorrow's old. It will also lessen the squeeze on those who feel responsible to supplement the incomes of their aging parents while also assisting their own children and grandchildren.

Moreover, increasing Social Security benefits will increase the benefits not just of retired workers but also of workers with disabilities, their families, and the families of deceased workers. This increase would occur automatically, without reference to specific groups, because nearly all Social Security's benefits are generated from the same formula.

## INCREASE BENEFITS FOR ALL CURRENT AND FUTURE BENEFICIARIES

In light of the looming retirement income crisis, which will affect most workers, Social Security's modest benefits should be increased for everyone.[2] Increasing everyone's benefits fits with the spirit of Social Security and could ensure that all workers and their families have, at least, a somewhat stronger and larger foundation when wages are gone, and, at best, enough guaranteed income to fully replace wages to allow the maintenance of workers' standards of living when those wages are gone.

And so the All Generations Plan proposes an increase in benefits for everyone who receives Social Security benefits now or will in the future. (See figure 8.1.) The increase is intended to make Social Security fully adequate for the vast majority of Americans with no need for supplementation.

As discussed in chapter 4, most experts believe that around 70 to 85 percent of preretirement wages is necessary for workers to maintain their standards of living in retirement, once wages are gone. Higher percentages are needed for low-paid workers, somewhat lower for the highest paid. Less than 100 percent is needed, because people no longer have work expenses and, instead of saving, start to spend their savings. The All Generations Plan is designed to provide average workers with that 70 percent replacement; those with lower incomes would receive higher percentages, those with higher, lower percentage replacements. For the wealthiest, just as Social Security has a minimum benefit and a maximum family benefit, we limit our plan's maximum benefit to $8,200 a month.

Some will charge that we are fundamentally changing Social Security, that it was intended to simply be a foundation on which to build. But those who claim that are wrong. There is no evidence that Roosevelt and his colleagues intentionally designed Social Security simply to be part of what is needed, with the expectation that individual employers would make up the difference through their own individual plans. Indeed, the legislative history indicates the exact opposite.[3] Increasing Social Security's benefits so they are fully adequate, without supplementation, is completely consistent with the original intent and structure of Social Security.

## REPLACEMENT RATES AND MONTHLY BENEFITS UNDER CURRENT LAW AND UNDER ALL-GENERATIONS PROPOSAL FOR LOW, MEDIUM, AND HIGH EARNERS

| Type of Scaled Hypothetical Worker | Career-Average Earnings in 2018 | AIME | Replacement Rate Under Current Law | Replacement Rate Under Proposed Law | Monthly Benefit Under Current Law | Monthly Benefit Under Proposed Law |
|---|---|---|---|---|---|---|
| Low Earner | $23,249 | $1,937 | 41% | 80% | $795 | $1,559 |
| Medium Earner | $51,665 | $4,305 | 31% | 72% | $1,309 | $3,098 |
| High Earner | $82,664 | $6,889 | 25% | 64% | $1,734 | $4,400 |

**Source:** "Fact Sheet on the Old-Age, Survivors, and Disability Insurance Program," Social Security Administration, February 4, 2014.

Figure 8.1

# IMPROVING ECONOMIC SECURITY FOR WORKERS CLAIMING BENEFITS EARLY

With the enactment of early retirement benefits for women, starting in 1956, and for men, starting in 1961, benefits claimed early were reduced.[4] The reason for the reduction was to make the age of claiming neutral from the perspective of Social Security. Early retirement was not to be subsidized nor penalized. If a person received benefits early—and therefore for more months prior to their deaths—they received a lower monthly amount than if they started receiving benefits later. When age sixty-seven is fully phased-in as the age of eligibility for full benefits for workers born after 1959, the monthly benefit for those accepting their retired worker benefits at age sixty-two will be 70 percent of a "full benefit." That is, the benefit will be 70 percent of what a retired worker would receive if benefits were not claimed when a worker turns sixty-seven.

As previously discussed, many persons who accept reduced retired worker benefits before the full retirement age do so because they have little or no choice. One study previously mentioned finds 27 percent of persons ages sixty-one to sixty-two reporting work-limiting health conditions, with higher proportions of African Americans and Hispanics so reporting.[5] A January 2020 Allianz Life study (of persons with household incomes of at least $50,000, if single, $75,000, if coupled, or with investable assets of at least $150,000) finds that more than half of the people surveyed "are being forced to leave the workforce earlier than expected because of reasons outside of their control, with 34% of survey respondents saying they had to leave the workforce because of unanticipated job loss and 25% cutting off their careers because of health issues."[6]

All things being equal, benefits regardless of when initiated were, on average, to be roughly the same over the remaining lives of beneficiaries. Of course, all things are not equal. African Americans and indigenous persons have shorter life expectancies at age sixty-two, as do people with less education, significant health problems, and functional disabilities. Life expectancies have increased since early retirement reductions were first employed, although not equally across various demographic groups. Thus, the gap in life expectancy between those who claim early retired worker benefits and those who are able to delay claiming benefits has grown.[7]

These reductions are large, especially for those with health, employment, and financial exigencies that result in their having limited control over when they leave the workforce *and* whether they must accept permanently reduced retired worker benefits.

Recognizing that many low- and modest-income workers face work-limiting health- and employment-related circumstances and that the actuarial reduction prior to the full retirement age is disproportionately burdensome for such workers who leave the workforce involuntarily, the All Generations Plan calls for:

- Liberalizing eligibility criteria for the Social Security and SSI programs so that greater weight is given for applicants aged fifty and older to age-related health limitations, partial disabilities, and vocational and educational factors when making disability eligibility decisions.
- Establishing 80 percent of the PIA as the benefit floor for persons first accepting benefits when they become sixty-two, by establishing a uniform benefit reduction factor of 4 percent per year for persons who accept benefits prior to the full retirement age (sixty-seven when fully phased in).

Figure 8.2 illustrates the impact of the proposed 80 percent benefit floor (assuming the worker would receive a monthly benefit of $1,000 at the full retirement age of sixty-seven, in 2022 and later).

Workers leaving work prior to age sixty-two due to factors beyond their control may also experience a second, less obvious

## PROPOSED CHANGES
## FOR EARLY ACCEPTANCE
## OF RETIRED WORKER BENEFITS

| Age worker first claims benefits | Current law % of PIA starting 2022 | Current law benefit amount | Benefit amount under proposal | Proposed % of PIA |
|---|---|---|---|---|
| 62 | 70% | $700 | $800 | 80% |
| 63 | 75% | $750 | $840 | 84% |
| 64 | 80% | $800 | $880 | 88% |
| 65 | 86.67% | $866 | $920 | 92% |
| 66 | 93.34% | $933 | $960 | 96% |
| 67 | 100% | $1,000 | $1,000 | 100% |

**Source:** "Fact Sheet on the Old-Age, Survivors, and Disability Insurance Program," Social Security Administration, February 4, 2014.

Figure 8.2

reduction. Lower earnings and time out of the labor force mean a worker is not getting credit for wages that would otherwise have raised their base benefit. This, too, is permanent and can be very large, especially for those leaving work in their fifties and not meeting Social Security Disability Insurance's stringent eligibility requirements. Recognizing this problem, Social Security Disability Insurance holds eligible persons with severe work disabilities harmless from this base reduction. Termed the "disability freeze," this provision eliminates years of low or no earnings when calculating a Disability Insurance beneficiary's average indexed earnings (AIME) beginning with the medical onset of disability.

Although not including the disability freeze concept in the All Generations Plan, workers leaving the workforce involuntarily between ages fifty and their full retirement age, we believe consideration should be given to such a proposal.

## ADOPT A MORE ACCURATE COST OF LIVING ADJUSTMENT

Having an automatic annual cost of living adjustment (COLA) is one of the most important features of our Social Security system. It is intended to ensure that benefits, once received, maintain their purchasing power no matter how long someone lives. That's why Social Security benefits are adjusted automatically virtually every January to prevent their erosion if and when there has been inflation.[8] Without accurate and timely inflation adjustments, retirees, people with serious and permanent disabilities, and other beneficiaries would see their Social Security lose value as they age.

To ensure that the value of Social Security's vital but modest benefits do not erode as people age, it is crucial that the automatic adjustment be as accurate as possible. Unfortunately, the current inflation index under measures how inflation eats away at the purchasing power of benefits. That's because it is calculated for urban workers. But seniors and people with disabilities spend more on health care—where prices rise faster—and less on clothing, recreation, and other items—where prices tend to rise more slowly—than younger, healthier Americans.[9]

When the automatic increase was enacted in 1972, the Department of Labor's Bureau of Labor Statistics produced only one measure of inflation, the Consumer Price Index for Urban Wage Earners and Clerical Workers (CPI-W). Even though the index measures the cost of living of workers, not retirees, it was the only measure available. In recognition, though, that seniors have very different expenditures from those of workers or the population as a whole, the Older Americans Act Amendments of 1987 mandated the Bureau of Labor Statistics to develop a consumer price index

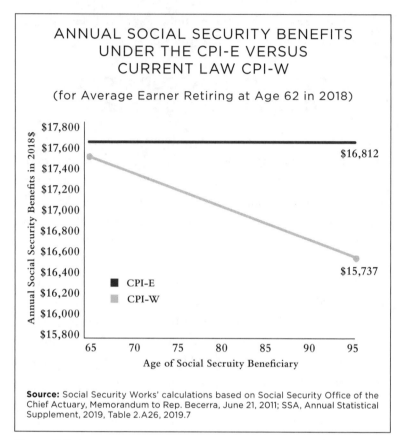

Figure 8.3

for older Americans. In response, the bureau created and continues to produce the Consumer Price Index for the Elderly (CPI-E).[10]

As figure 8.3 illustrates, because the erosion of the benefits compounds over time, the largest impact falls on the oldest old and those disabled for the longest time. Distressingly, this occurs as other resources are exhausted and health costs are increasing on average.

The intent of the cost of living adjustment is to allow beneficiaries to tread water; instead, they are slowly sinking. That is why it is so important to adopt the Consumer Price Index for the Elderly as the basis of the annual cost of living adjustment.

# INCREASE BENEFITS TARGETED TO ALLEVIATING POVERTY

In addition to a better Consumer Price Index and a substantial benefit increase, the All Generations Plan calls for targeted benefit increases to alleviate poverty. As chapter 4 explains, poverty among seniors has declined sharply over the past half century. Nevertheless, some serious pockets of poverty remain. Frequently, people who were poor at younger ages remain poor in retirement. Low-wage workers, as well as workers who were disadvantaged during their working years—disproportionately, people of color, women, and members of the LGBTQ+ community—are likely to have disproportionately high rates of poverty in old age. Indeed, many women who were secure at younger ages find themselves financially strapped as they grow older.[11] Women live longer on average than men, are less likely to have supplemental pensions, and, as chapter 6 details, often are the ones to take time out from the workforce for the essential but uncompensated job of caring for family members.[12]

Social Security is by no means a total solution to the various risks faced by everyone over their lives. People must earn a living wage when they work full-time. Workers must not be victims of wage theft or denied overtime or other benefits to which they are entitled by law. No one in this country should be penalized in the workplace for their race, gender, sexual orientation, religion, or ethnicity. Caregivers should receive the economic and emotional support they deserve. But Social Security, because of its ingenious structure, helps those workers and their families when they reach old age. It could easily do even more.

One of the fundamental values underlying Social Security is that workers who retire after a lifetime of work should not retire into poverty. Moreover, the architects of Social Security believed that workers who contributed to Social Security should receive benefits larger than they could receive simply by applying for means-tested welfare. Thus, Social Security provides benefits that are dispropor-tionately larger for those who have experienced lower wages over their careers. The All Generations Plan maintains this feature with its universal benefit increase.

In addition, Social Security has included a minimum benefit since 1939. The minimum benefit originally did not differentiate between high-paid workers who worked relatively briefly in cov-ered employment  and low-paid workers with long work histories, Congress in 1972 introduced the so-called special minimum for low-income workers with many years of work. Because the special minimum is only indexed to the rise in prices, not wages, it has not kept pace with the nation's rising standard of living and 1998 is the last year a worker actually received the special minimum.[13]

It is time to update the special minimum benefit so that those working full-time for at least thirty years and retiring at their full retirement age will receive a benefit equal to 125 percent of the federal poverty line. The All Generations Plan proposes to do just that.

As chapter 4 explains, another area of disproportionate pov-erty occurs among the very old, who likely have exhausted oth-er resources. Those disproportionately poor at very old ages are more likely to be women, who may be widowed, divorced, or never married, and who may never have earned much during their younger years. To address this issue, some have proposed increasing benefits at an advanced age, such as eighty-five. Some colloqui-ally refer to these proposed increases as birthday bumps. Another proposal is to increase benefits for widows, who have dispropor-tionately high rates of poverty. Although the All Generations Plan does not include these specific, targeted reforms, we applaud them. We think they would help many who are disadvantaged, while remaining consistent with Social Security's overall structure and conceptual underpinning.

# A SERIOUS CAUTION ABOUT THE GOAL OF ANTIPOVERTY AND SOCIAL SECURITY

While targeted increases (like the ones just highlighted and discussed in more detail in appendix B) are valuable and relatively inexpensive, they should not be done while scaling back, or worse, eliminating benefits for others. Some who don't like Social Security, or simply don't understand it, have proposed enacting these targeted expansions while scaling back on benefits for what they call higher-income workers.

Although it is a clever sound bite to ask why billionaires should get Social Security, there are practical as well as conceptual reasons why everyone should receive the benefits they have earned. Scaling back or eliminating the benefits of millionaires and billionaires would produce relatively minute savings, since there are so few billionaires and their benefit levels are low already in relation to their contributions, as a result of Social Security's progressive benefit formula. That is why every proposal put forward to scale back benefits for "higher-income" individuals that has any noticeable cost savings involves reducing the benefits of middle-class Americans, sometimes those with annual incomes as low as $25,000.[14]

While eliminating the benefits of the very rich would not produce much in the way of savings, means-testing Social Security would create enormous problems for the program and the people it serves. It would create administrative problems and be costly. It would require everyone to prove to the Social Security Administration that their yearly income would be low enough to receive benefits—a process that many would find distasteful and undermining of their dignity. If lawmakers also deemed it desirable to reduce or eliminate benefits for those who "owned too much," then we would have to provide information about the value of our assets (e.g., homes, cars, bank accounts, stocks), again to prove that we are not too rich to receive Social Security.

Taking away benefits from the wealthiest, who have nonetheless earned those benefits, would discourage and penalize savings. More importantly, it would subtly but fundamentally undermine the core structure and popular support of this widely popular insurance that has done more to prevent and eradicate poverty in this country than any other program, while also helping to stabilize household incomes when wages are lost. And its benefit levels would be more difficult to sustain because it would no longer be seen as a program benefiting all income groups.

Welfare is necessary as long as there is poverty. But, as we discuss further in chapter 11, supporters of Social Security, which prevents poverty in the first place, should be alert to changes that would transform Social Security from insurance into welfare.

## TO FURTHER ALLEVIATE POVERTY, IMPROVE THE SUPPLEMENTAL SECURITY INCOME PROGRAM

SSI, which currently serves 8.1 million low-income aged, blind, and disabled Americans, is an important complement to Social Security, but its extremely modest benefits and very restrictive eligibility criteria are in desperate need of updating.

That's why, in addition to expanding Social Security, it is time to increase SSI's meager benefits as well as its income and assets limitations.[15] At a minimum, the SSI benefit should be set at the official poverty level (inadequate as that is, as we discuss in chapter 4). If that were done, the federal benefit,[16] in 2020, would have been a still meager $1,041 a month rather than the actual level of $783 a month for individuals, and $1,409 a month rather than the actual $1,175 a month for couples. The assets limit, which is $2,000 for individuals and $3,000 for couples, has only been updated once, in

1989. It should be updated and then increased automatically each year to offset changes in the cost of living. The same should be done for the earnings limitations, which have not been increased since the program's enactment in 1972![17]

## STRENGTHENING FAMILY PROTECTIONS AND REINFORCING CAREGIVING

Although Social Security is often thought of as a program for the old, it is more accurately a family protection program. One in four beneficiaries receive disability or survivor benefits. As described above, the large benefit expansion we propose will increase benefits for tens of millions of younger Americans.

Moreover, increasing Social Security benefits reduces the burden on adult children to care for aged parents. Throughout history, adult children have cared for aging parents. One way to think about Social Security is as an institution that routinizes and streamlines that age-old transfer, allowing seniors to have the dignity that comes with having earned their support, and the autonomy provided by an independent source of income—all while alleviating the pressure on younger family members.

But expanding Social Security in targeted ways, beyond increasing benefits for everyone, is important, as well.

## SUPPORT CARE GIVEN TO OTHERS

In addition to death, disability, and old age, other times that wages may disappear are when a child is born, when a worker becomes sick, or when a worker leaves paid employment to care for a sick or functionally disabled relative. Federal law already mandates that workers may take up to twelve weeks of leave without losing employment.[18] It is a simple step to say that the wages lost during those weeks should be insured and replaced through Social Security. The All Generations Plan takes that simple step and adds these circumstances as insurable events that Social Security covers.

We base our proposal on the Family and Medical Insurance Leave (FAMILY) Act, which Representative Rosa DeLauro (D-CT) has introduced in the House of Representatives, with 203 cosponsors, all but one Democrats, at the time of this writing,[19] and which Senator Kirsten Gillibrand (D-NY) has introduced, with 34 cosponsors, in the Senate.[20] Our proposal is nearly identical to theirs but simply adds these circumstances as insurable events under Social Security, while the FAMILY Act designates its own earmarked contribution, separate and apart from what is now paid for Social Security's old age, survivors, and disability insurance.[21] We believe that simply adding family leave to Social Security, paid from out of the same trust fund that other benefits are paid, is a far better approach. (As a related matter, we propose combining Social Security's Old Age and Survivors Insurance Trust with its Disability Insurance Trust for the same reasons of administrative ease and to ensure that artificial shortfalls are not produced, as discussed in chapter 9 and appendix B.)

We think it is important to distinguish between real paid family leave proposals, such as the DeLauro/Gillibrand bills and our slight modification of theirs, and those that undermine economic security. For example, Senator Marco Rubio and Ivanka Trump have been advancing such a proposal, despite Republican pro-family rhetoric. As described in chapter 12, the Rubio-Trump proposal would allow new parents to take up to three months of paid leave but only in exchange for a cut to their Social Security retirement benefits.[22] Sounds good to some, but it's stingy and it amounts to paid leave on the cheap, with virtually no public support for the young families. Hardly the way to go, with today's young workers already facing a retirement income crisis in their futures.

In addition to the income lost when a child is born or adopted, which the All Generations Plan's paid family leave proposal addresses, family expenses also increase. That's why many other industrialized countries provide not only paid family leave but also children's allowances.[23] The All Generations Plan proposes a $2,000 allowance at the birth or adoption of a child.

Moreover, when workers take time out from the workforce to care for family members, they not only lose wages, but also fail to earn credit toward their own Social Security benefits in the event of old age, disability, or premature death. As we discuss in chapter 6, many people, disproportionately women, withdraw from or reduce their paid work to undertake this enormously important unpaid work. In order to increase the economic security of those who engage in this invaluable labor, the All Generations Plan provides credit toward Social Security benefits when caregivers leave or reduce paid work to care for family members.

Along with these other expansions, sick leave and other short-term disabilities should be an insured event under Social Security. This coverage has been discussed as far back as the 1930s.[24] It is time to take this step as well.

# RESTORE STUDENT BENEFITS FOR CHILDREN OF DECEASED, DISABLED, OR RETIRED WORKERS

Many younger Americans are either finding advanced education out of their financial reach or taking on huge amounts of debt to continue to attend school. While the major solution to this challenge lies outside of Social Security, the program can do its part.

As chapter 3 has described, Social Security provides benefits to minor children whose parents have died or become disabled or retired.[25] The concept is that if those events had not occurred, those workers' wages would have provided their support. At one time, those children's benefits continued until age twenty-two for those who attended postsecondary colleges, universities, or vocational schools. But at the beginning of the Reagan administration—when the current campaign against Social Security was just getting under way—those benefits were repealed.[26] At that time, the cost of that education was more affordable, and government-provided student loans and grants were more readily available.

Children's benefits, received when a worker has died, become disabled, or retired, should continue beyond high school—as they did for many years—if those children attend college or vocational school. Responding to these concerns, Representative Gwen Moore included a proposal in the Social Security Enhancement and Protection Act of 2019 to restore and make available until age twenty-six these benefits to all full-time high school, college, and advanced vocational education program students. The All Generations Plan restores and extends student benefits to age twenty-six for children of deceased, disabled, and retired workers—a disproportionate number being racial and ethnic minorities or coming from low- or moderate-income households.[27]

## ENHANCE PROTECTIONS FOR WORKERS WITH DISABIILITES, DISABLED ADULT CHILDREN, AND DISABLED WIDOW(ER)S

The large benefit increases that the All Generations Plan proposes expand benefits for workers with disabilities and survivors, as well as for retirees. In addition, though, targeted improvements are important to increase the economic security of workers and their families when disability strikes. Even when workers satisfy the rigorous test of qualifying for disability benefits, they do not begin to receive benefits for five months following the onset of the disability. Moreover, these out-of-work and disabled workers do not receive health insurance in the form of Medicare for two years! Both these waiting periods should be eliminated; the All Generations Plan proposes to do just that.

Other targeted reforms are warranted, as well. Disabled adult children (DACs) are adults who became disabled before age twenty-two and who, as a result of a parent's eligibility for Social Security benefits, can, as adults, receive Social Security children's benefits, even though they haven't qualified based on their own contributions.[28]

Parents generally worry especially about children with disabilities and want to make sure that they are cared for after the parents have died.[29] Parents also want those children to have as independent and productive lives as possible. Social Security helps with these concerns, but there is much need—and room—for improvement.

Social Security has a family maximum, which limits the amount that can be paid based on a worker's earnings record. This may apply even if the disabled adult child is able to live independently. This can have the unfortunate side effect of reducing monthly benefits for the family unit. While this limitation may make sense when a disabled-adult-child beneficiary lives in the family home and shares household expenses, it makes no sense when those beneficiaries do not live with their parents. Although the number is small, the limitation poses a significant barrier for disabled-adult-child beneficiaries who wish to live more independently. This provision potentially penalizes people who adopt children with disabilities. If an adopted child later receives DAC benefits, then the family maximum might reduce benefits for other members of the family.

The DAC benefit also discourages marriage. A disabled adult child loses their benefit if they get married. (There is one strange exception to this: if they marry another person who receives DAC benefits, then both can continue to receive benefits.[30] The All Generations Plan addresses these shortcomings.)

Social Security also recognizes the special hardship faced by people with disabilities who are widowed. While widow(er)s cannot receive survivor benefits until age sixty at the earliest (unless they are caring for dependent children), widow(er)s who are disabled can receive benefits at younger ages, in recognition of their inability to work. But there is an arbitrary age, fifty, for the start of these benefits and a requirement not applied to other persons with disabilities about how recent the onset of the disability must be. Moreover, unlike disabled workers, their benefits are reduced substantially, to 71.5 percent of a full benefit, when they are received at age fifty. The All Generations Plan proposes to drop these arbitrary restrictions and harsh reductions. Like the disabled–adult-child proposal, relatively few people are affected and so the cost is relatively low, but the importance to those who would benefit is substantial.

## NOW IS THE TIME TO EXPAND SOCIAL SECURITY

All of the expansions highlighted in this chapter and discussed in appendix B fit within the solid structure of Social Security, the cornerstone of which was laid eighty-five years ago. We are the wealthiest nation in the world, much wealthier than we were when Social Security was created, and much wealthier than when it was expanded in the past. [31]

The last major legislative expansion occurred in 1972.[32] That was a half century ago; it is time to expand it again. Expanding Social Security, where the benefits go largely to lower-, moderate-, and middle-class families, and paying for those expansions by requiring the wealthiest among us to pay their fair share, will reduce the growing income inequality discussed in chapter 7. The next chapter and appendix B explain just how affordable these expansions are. But we believe the right question to ask is not can we afford these expansions. Rather, the question we should ask is how can we afford not to expand Social Security in these ways. The results will be greater economic security for America's working families and a fairer distribution of the nation's bounty.

# 9

## PAYING THE BILL

HOW SHOULD THE COSTS OF AN EXPANDED SOCIAL SECURITY be shared without unduly burdening anyone? As we explain in this chapter, there are numerous options, all of which are affordable, reasonable, good policy, and fair. Drawing on these options, the All Generations Plan illustrates how our nation can build on the existing financing of Social Security in a manner that not only is fair but will alleviate the perilous upward redistribution of income and wealth.

This chapter explains the nuts and bolts of how to finance an expanded Social Security system.

## MEASURING PROGRAM COSTS AND REVENUES

Opponents of Social Security like to throw around large incomprehensible numbers—billions and trillions of dollars—to make even today's modest benefits sound unaffordable. That is a tactic, a trick, an obfuscation that needs to be understood as such to make reasoned decisions about the future of Social Security. Moreover, talking about trillions of dollars over decades is not only largely incomprehensible but also meaningless because there is no perspective or frame of reference.

Human understanding is sharper and deeper if, instead of using large, unwieldy numbers with which none of us have real-world experience, we work with numbers that are more human in scale. Astronomers do not describe most astronomical distances in miles or kilometers, but rather in terms of the distance light travels in a year, or light-years. It is much easier to understand the relative distances from the Earth to, for example, the stars Sirius and Polaris by comparing 8.6 light-years and 323 light-years, as opposed to approximately 50,600,000,000,000 miles to approximately 1,890,000,000,000,000 miles. The use of the more human-scale numbers allows an easier and clearer understanding of the magnitude of the relative distances.

Fortunately, rather than talking about the cost of Social Security in terms of hundreds of billions and trillions of dollars, there are two more comprehensible measures: "Percent of gross domestic product" (GDP) measures Social Security's costs and expenditures against the total value of all goods the nation produces and all paid services it provides in a single year.[1] Likewise, "percent of taxable payroll" is a measure of what payroll contribution rates would need to be to bring Social Security into actuarial balance over its seventy-five-year estimating period, the cost of any proposed expansion of benefits or revenues, and the cost of any proposed reduction. (The percent is of "taxable" payroll because, as chapter 3 explains, current law applies the current FICA rate only up to a maximum annual earnings level, which is $137,700 in 2020. If that maximum were eliminated, the phrase would simply be "percent of payroll.")

Besides being more understandable than huge dollar amounts, these two approaches address measurement problems that arise as face values change when comparing large dollar amounts over many decades. For example, in 1935, when Social Security was enacted, gasoline cost 19¢ a gallon, a loaf of bread was 8¢, the average home price was $6,300, and the average annual salary was $1,500.[2] Today's prices and salaries would have sounded astronomically large back then. And future prices sound astronomically large to us. Seventy years from now, a loaf of bread is projected to cost around $35, average homes $12 million, and the lowest paying jobs will pay hundreds of thousands of dollars a year.[3]

Talking in terms of percentage of GDP or percent of taxable payroll is much more understandable and meaningful. Percent of GDP provides not only a frame of reference but human-scale numbers. Percentage of GDP allows us to see the cost of Social Security in terms of the nation's total annual income. Percent of taxable payroll can be easily translated into the extent to which the FICA contribution rate would need to be increased to bring the program into actuarial balance over the next three-quarters of a century, as well as the cost or savings of various proposals.

## SOCIAL SECURITY IS FULLY AFFORDABLE

So what will our current Social Security system cost in the future? As figure 9.1 shows, the cost of Social Security as a percentage of GDP is close to a straight, horizontal line for the next three-quarters

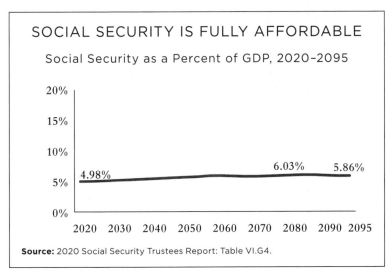

Figure 9.1

of a century and beyond. Social Security currently accounts for around 5 percent of GDP. That percentage is projected to slowly rise to 5.91 percent in 2040, when the youngest Baby Boomers, those born in 1964, reach their 76th birthdays, decline for the next fifteen years, increase a bit, peaking at 6.03 in 2075, and then decline again to around 5.85 percent at the end of the century.[4]

To put those percentages into perspective as figure 9.2 highlights, a number of other industrialized countries spend considerably

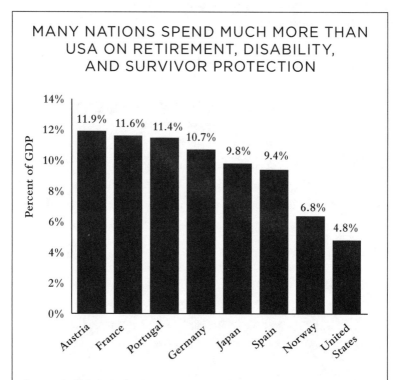

**MANY NATIONS SPEND MUCH MORE THAN USA ON RETIREMENT, DISABILITY, AND SURVIVOR PROTECTION**

**Source:** Analysis by Benjamin W. Veghte of OECD Social Expenditure Database.

**Note:** All data are for 2009 (most recent comparative data available). All countries compared have similar, defined-benefit pension systems. Private systems are excluded, as are targeted social assistance programs. To increase data comparability, only half of spending was counted for program components in other countries that cover all government employees (and only a quarter of spending on those that cover a combination of government employees and members of the military/veterans), as only roughly half (a quarter) of such spending in USA is Social Security spending.

Figure 9.2

higher percentages of their GDP on public pensions—primarily the part of their social security systems that provides old-age, survivors, and disability benefits plus pensions for government workers.[5] Moreover, they spend more today, as a percentage of GDP, than we will spend in 2035, when the entire Baby Boom will be over age seventy. Indeed, we will even spend less at the end of the century on OASDI than those nations spend today on their parallel retirement and disability pension programs![6] Even the expanded system described in chapter 8 will not cost more, in terms of GDP, than those other countries spend![7]

And our nation will be much wealthier in coming decades, just as we are wealthier now than we were seventy-five years ago, before computers, smartphones, and other technological advances. Economists project that our GDP will be much larger than it was seventy-five years ago—and that is using inflation-adjusted numbers, so the growth is real growth. That means that the 5.86 percent of GDP at the end of the century will be easier to afford, just as 10 percent is a larger amount, but more easily afforded, if you are earning $100,000 than if you are earning $10,000. In one case, you have $90,000 remaining; in the other, just $9,000.

Nor should the increase from 4.98 percent to 6.03 percent of GDP over the next half century produce an impact that anyone is likely to notice. Just between 2000 and today, we have experienced almost a one percentage point of GDP increase in the cost of Social Security, from 4.03 to 4.98 percent of GDP.[8] But did you notice?

To put that projected increase between now and 2075 of 1.05 percent of GDP in perspective, military spending after the 9/11 terrorist attack increased 1.1 percent of GDP, as a result of the Iraq and Afghanistan wars—and that increase was the result of a surprise attack, with no advance warning.[9] As another example, spending on public education nationwide went up 2.8 percent of GDP between 1950 and 1975, when the Baby Boom generation showed up as schoolchildren, without much advance warning.[10]

In contrast to the wars that followed the surprise 9/11 attack and the increased numbers of kindergartners who started showing up in 1950, Social Security's actuaries and policymakers knew, shortly after the Baby Boomers were born, that they would someday retire and claim benefits. The actuaries knew that life expectancies would increase. They have been preparing for the eventuality of larger numbers of retirees, living longer, for at least a half century. And they are good at their projections.

From the beginning, the actuaries working on Social Security have made careful, educated projections. In 1934, the actuaries working on President Roosevelt's Committee on Economic Security, the group that devised the Social Security program, made projections about what the world would look like in the year 2000, sixty-six years into the future. In 1934, they projected that the percentage of the population that would be sixty-five or older in 2000 would be 12.7 percent.[11] How accurate were they? Extremely accurate. According to census figures from year 2000, the actual percentage was 12.4 percent.[12] So it is unlikely that today's actuaries are wildly off, despite all the hype that Social Security is unaffordable.

Not only can we afford a larger Social Security program, but it is completely appropriate. In 2020, about 17 percent of our nation consists of people sixty-five and older.[13] By 2060, that percentage is projected to rise to about 23 percent.[14] It is only reasonable that a somewhat greater percentage of the nation's goods and services should be consumed by seniors as their numbers increase. (In chapter 11, we will explain why this increased spending does not hurt young people, despite claims of intergenerational unfairness.)

As a prudent insurer, the Social Security Administration employs more than forty actuaries whose job it is to make those projections. Moreover, Social Security makes those projections out for three-quarters of a century. This is a longer valuation period than that used by private pension plans or by the Social Security programs of most all other industrialized countries. The projections appear in public trustees reports to the Congress.

Whenever projections are made over such a long time horizon, they will rarely show perfect balance.[15] Rather, they may show a surplus, or they may show a deficit. That is unremarkable. The question is, how large is the shortfall and how imminent?

Today, Social Security is projecting a deficit, but that deficit is manageable in size and still about fifteen years away. The 2020 annual report of Social Security's Board of Trustees indicates that the program can meet all its obligations through 2035 and is 3.21 percent of taxable payroll short over the seventy-five-year valuation period. The payroll contribution rate would need to be raised, beginning in 2020, by 3.21 percentage points (1.605 percent on employers and employees each) or program benefits decreased by an equivalent amount to achieve actuarial balance.[16]

These projections should provide Americans with a sense of confidence, because Social Security is being so carefully monitored and managed. Instead, the annual trustees reports have been turned on their heads, creating hysterical cries of bankruptcy every time a distant shortfall is projected.

The remainder of this chapter describes the wide range of options available, not only to eliminate the projected shortfall that recent reports have forecast, but also to pay for all expansions. It identifies those revenue sources proposed as part of the All Generations Plan, as well as some other reasonable funding sources. At the conclusion of the chapter, we summarize the All Generations Plan, including all the expansions and all the revenue sources. Appendix B includes the cost and revenues of the individual elements in the plan. Spoiler alert: Under the All Generations Plan, Social Security will be in surplus for the next seventy-five years and beyond!

## TIME TO INCREASE REVENUES FROM PREMIUMS

As chapter 3 explains, Social Security's wage insurance has been financed, from the beginning, primarily from premiums split evenly between employees and employers. Those premiums today are 12.4 percent of wages, equally divided between employer and employee, up to a maximum salary amount.[17] The 12.4 percent rate has not increased since 1990.[18]

If the rate were to be gradually increased by 0.05 percent on employers and employees each, over a three-decade period, from 2025 to 2054, as the All Generations Plan proposes, that would translate to an average increase of about 50¢ a week each year.[19] It is an annual increase of just a nickel on every hundred dollars of salary or wages. Just that gradual increase would bring in substantial revenue, as appendix B details.[20]

As a fail-safe, the Plan also proposes a one-time contribution increase of 0.50 percent on employers and employees, contingent on whether additional revenues are needed sixty years from now.

The maximum amount of wages on which Social Security contributions are made—$137,700 in 2020—increases every year by the percentage that average wages nationwide increase.[21] However, because wages at the top have gone up rapidly over the past nearly forty years, while nearly everyone else's have stagnated, the impact is that more and more wages at the top escape from being assessed for Social Security.[22] That's why, in contrast to 1982 when Social Security covered 90 percent of all earnings, today it now covers about 83 percent, resulting in a loss of roughly $83 billion in revenues in 2020.

The revenue produced by increasing the Social Security contribution rate would be substantially larger if combined with gradually eliminating the payroll contribution ceiling. Some have argued that instead of just restoring the maximum to 90 percent of all earnings where Congress intended—which should have been done years ago—it should be scrapped altogether. This would result in workers all paying the same rate on all their wages whether they earn the minimum wage or are CEO of a Fortune 500 company.

Only 6 percent of the workforce earns in excess of the maximum.[23] The All Generations Plan gradually phases out the maximum, so that all workers would contribute to Social Security at the same rate on all their cash compensation. The Plan proposes that premium contribution made above the existing ceiling would result in somewhat larger benefits, but that monthly benefits would not exceed $8200. (It is instructive to note that Congress eliminated the maximum with respect to the hospital insurance part of Medicare, starting in 1994.)[24] Those 6 percent, who would under the proposal make larger contributions, would also receive somewhat higher benefits. Nevertheless, the net revenue produced would be substantial.[25]

Obviously, there are other ways of achieving similar revenues. For instance, there is no reason that employers and employees have to pay the same rate or cover the same wages. Employers could pay premiums on their entire payroll, while employees could continue to pay only up to a maximum wage amount. Employees earning at the top 1 percent of the wage scale and their employers could pay premiums on their highest earnings at a higher rate. Although the All Generations Plan does not include these types of proposals, they are all reasonable and would produce substantial revenues to pay for expanded benefits.

Because employee compensation consists of cash earnings and fringe benefits, it matters, for Social Security purposes, that the cost of the civilian workforce's fringe benefits has grown as a percent of total compensation—from 15.8 percent in 1980[26] to 27.4 percent in 2000[27] and 31.4 percent in December 2019.[28] In terms of Social Security's revenues, it's unfortunate that a larger and larger proportion of compensation is paid not as cash but as deferred or noncash compensation, such as health insurance and so-called flexible spending accounts. This compensation is generally not treated as compensation covered by Social Security.[29]

The failure of employer-provided health insurance and other noncash compensation to be counted for Social Security purposes has serious consequences, not just for Social Security's income. It also means that those noncash wages are not insured against loss in the event of death, disability, or old age. Moreover, that failure may encourage employers and employees to set up deferred or noncash compensation plans for the express purpose of avoiding part of the cost of the mandatory Social Security premiums. If just payments to flexible spending accounts were considered wages for Social Security purposes—as contributions to 401(k) plans already are, and as the All Generations Plan advocates—that change alone would generate meaningful new revenue.[30] Moreover, if Medicare for All were enacted and financed through progressive revenues, as it should be, the current 2.9 percent of FICA payments now going to Medicare's Hospital Insurance Trust Fund could be redirected to Social Security's Old-Age, Survivors, and Disability Trust Funds, providing substantial revenue for expansion.

## DIVERSIFY SOCIAL SECURITY'S INVESTMENT PORTFOLIO

In addition to premiums, Social Security has other sources of income. In any year that Social Security has more income than outgo, the surplus is held in trust and invested in interest-bearing treasury bonds backed by the full faith and credit of the United States.[31] These are the safest investment on the planet. (If you have heard that the trust funds aren't real and the bonds are worthless IOUs, you will learn the truth in chapter 11.)

Thanks to past surpluses, the Social Security trust funds have accumulated reserves of $2.9 trillion.[32] The interest from the investments of these funds accounted for about 8 percent of Social Security's total income in 2019, or about $81 billion in that one year alone.[33] By law, these funds can only be invested in interest-bearing United States' obligations or in entities whose principal and interest are guaranteed by the United States. While Social Security's principal is secure and its income is fixed, bonds tend to produce less income over time than investment in stocks. To get a higher return, Social Security could diversify its portfolio by investing a portion of its assets in broad-based stock funds. Virtually all other pension funds have this kind of diversified investment portfolio, including most public pensions because higher market returns can be realized.

The All Generations Plan advocates diversifying Social Security's portfolio by investment in broad-based equity funds, with appropriate safeguards to ensure no improper interference in the governing of the businesses or markets. This is a very different proposal from simply placing contributions in individual retirement accounts, which subject individuals to the vagaries of the stock market. Regardless of whether the stock market went up or down, Social Security benefits would remain guaranteed. Retirement income would continue to be based on earnings records, not stock market fluctuations.

## INCREASE PROGRESSIVE REVENUES

Even if Social Security's premiums were assessed against all wages and salaries, not just those up to the maximum, the structure would simply be proportionate—everyone would pay the same flat percentage. Social Security's investment income is similarly proportionate. Social Security's premium income and investment earnings, which make up around 96.5 percent of Social Security's annual revenue,[34] do not require the wealthy—no matter how many hundreds of millions of dollars they earn each year—to pay a larger percentage of their earned income than anyone else. And no matter how much unearned income and wealth they have—perhaps billions of dollars—they contribute not a penny of that to Social Security.

Historically, Americans have believed that those who have more should contribute more to the common good. This is even more true, given the rising and perilous income and wealth inequality the nation has experienced in recent decades. And, as explained in chapter 7, that income and wealth inequality has cost Social Security many billions of dollars of revenue.

Having the wealthiest bear a greater burden of expenses for the common good is as American as apple pie, and for good reason. All of us benefit from public expenditures, but the wealthy benefit the most. Since they have the most property, they are arguably disproportionately advantaged by having police, military, court systems, fire departments, and other public services designed to protect us and our property. The accumulation of large estates is dependent, in part, on the general productivity of the American economy and its infrastructure—including, for example, roads, police, and education. Also, the very well-off benefited far more than others from large tax cuts, initiated during Ronald Reagan's, George W. Bush's, and Donald Trump's presidencies. Further, as chapter 7 highlights, since the mid-1970s, a dramatic increase has taken place in the share of income going to the top 1 percent of American households, and there has been an enormous concentration of wealth. It is reasonable to ask of those who have benefited so greatly from the commonwealth (i.e., common wealth) to contribute more to the common good, specifically more to Social Security.[35]

Taxation of earned income is currently the primary source of revenue to fund the government. Federal income tax is intended to be progressive, with increasing marginal rates. In theory, the more income you have, the higher percentage you pay. Yet, thanks to all of those tax cuts and enormous so-called tax "expenditures," the federal income tax increasingly favors the richest Americans and corporations.

Though the phrase "tax expenditures" sounds oxymoronic, it is a crucial concept to understand. Spending through the Internal Revenue Code—giving tax breaks for inducing action (as opposed to simply spending in a more direct, straightforward, and often more efficient way)—is called tax "spending" or tax "expenditures" by policymakers and tax experts. Those receiving tax expenditures pay significantly lower taxes. And those who don't must make up the difference, if the federal deficit and debt are not to grow.

The nation currently spends literally trillions of dollars through our federal income tax laws. Some of this spending is for important and popular uses, such as the charitable contribution deduction to encourage charitable giving and the deduction of home mortgage payments to encourage home ownership. But others benefit special interests that harm the public or certainly don't benefit it, such as special breaks for fossil fuel companies—which add to extreme weather—and for real estate developers like the Trump family.

Requiring the wealthiest among us to pay more, while still retaining the great bulk of their fortunes, has precedent. In fact, it was the norm for most of the past one hundred years. The top marginal income tax rates were 70 percent or higher each and every year between 1936 and 1980, before dropping to today's low rates.[36] Indeed, even during the relatively conservative administration of President Eisenhower from 1953 to 1961, the highest marginal personal income tax rates exceeded 90 percent. Today, the top rate is only 37 percent.[37] As figure 9.3 shows, a top marginal rate ten, twenty, even fifty percentage points higher would still be below what it was in the 1950s and 1960s, when the nation had a thriving middle class and much greater income and wealth equality.

Moreover, the wealthiest among us receive most of their annual incomes from earnings on assets—so called unearned income which is subject to substantially lower income tax rates than income earned by hardworking middle- and lower-income workers.

Eliminating special interest tax expenditures while treating unearned income like earned income for income tax purposes and requiring those who make up the top 1 percent of wealth to pay higher marginal tax rates will, together with other revenue sources described in this chapter, pay for making Social Security fully adequate, as described in chapter 8. As an important by-product, it will make our system of taxation much fairer. That is something fair-minded policymakers have tried to achieve, but special interests have always thwarted their efforts. Dedicating the revenue gained from this fairer income tax system makes reform much more likely to succeed.

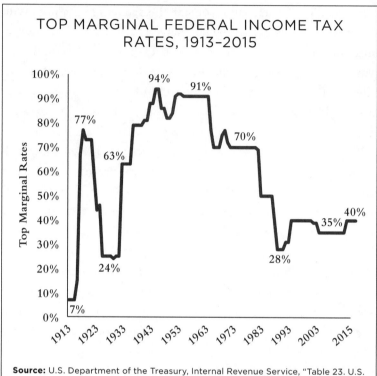

## TOP MARGINAL FEDERAL INCOME TAX RATES, 1913–2015

Source: U.S. Department of the Treasury, Internal Revenue Service, "Table 23. U.S. Individual Income Tax: Personal Exemptions, and Lowest and Highest Bracket Tax Rates, and Tax Base for Regular Tax, Tax Years 1913–2015," https://www.irs.gov /statistics/soi-tax-stats-historical-table-23 (accessed March 3, 2020).

Figure 9.3

Even more progressive tax could be used to contribute a small percentage of progressive revenue to help fund Social Security. The income tax, by definition, focuses only on income, not wealth. Senators Elizabeth Warren (D-MA) and Bernie Sanders (I-VT) have each proposed annual wealth taxes on multimillionaires. It is noteworthy that the top 1 percent owns more wealth than the bottom 90 percent combined.[38] Some or all of the proceeds from that proposed tax could be dedicated to Social Security.

Similarly, the federal estate tax is the nation's most progressive tax. Estates left to spouses are not subject to tax. More than $11 million of wealth can be left tax-free to other heirs, meaning couples can bequeath $23.16 million tax-free to non-spouse heirs in 2020. In 2018, only the top 0.2 percent of people who died had estates large enough to pay even a penny in estate taxes. That was just around 1,900 of the more than 2.8 million deaths that year.[39]

The estate tax should be preserved as a matter of principle. Inherited wealth undercuts the democratic ideal of a meritocracy. Imposition of a tax upon the transfer of huge estates from one generation to another is consistent with basic democratic principles, as was recognized by, among others, Thomas Paine, one of the leading intellectuals behind the American Revolution and an advocate of an inheritance tax.[40] Requiring the very wealthiest Americans to contribute a portion of their fortune to the common good seems a reasonable minimum to ask of those who have benefited so greatly from living in the United States. And dedicating those funds to Social Security makes perfect sense.

Another progressive tax, also with a good policy impact, is a financial speculation tax, which arguably could be dedicated to Social Security, though we recognize that there are other critical needs that revenues from such a tax could fund. Speculation in stocks, derivatives, and other financial instruments has no economic benefit. Indeed, irresponsible speculation and defaults on exotic financial instruments are what brought our economy to its knees in 2008. A tax on Wall Street speculation, a so-called financial transactions tax, imposed at a very low rate and primarily levied on large banks, would, if its proceeds were dedicated to Social Security, together with the other taxes described in this chapter, allow benefits to be expanded substantially.

England has had such a tax since 1694. The United Kingdom imposes a modest tax of 0.5 percent on stock transfers—0.25 percent on the purchaser and 0.25 percent on the seller.[41] If the United States had a financial transaction tax equal to what the United Kingdom assesses—just 0.5 percent on stock transfers—and imposed it on the sale and purchase of stocks, credit swaps, and other exotic financial instruments, it would fall mainly on large banks that engage in proprietary, speculative trading and serve the public goal of reducing stock market speculation by large Wall Street banks. As stated elsewhere, the United States is the wealthiest nation in the world at the wealthiest moment in its history.[42] It may not feel that way to most readers because that wealth is highly skewed. A fairer system of taxation, with revenue dedicated to Social Security, would allow all of us to share the wealth that all of us have created.

# REVENUE SOURCES THAT REQUIRE NO ONE TO PAY MORE

### Increase Immigration

Contrary to another popular belief—that immigrants are a drain on the economy—decades of economic research reveal that immigration *benefits* U.S. aggregate economic growth.[43] Social Security's financing shares in this economic benefit because, on average, immigrants are younger than the general population, so they will work and contribute to Social Security for more decades than the nation's American-born, aging population. If immigration were doubled, Social Security would gain around $5.5 trillion over the next seventy-five years.[44]

The projected increased revenue from doubling immigration is about fifteen times the cost of restoring an important part of Social Security that was wrongfully eliminated in 1981: benefits to students between the ages of eighteen and twenty-two, discussed in the previous chapter. Indeed, it is substantially more than the cost of giving all current and future beneficiaries a 5 percent increase starting today.

Because immigrants to the United States tend to be younger and may, as a matter of culture, have larger families, they increase the ratio of working-age population to retirement-age population in much the same way as higher fertility rates do. In congressional testimony, the chief actuary of the Social Security Administration explained the benefit to Social Security of increased immigration:

Immigration has played a fundamental role in the growth and evolution of the U.S. population and will continue to do so in the future. In the 2014 Trustees Report to Congress, we projected that net annual immigration will add about 1 million people annually to our population. With the number of annual births at about 4 million, the net immigration will have a substantial effect on population growth and on the age distribution of the population. Without this net immigration, the effects of the drop in birth rates after 1965 would be much more severe for the finances of Social Security, Medicare, and for retirement plans in general.[45]

Another fact contrary to common belief is that undocumented workers benefit Social Security, even more than documented workers. This is because they contribute but are prohibited from receiving benefits. The actuaries at the Social Security Administration have estimated that unauthorized immigrants were responsible for a $12 billion revenue increase for Social Security in 2010 alone.[46]

Donald Trump has demonized hardworking immigrants who have come to the United States in search of a better life for themselves and their families. Trump's treatment of them and his rhetoric are a moral disgrace. It is also economically foolhardy. Even those who are not moved by the morality of the issue should understand that it is in their—and all of our—self-interest to once again be the welcoming nation that the Statue of Liberty symbolizes and greatly expand immigration. The All Generations Plan provides for just that.

## Peace Dividend

The United States spends more on the military than the next seven highest-spending countries combined.[47] When all the monies from different corners of the federal budget are added together—fighting current wars, preparing to fight wars, dealing with the consequences of wars, as well as spending on homeland security—the *annual* spending amount totals more than $1.25 trillion.[48]

With the end of the Cold War and the fall of the Soviet Union, there was much talk of a peace dividend. At the end of other American wars, the military was reduced and war funding was spent on domestic needs.[49] One way finally to make that peace dividend a reality would be to simply allocate a small percentage of funds now spent on the military and related activities and instead dedicate that percentage to Social Security. If 10 percent of that $1.25 trillion were dedicated to Social Security, that would amount, over the next seventy-five years, to about 1.7 percent of taxable payroll or 0.61 percent of GDP.

Although many of the benefit expansions and revenue enhancements discussed in chapters 8 and 9 are not part of the All Generations Plan, we believe they, too, deserve consideration in the context of the next major Social Security reform. The All Generations Plan is not the only approach to expanding Social Security. We believe many other excellent legislative and policy proposals fully deserve careful consideration. Still, we share our plan as an example of what a major Social Security expansion could be, inclusive of large benefit improvements and sufficient revenues to achieve solvency over the next seventy-five years.

Here we present a brief summary of the All Generations Plan. The specifics of the plan are discussed in much greater detail in appendix B.

## SUMMARY OF THE SOCIAL SECURITY WORKS ALL GENERATIONS PLAN

To strengthen retirement security and address the retirement income crisis, the All Generations Plan would:

- Increase benefits for all current and future beneficiaries so the vast majority of Americans can maintain their standards of living without supplementation in old age or if tragedy strikes in the form of disability or death. Just as Social Security currently has a minimum benefit and a maximum family benefit, the All Generations Plan provides a maximum individual benefit of $8,200 a month.

- Reduce early retirement reductions for every month benefits are claimed before the statutorily defined retirement age, so that those claiming benefits early will receive more than current law provides.

- Change disability eligibility criteria for older workers, ages fifty to sixty-six, whose employment possibilities and earnings potential are greatly limited due to health, functional disability, and availability of suitable employment. (And do the same for SSI.)

- Eliminate five-month and twenty-four-month waiting periods for people with disabilities. The time it takes to determine eligibility for disability insurance benefits can stretch to more than two years. That's obviously a huge problem in itself and there is much to be said about it. But here we want to raise the profile of two lesser known problems that persons deemed eligible for benefits experience—a five-month waiting period after being determined eligible before their monthly cash benefits begin and a twenty-four-month waiting period before their Medicare health benefit protections begin. It almost seems like a bad joke, but it is not. It's just plain wrong that persons with potentially great needs to access health care should have an additional barrier to such care or for them not to have immediate access to their monthly benefits. Removal of these barriers to benefits would cost 0.12 percent of taxable payroll or 0.04 percent of GDP. Cost would also accrue to the Medicare program.

We also include changes in the All Generations Plan that would

- Ensure that benefits do not erode over time by using the more accurate Consumer Price Index for the Elderly (CPI-E).
- Provide a minimum benefit of 125 percent of poverty at full retirement age with thirty years of work.

To strengthen family protections for all generations and to reinforce the caregiving functions of the family, the plan would:

- Provide up to twelve weeks of paid family leave and paid sick leave.
- Provide up to five years of Social Security benefit credits for caring for children or other family members who need care.
- Provide a new child benefit of $2,000 upon the birth or adoption of a child.
- Facilitate higher education by restoring and extending student benefits for dependent children up to age twenty-six whose covered parents have died, retired, or become disabled.
- Provide equity for disabled widow(er)s by eliminating both the age fifty requirement and the seven-year rule and by providing unreduced benefits.
- Encourage work and support family caregiving by not applying the Family Maximum when Disabled Adult Children do not live at home and by eliminating the marriage penalty.

To secure Social Security's financing for generations to come, the plan would:

- Gradually, increase the Social Security contribution rate from 2025 to 2054, until the rate reaches 7.7 percent on both employers and employees in 2054 and later; and then include a one-time contribution increase of 0.50 percent on employers and employees, contingent on whether additional revenues are needed sixty years from now.

- Gradually eliminate the maximum taxable wage base, giving credit for these contributions.
- Treat capital gains as ordinary income, reported and taxed annually with proceeds dedicated to Social Security.
- Restore the federal estate tax to the way it was in 2000 and dedicate proceeds to Social Security.
- Dedicate a modest financial transaction tax of 0.25 percent on both the sale and purchase of stocks and exotic financial instruments such as credit swaps.
- Invest in well-being of future generations by repealing tax expenditures enjoyed by the fossil fuel industry and activities destructive to the environment and civil society (for example, private criminal justice facilities). As the long-delayed peace dividend, reallocate 10 percent of military expenditures to Social Security.
- Double the rate of immigration to the United States.
- Restore the federal estate tax to the 2000 level.
- Diversify Social Security's trust fund portfolio by investing 40 percent of its reserve in broad-based equity funds (phased in over fifteen years).
- Require Social Security contributions to be assessed on all salary reductions, as they now are on 401(k) plans.
- Combine the OASI and DI trust funds into a single OASDI trust fund. (See chapter 11 and appendix B for additional information about these two trust funds.)

In addition to a more detailed discussion of the All Generations Plan, readers can find estimates of the costs of benefit expansion and financing proposals in appendix B. Taken together, the increased revenues from our expansion plan fully pay for the benefit improvements and leave Social Security in long-range actuarial balance for the next three-quarters of a century and beyond.

## CONCLUSION

The United States is the wealthiest nation in the world.[50] It may not feel that way, because most of the recent gains in income have gone to those at the very top of the economic ladder. Nevertheless, together all of us who are part of the United States are wealthy enough to afford the expanded Social Security system we advocate.

Means-tested programs, including the Supplemental Security Income program, should be expanded and its recipients held harmless, so that expanding Social Security doesn't result in the loss of Medicaid benefits. (Indeed, Medicaid should be folded into a universal Medicare for All program.)

As an important by-product, the revenue sources included in the All Generations Plan make the system of taxation in this country much fairer. While solving the nation's retirement income crisis, the All Generations Plan addresses the past few decades' upward redistribution of wealth and takes a step toward ameliorating the nation's caregiving needs.

Yes, we can expand our Social Security system and address the nation's challenges outlined in previous chapters. Yes, we can afford to do it. Unfortunately, it is not as simple as these last two sentences sound. Standing in the way are determined, powerful, and well-financed foes. The next chapter reveals who they are.

PART FOUR

# THE THREATS TO OUR SOCIAL SECURITY

# 10

## THE BILLIONAIRES' WAR AGAINST SOCIAL SECURITY

OUT OF SIGHT FROM MOST AMERICANS, POWERFUL, ORGA-nized, and determined moneyed interests have waged a more than three-decade-long campaign to dismantle Social Security. That campaign has enjoyed some success. And it is with us still.

It is not hard to see the successes of that campaign. Many have been persuaded that Social Security is unaffordable, in crisis, and must, at the very least, be scaled back. But while the campaign has succeeded in undermining confidence in the future of Social Security, it has failed in scaling back Social Security's modest but vital benefits or, worse, radically transforming Social Security, ending it as we know it. And over the past few years, the movement to expand Social Security with no cuts has been growing.

This chapter tells the story of the billionaires' campaign and the progressive effort to defeat it. And, as lead-in to a more extensive discussion in chapter 12 of why Social Security's supporters must remain vigilant, we end this chapter with a teaser about a new billionaire (well, maybe billionaire) who rode into the White House in January 2017 promising that, believe him, he would never, ever cut Social Security—but whose words and actions before running for office and once in power put the lie to that promise.

Even today, prominent Republicans and major media outlets continue to buy the billionaire-funded campaign's propaganda. They continue to claim that Social Security must be cut. On July 23, 2019, for example, Senator Lindsay Graham argued, "We've gotta fix entitlements. We're in debt because we made promises we can't keep to Medicare, Social Security, and Medicaid."[1] Similarly, cohost Joe Scarborough of the MSNBC show *Morning Joe*, retweeted an article about the growing federal deficits and commented:

> Umm, this is what happens when you pass massive tax cuts for the rich, bust the Pentagon budget, and *refuse to stop entitlement programs from spiraling toward bankruptcy* [emphasis added].[2]

And these supposedly Very Serious People[3] scheme over how to force action, in light of the overwhelming opposition of the American people to cutting Social Security.[4] Senator Joni Ernst (R–IA), when asked by a constituent about Social Security at an August 31, 2019, town hall meeting, said, in a burst of candor, that Congress should act "behind closed doors."[5] Similarly, Senator Mitt Romney (R–UT), joined by a few conservative Democrats and other Republicans, has introduced the TRUST Act, which calls for a commission to develop Social Security recommendations that would be forced through Congress with limited debate and other rules that would make stopping the measure more difficult than it would be for regular legislation.[6]

These efforts are only the latest in a long-running narrative that Social Security is unaffordable and must be cut, but politicians lack the political courage to do so.

In her important article "How the Media Has Shaped the Social Security Debate," Trudy Lieberman—a highly regarded, award-winning journalist of more than four decades—highlights the distortions that have characterized the mainstream-media reporting on Social Security: "For nearly three years CJR [the *Columbia Journalism Review*, where Lieberman was a contributing editor] has observed that much of the press has reported only one side of this story using 'facts' that are misleading or flat-out wrong while ignoring others."[7]

It is no accident that the media and political elite discussions have had this flavor. It has resulted from a deliberate campaign, backed by hundreds of millions of dollars and a cottage industry of academics who have built their careers on criticizing Social Security. Together, those forces have brought a veneer of respectability to claims that Social Security is unaffordable, in crisis, and spawning competition and conflict between generations.[8]

Abetting the effort have been journalists and politicians who have either willingly advanced an anti–Social Security agenda or fallen prey to myths, misunderstandings, half-truths, and a few outright lies that have been masquerading as incontrovertible facts. Perhaps unwittingly, they have advanced policy changes that would render Social Security unrecognizable and undermine the economic security of the American people.

The next chapter will explode the pervasive myths, half-truths, and mischaracterizations that have been put forward by this well-financed campaign and that have gained such traction in the public discourse. But first, in this chapter, we pull back the curtain and reveal the campaign itself.

The three-decade-long period is bookended by two commissions, whose differing approaches and recommendations reveal just how successful the campaign was in shaping the recent debate.[9] A third commission, about halfway through the period, provides an informative and inside look at one of the least well known, but most influential, billionaires, who until his death helped drive the campaign.

## A TALE OF THREE COMMISSIONS

The first commission was the National Commission on Social Security Reform—often referred to as the Greenspan Commission in reference to the economist Alan Greenspan, who chaired it. (Both authors of this book served as staff to the commission.) The Greenspan Commission has been touted as an enormous success and a shining example of bipartisanship at its best.[10] What is largely forgotten is that it was born out of a failed attempt in 1981 to undermine the program by determined opponents.

As explained in the previous chapter, Social Security is extremely conservatively managed. Unsurprisingly, as good as actuaries are, and as hard as they work, projections are just that: projections, not crystal balls. Consequently, they may not be right on target, and, indeed, may be way off the mark on occasion. This is why projections are made every year. In response to a projected shortfall, Congress took action in 1977,[11] and the subsequent Trustees Report showed that the legislative changes had accomplished their intended purpose.[12] Accordingly, Social Security's 1979 Trustees Report projected that the program could pay all benefits through 2032.[13]

But the very next year, thanks to a continued bad economy and a technical problem with the 1977 legislation, the 1980 Trustees Report projected a shortfall just three years away, in 1983.[14] Despite claims after the 1977 amendments that Social Security had been restored to balance, it was once again projecting an immediate deficit. In addition, much like today, there was concern in Washington about federal deficits in the nation's general operating fund. In those twin deficits—one in the government's operating budget, the other in Social Security—opponents saw an opportunity.

One of those opponents was David Stockman, who was appointed budget director by the newly elected president Ronald Reagan. In his memoir, written a few years later, after leaving government, Stockman admitted that he considered Social Security "closet socialism."[15] He had earlier confided in an interview with journalist Bill Greider that Social Security's projected deficit would "permit the politicians to make it look like they're doing something *for* the beneficiary population when they are doing something *to* it, which they normally wouldn't have the courage to undertake [emphasis added]."[16] But Stockman was too clever for his own good.

Congress was well on its way to passing legislation in 1981 to eliminate the new projected shortfall, when Stockman inadvertently derailed the process. In the midst of congressional deliberations, the Reagan administration, at Stockman's urging, unveiled a Social Security package that called for draconian benefit reductions.[17] One reduction would have fallen very heavily on workers reaching retirement age the very next year, workers who were counting on that income to be able to retire.[18]

Not surprisingly, the proposal set off a political firestorm. The proposal, and, indeed, the entire package, had little to do with good Social Security policy and everything to do with diminishing the size of the program. It is that episode that gave rise to the now-famous expression that Social Security is the third rail of politics—mess with it at your peril.[19] The strong negative public outcry forced the administration to withdraw the not-yet-submitted package, but that was not enough.

The outcry was so great that President Reagan, in a face-saving move, announced that he, together with the leaders in Congress, would appoint a bipartisan commission. The ensuing Greenspan Commission was hastily conceived to quench the political firestorm.[20]

Fast forward thirty years. The commission that enters the story more recently is President Obama's National Commission on Fiscal Responsibility and Reform. Like the Greenspan Commission, it is best known by the name of its chairs. As a sign of the times, President Obama selected not one but two chairs, one from each political party: a center-right Democrat and a Republican, both of whom had long sought to cut Social Security.[21] They were Erskine Bowles, businessman and former chief of staff to President Clinton, and former Republican senator Alan Simpson.

The executive orders establishing these two commissions reveal how attitudes changed over those thirty years, thanks to the intervening billionaire-funded campaign. President Reagan's December 16, 1981, Executive Order 12335 defined the Greenspan Commission's task as recommending solutions "that will both assure the financial integrity of the Social Security System and the provision of appropriate benefits."[22] President Obama's February 18, 2010, Executive Order 13531 defined the task as proposing recommendations that "balance the budget, excluding interest payments on the debt, by 2015," and "that meaningfully improve the long-run fiscal outlook, *including changes to address the growth of entitlement spending* and the gap between the projected revenues and expenditures of the Federal Government [emphasis added]."[23]

Note the difference in substance and language. By the very terms of the Reagan executive order, the commission was required to focus not just on solvency but also on the provision of adequate benefits. And Reagan's order instructed the commission to limit its focus to Social Security on its own, apart from general budgetary concerns. Early on, the commission members agreed to limit their focus even more by excluding Medicare from consideration. They recognized that Medicare was a very different program from Social Security's cash benefits and required different expertise and different solutions.

Also ruled off the table were proposals to means-test, privatize, or otherwise fundamentally change Social Security.[24] Indeed, the Greenspan Commission's very first recommendation stated that Congress "should not alter the fundamental structure of the Social Security program or undermine its fundamental principles."[25]

The 1982 commission and its staff functioned within the framework of serious knowledge and support for Social Security. Appointments on the Greenspan Commission epitomized Republican and Democratic commitment to the institution of Social Security. Alan Greenspan appointed Robert J. Myers, chief actuary of Social Security from 1947 to 1970, as executive director, and House Speaker Tip O'Neill (D-MA) appointed, as a member of the commission, Robert M. Ball, Social Security commissioner from

1962 to 1973. The commission's membership included senators and representatives, and public representatives from business and labor, from both parties, the majority of whom had significant expertise in Social Security. Thus, it is not surprising that substantial analytic attention was given to the consequences of reform options on workers and future Social Security beneficiaries, including implications across income classes.[26]

In contrast to the limited scope of Reagan's executive order, President Obama's executive order was expansive, covering all of the federal government's expenditures—other than interest on the debt—and all of its revenue. Unlike the Greenspan Commission, which explicitly separated the discussion of Social Security's cash benefit programs from Medicare, the Obama order lumped together Social Security, Medicare, and Medicaid under the rubric of "entitlement spending." Moreover, there were few members and staff with in-depth understanding of Social Security. And while some members sought to include information about the distributional impact of various policy options or of what the benefit reductions might mean to individuals and their families, for the commission as a whole such information appeared to be little more than an afterthought.[27]

Let's pause for a moment on the language of the Reagan and Obama executive orders. They offer an important insight into a crucial tactic of the long-standing campaign against Social Security.

President Reagan's executive order refers straightforwardly to "the Social Security System." In stark contrast, President Obama's executive order refers opaquely to "entitlement spending," a budgetary term that could include numerous mandatory spending programs, as well as provisions in the Internal Revenue Code, sometimes referred to as tax entitlements. But the reference is well understood as Washington-speak referring to Social Security, Medicare, and Medicaid—three extremely different programs with different structures, goals, budgetary impacts, and financial outlooks.

Indeed, the change in terminology—the fact that many policy-makers now call Social Security an entitlement—is part of the story. The popularization and promulgation of the terms "entitlement" and "entitlement crisis" as political tools to strengthen the hand of those wanting to cut Social Security was the handiwork of yet another commission, this one established by President Clinton's November 9, 1993, executive order—the Bipartisan Commission on Entitlement and Tax Reform.[28] (Coauthor Eric R. Kingson was on staff to this commission.)

This commission never produced recommendations that garnered even a majority of votes.[29] While never achieving consensus, the commission, by lumping Social Security, Medicare, and Medicaid together as part of a unified entitlement crisis, helped set the terms of the Social Security debates that would follow.

Pity the poor word "entitlement." In less than a year, this eleven-letter term migrated from being perfectly respectable budget jargon—though boring, wonky, and technical—into the proverbial four-letter word, used to suggest that the benefits Americans earned were less than deserved, and to obfuscate the goals of those who sought to radically diminish social protections.

Focus groups indicate that most people equate the word "entitlement" with a government handout—receiving something for nothing. But here's the catch that pollster Celinda Lake uncovered: when participants in focus groups are told that the term "entitlement" includes Social Security, they vigorously disagree. Social Security can't be an entitlement, focus group members say, since they have earned their benefits, just as they earn their other compensation for work performed.[30] When they are told that, in Washington, entitlement does indeed refer to Social Security, as well as to Medicare and Medicaid, they are often angry and insulted.[31]

The American people do not like the change in language, but the media loved the story line that entitlement spending on the old was crowding out spending on the young and ruining the country. When the Entitlement Commission released an interim report identifying the size of the so-called problem,[32] front-page newspaper stories appeared, and network news shows ran major segments on the problems caused by out-of-control entitlement spending. A headline in the *Los Angeles Times* alarmingly trumpeted, for example, "Entitlements Seen Taking Up Nearly All Taxes by 2012."[33]

But the reach of some of the Entitlement Commission's members was greater than simply the commission's legacy of making the word "entitlement" a pejorative label. Alan Simpson—who later became the cochair of Obama's commission—was a member of the Entitlement Commission. The final report[34] was released two months after Erskine Bowles—the other future Obama Commission cochair—became President Clinton's deputy chief of staff.[35] Presumably, Bowles read it, and, based on his subsequent actions, it seems likely that he was influenced by it.

President Obama gave both men considerable prominence by naming them as cochairs to his commission, notwithstanding the hostility that both had displayed to Social Security in the past. Indeed, the outspoken Simpson has helped popularize the phrase "greedy geezers"[36] and once referred crudely to Social Security as "a milk cow with 310 million tits!"[37] Not surprisingly, the cuts proposed for Social Security by Bowles and Simpson not only were deep, but would radically transform the program, gradually but inexorably, from wage insurance—where benefits are designed to replace a set percentage of wages—to a program where all beneficiaries receive about the same subsistence level benefit amount, largely unrelated to wages.

The overall Bowles-Simpson deficit reduction proposal was widely lauded in the mainstream media but has thankfully faded from view. There was another member of the Entitlement Commission whose money and activities have been largely responsible for the change over the past thirty years so well exemplified by the Greenspan and Bowles-Simpson commissions.

# MONEY, MONEY, MONEY

He is the late Peter G. Peterson, an investment banker who was ranked during his lifetime as one of the richest men in America.[38] His billions provided most of the money behind the campaign. He created a number of supposedly independent think tanks—all of which, no surprise, assert through their work that Social Security is unaffordable and must be cut—culminating in the creation of the Peter G. Peterson Foundation, which he endowed with $1 billion.[39]

Peterson formed the foundation in 2008 but had been pushing the issue, spending time and money on his crusade to cut Social Security, for more than thirty years. In 1982, Peterson—then the chairman and CEO of Lehman Brothers, and former secretary of commerce in the cabinet of President Richard Nixon—wrote two articles for the *New York Review of Books*, both published shortly before the Greenspan Commission issued its report. The first appeared on December 2, 1982, and was titled "Social Security: The Coming Crash." It began: "Social Security's troubles are fundamental. Its financial problems are not minor and temporary, as most politicians, at least in election years, feel compelled to insist. Unless the system is reorganized, these problems will become overwhelming. To put the matter bluntly, Social Security is heading for a crash." [40]

The second article, titled "The Salvation of Social Security," appeared two weeks later, and asserted:

> Social Security . . . threatens the entire economy. In the recent election campaign, practically all the candidates promised to "preserve Social Security," to "resist any cuts in benefits," and to "protect the elderly poor." No one dared to say that without major reforms—including "cuts"—the Social Security system will run huge deficits, that these deficits will push our children into a situation of economic stagnation and social conflict and

create a potentially disastrous situation for the elderly of the future. [41]

This was one of the very first times anyone claimed that Social Security is hurting young people.[42] Ironically, Peterson's own children (and the authors themselves) were young adults when he first began making the intergenerational theft claims.[43] Now, all of us are approaching or have reached old age and are the ones supposedly threatening the well-being of today's children and young adults. Fast forward twenty-five years from now. No doubt Peterson's ideological progeny will be claiming that Gen Xers, persons born from 1965 to 1980, are stealing from Millennials and those who follow! (For more on the campaign's efforts to ignite intergenerational warfare and why seniors are not robbing children, see the next chapter.)

In yet another *New York Review of Books* article that appeared shortly after the Greenspan Commission had reported in 1983, but before Congress had taken action, Peterson wrote, "[I]f, as with past reforms, we pretend that the report has restored long-term solvency to the system, we will find that it has become simply another example of unjustified optimism."[44] Peterson was dismayed that the Greenspan Commission's recommendations, which were largely enacted as the Social Security Amendments of 1983, did not fundamentally restructure Social Security.[45] Despite Peterson's alarmist warnings, all benefits have been paid in full and on time to this day.

Over the years, starting when those articles were published, Peterson funded numerous nonprofit organizations, all working to convince politicians and the mainstream media that the federal deficit must be reduced by cutting entitlements. In 1981, for example, he helped to form the Committee for a Responsible Federal Budget, which has been a major player in arguing for the need to cut Social Security. In 1992, he was the founding president of the Concord Coalition,[46] whose mission, according to its website, includes "educating the public about . . . the long-term challenges facing America's unsustainable entitlement programs."[47] More recently, in 2010, he funded the development, by Columbia Teachers College, of a high school curriculum on fiscal issues, which was distributed free of charge to high schools around the country.[48]

Around the same time, his Peterson Foundation promoted a movie, called *I.O.U.S.A.*, which opened in four hundred theaters[49] and was broadcast on CNN.[50] The movie starred David Walker, the then-president and CEO of the Peterson Foundation, and Robert Bixby, the executive director of the Concord Coalition.[51] The foundation also gave out a number of grants to produce guides and other teaching tools to accompany the movie.[52]

Walker left the Peterson Foundation in 2010 to head his own organization, Comeback America, which received a $3.1 million grant from the Peterson Foundation,[53] and, for three years, supported an agenda closely aligned with the Peterson Foundation's. (Comeback America ceased operations in September 2013.[54]) Peterson was a key player in the deficit debates that consumed much of the Obama presidency. During that period, his foundation hosted annual high-profile fiscal summits where former president Clinton and other luminaries spoke.[55] Prior to the 2008 election, he bought two full pages in the *New York Times* urging the creation of a "bipartisan fiscal responsibility commission" by whomever was elected.[56]

His son, Michael Peterson, carries on the family tradition as president and CEO of the Peter G. Peterson Foundation. [57] The foundation continues to fund organizations advocating cutting Social Security, Medicare, and Medicaid in the name of deficit reduction. The past and current leadership of Fix the Debt, a spin-off of the Committee for a Responsible Federal Budget (CRFB) (which ironically was gestated by the New America Foundation, yet another Peterson-funded organization), includes the younger Peterson. Other veterans of the deficit wars with close ties as cofounders and board members of CFRB and related organizations have served in similar roles with Fix the Debt—including multi-billionaire and former New York City mayor Michael Bloomberg, Deficit Commission co-chairs Alan Simpson and Erskine Bowles, former Honeywell CEO David Cote, and Maya McGuineas, CRFB president and formerly director of the New America Foundation's Fiscal Policy Program.

The hypocrisy of Fix the Debt is remarkable. Fix the Debt claims to want to reduce the federal deficit, but nearly half of its board and steering committee members have ties to companies that lobby hard to preserve corporate tax breaks.[58]

Peterson and the Fix the Debt crowd have not been the only tycoons involved in this debate. One of the conservative Koch brothers, Charles Koch, for example, used a drop of his vast fortune to found the Cato Institute, a libertarian think tank. (It was founded in 1974 as the Charles Koch Foundation but changed its name to the Cato Foundation in 1976.[59])

## THE FOOT SOLDIERS IN THE WAR AGAINST SOCIAL SECURITY

In 1980, Cato published *Social Security: The Inherent Contradiction*, which argues that Social Security should be replaced with a system of private accounts.[60] The author, Peter Ferrara, then just out of law school, made a career out of pushing his Social Security views (though, more recently, he has ventured into the area of climate change denial[61]). He is currently a senior fellow at the Heartland Institute, a self-described "free market think tank," and an adviser for entitlement and budget policy at the National Tax Limitation Foundation.[62] In the more than thirty years since the publication of his book, Ferrara has also spent time at the Heritage Foundation, another conservative think tank. The Heritage Foundation was started in 1973 by another tycoon, beer magnate Joseph Coors, together with two young congressional aides.[63]

The determined foes of Social Security redoubled their efforts in the wake of their disappointment that their hero Ronald Reagan had not dismantled Social Security, the crown jewel of the New Deal. Just a few months after the enactment of the recommendations of the Greenspan Commission, the Koch-funded Cato Institute devoted its entire fall journal to criticizing Social Security and plotting its demise through the substitution of private accounts.[64]

Two employees of the Heritage Foundation coauthored one of the articles, mentioned earlier in this book, provocatively titled "Achieving Social Security Reform: A 'Leninist' Strategy." The authors chose that title because, they explained, they advocated adopting Lenin's insight "that fundamental change is contingent both upon a movement's ability to create a focused political coalition and upon its success in isolating and weakening its opponents."[65] The authors encouraged their comrades to prepare for the long haul, concluding, "as Lenin well knew, to be a successful revolutionary, one must also be patient and consistently plan for real reform."[66]

The next thirty-five years after the publication of the "Leninist Strategy" played out much as the revolutionaries envisioned it might. It was aided by academics, some of whom were just starting out in the 1970s, when Social Security was first trumpeted in newspaper headlines as going bankrupt. Laurence J. Kotlikoff, professor of economics at Boston University, for example, published his very first professional article, titled "Social Security: Time for Reform," in June 1978.[67] It was published by the Institute for Contemporary Studies, a think tank established in 1974 by associates of then–governor Ronald Reagan. Since the publication of that first article, Kotlikoff has spent the rest of his professional career arguing that Social Security is unfair to younger generations.[68]

Journalist Trudy Lieberman illuminates the access to media and the interlocking strategies employed by those dedicated to pulling Social Security apart brick by brick. Commenting on a lengthy *Esquire* piece titled "The War Against Youth," and subtitled "The recession didn't gut the prospects of American young people. The Baby Boomers took care of that,"[69] she observes:

> The argument that fat-cat elders are shafting young people follows from [the title and subtitle]. The author, Stephen Marche, writes: "The biggest boondoggle of all is Social Security," and he goes on to explain that the Baby Boomers are to blame.
>
> What readers of Esquire may not know is that, two years ago, the magazine assembled a bipartisan commission, similar to Obama's Simpson-Bowles Commission, that—in three days' time—came up with a plan to balance the federal budget. The Esquire group's recommendations were similar to those made by Simpson-Bowles.
>
> At the end of its report, the Esquire panel thanked the Committee for a Responsible Federal Budget and its president, Maya MacGuineas, "for their invaluable assistance in providing the commission with accurate data and budget options."[70]

Thanks to all of these forces, media elites and both political parties lost an understanding of the conceptual underpinnings that have led to Social Security's popularity, and have been convinced to see Social Security as a problem rather than the solution that it is.

This failure of both political parties with respect to challenging misinformation and false narratives about Social Security was perhaps best illustrated in the 2012 presidential election between President Barack Obama and former governor (and now Republican senator from Utah) Mitt Romney. In their October 3, 2012, televised debate, Obama was asked, "Mr. President, do you see a major difference between the two of you on Social Security?" His response: "You know, I suspect that on Social Security, we've got a somewhat similar position."[71] This about an opponent who had supported Social Security privatization and had picked as his running mate Paul Ryan, who was, until his retirement from Congress in 2019, top contender for the label of most enthusiastic and aggressive opponent of Social Security in the Republican Party![72]

But then the Democratic Party woke up and rediscovered its values. It started with then–Senator Tom Harkin (D-IA), who focused on the retirement crisis highlighted in chapters 3 and 4. He saw that the solution was to expand Social Security and in 2013 introduced legislation to do just that.[73]

Harkin's insight woke his colleagues. That fall, the authors, in their capacity as cochairs of a broad-based, diverse coalition, sponsored a one-day conference on expanding Social Security. The conference, which was held on Capitol Hill, concluded with numerous Democratic senators and congresspeople speaking about the importance of Social Security and their support for expanding, not cutting, it.[74] Not surprisingly, one of those senators was Bernie Sanders, the self-proclaimed democratic socialist from Vermont. (It should be noted that Sanders never bought into the conventional thinking pushed by the billionaire-funded campaign against Social Security. When others sought a bipartisan compromise that included benefit cuts, Sanders always stood firmly against all cuts.)

In 2016, Sanders, among the strongest champions of Social Security, decided to challenge Secretary Hillary Clinton for the Democratic nomination. On February 5, 2015, just after the closest of primaries in Iowa and just days before the New Hampshire primary, Sanders tweeted, "I urge Sec. Clinton to join me in saying loudly and clearly that we will never cut Social Security."[75] Though Clinton had been part of the administration that had established the Bowles-Simpson Commission and worked with Republicans on a so-called Grand Bargain that exchanged cuts to Social Security for tax increases, Clinton tweeted back, "I won't cut Social Security. As always, I'll defend it, & I'll expand it. Enough false innuendos."[76]

That caused virtually the entire Democratic establishment to fall in line behind this return to fundamental support for protecting and expanding Social Security, with no cuts. As detailed at length in chapter 12, the Republicans cling to the billionaires' playbook, continuing to claim that Social Security is unaffordable, is unfair to future generations, and must be cut. A comparison of the 2008 Party Platforms reveal that playbook.[77] The change in the Democratic Party Platform language between 2012 and 2016 spotlights the return of the Democratic Party to unequivocal support for Social Security, for its expansion-without-cuts story.

The 2008 Democratic Party Platform promised in its preamble to "protect Social Security, and help Americans save for retirement."[78] Despite the title of the plank, "Retirement and Social Security," the phrase Social Security was not even mentioned until the 258th and 259th words of the 300-word section. Its 53 words about Social Security offered only the vague promise to "fulfill our obligation to strengthen Social Security."[79]

The Social Security plank of the 2008 Republican Party Platform, like the Democratic plank, asserted vaguely, "We are committed to putting Social Security on a sound fiscal basis."[80] While the 2008 Democratic plank included the defensive promise, "We will not privatize Social Security," it asserted, near the outset, "In the 21st Century, Americans . . . need better ways to save for retirement." And, in contrast to its vague Social Security promise to "strengthen it," the plank followed the assertion about "better" ways for saving in the twenty-first century with the specific proposal: "We will automatically enroll every worker in a workplace pension plan that can be carried from job to job and we will match savings for working families who need the help."[81]

Notwithstanding the 2008 Democratic line expressing opposition to privatization, the Republican plank that year did not use the words, "privatize Social Security." Muddying the distinction between what the two parties supported, the Republican plank deftly promised, "Comprehensive reform should include the opportunity to freely choose to create your own personal investment accounts which are distinct from and supplemental to the overall Social Security system."[82]

To the careful reader, the two planks read very differently. The 2008 Republican Platform entitled its Social Security, Medicare, and Medicaid plank "Entitlement Reform." It claimed, falsely, that "younger workers will not be able to depend on Social Security as part of their retirement plan." Following the Leninist strategy, it reassured, "No changes in the system should adversely affect any current or near-retiree." Moreover, it hinted at privatization, asserting, "We believe the solution should give workers control over, and a fair return on, their contributions."[83] In contrast, the 2008 Democratic plank stated that it believed Social Security to be indispensable and promised "to make sure that it provides guaranteed benefits."[84]

But on a quick read, the distinctions were easily overlooked. Though the Republicans devoted twice as many words to Social Security in 2008, the specifics were similar. Vaguely promising to "strengthen" Social Security, in the case of the Democrats, or "putting Social Security on a sound fiscal basis," in the case of the Republicans, most of the focus of both was on saving for retirement.

The 2016 Democratic Platform illuminates the sea change in the party. It is worth reading in its entirety:

## Protecting and Expanding Social Security

Democrats are proud to be the party that created Social Security, one of the nation's most successful and effective programs. Without Social Security, nearly half of America's seniors would be living in poverty. Social Security is more than just a retirement program. It also provides important life insurance to young survivors of deceased workers and provides disability insurance protection. We will fight every effort to cut, privatize, or weaken Social Security, including attempts to raise the retirement age, diminish benefits by cutting cost-of-living adjustments, or reducing earned benefits.

Democrats will expand Social Security so that every American can retire with dignity and respect, including women who are widowed or took time out of the workforce to care for their children, aging parents, or ailing family members. The Democratic Party recognizes that the way Social Security cost-of-living adjustments are calculated may not always reflect the spending patterns of seniors, particularly the disproportionate amount they spend on health-care expenses. We are committed to exploring alternatives that could better and more equitably serve seniors.

We will make sure Social Security's guaranteed benefits continue for generations to come by asking those at the top to pay more, and will achieve this goal by taxing some of the income of people above $250,000. The Democratic Party is also committed to providing all necessary financial support for the Social Security Administration so that it can provide timely benefits and high-quality service for those it serves. Our plan contrasts starkly with Donald Trump. He has referred to Social Security as a "Ponzi scheme" and has called for privatizing it as well as increasing the retirement age.[85]

Revealingly, the 2016 Republican Party Platform continued to employ deceptive tactics. The platform falsely asserts that "[E]veryone knows that [Social Security's] current course will lead to a financial and social disaster." Employing the Leninist strategy, the Republican plank immediately reassures older Americans: "Current retirees and those close to retirement can be assured of their benefits." Asserting that "all options should be considered to preserve Social Security," [86] it then immediately contradicts itself by stating opposition to tax increases.

Thanks to the Democratic Party awakening from its Leninist strategy–induced slumber, the debate over Social Security has become more evenhanded. Do we cut Social Security or expand it? And what is the fairest way, consistent with the program's fundamental structure, to pay for Social Security's earned benefits? When those are the questions, there is no need for secrecy, for fast tracks, for undemocratic processes, for gridlock. No need, because, as polarized as the American people are over many issues, we are united in our support for Social Security.

But don't bet on the Republicans and their billionaire donors going quietly into the night. When one strategy to cut and destroy Social Security fails, another appears.

While Donald Trump ran on a promise not to cut Social Security, once he got into power he immediately took steps to harm it. All of that will be documented in chapter 12. Supporters of Social Security need to understand the tactics of those who want to undermine Social Security and be constantly vigilant—topics we elaborate on in chapter 12. But first, the next chapter will dissect the conventional thinking—so prevalent, so embedded, but so wrong.

# 11

## THE CONVENTIONAL WISDOM IS JUST PLAIN WRONG

TALKING WITH FAMILY AND FRIENDS, LISTENING TO CNN AND FOX News, or following public debate about the future of Social Security, you've likely heard one or more of the following comments asserted as incontrovertible fact:

- Social Security is going bankrupt, going broke, in crisis; young people will never see a penny in benefits.[1]
- Social Security's trust funds are simply an accounting gimmick, worthless IOUs.[2]
- Social Security is unsustainable. There just will not be enough working-age people to support retired Baby Boomers.[3]
- A demographic tsunami is on its way, threatening to drown our children and grandchildren.
- Spending on entitlements—Social Security, Medicare, and Medicaid—is by far the major cause of federal deficits and debt.
- Everyone's living longer; it only makes sense to raise the retirement age.[4]
- Social Security is unfair to younger Americans.
- Social Security is unfair to African Americans.
- You could do better investing on your own.[5]

- People should be able to take money from Social Security just as they can from their 401(k)s.[6]
- Rich people should not get Social Security.[7]
- Cutting payroll taxes is an important tool for stimulating the economy and quickly putting money into the hands of people.

There are other claims, which sometimes appear in one's email inbox or in discussions with friends and family. They include:

- Social Security is a Ponzi scheme.[8]
- Senators and members of Congress should pay into Social Security, but they don't.
- Undocumented workers get benefits without paying in. They should not get Social Security.[9]

This chapter offers a point-by-point refutation of each of these assertions. We then step back and put each point/counterpoint into perspective, showing how these claims undermine confidence in the future of Social Security and distract attention from what is really going on. But first, the facts:

**CLAIM:** *Social Security is going bankrupt, going broke, in crisis; young people will never see a penny in benefits.*

**TRUTH:** As long as there are Americans who work, there is simply no way that Social Security can run out of money. Social Security has a dedicated revenue stream that is not going away. Its major source of income—$948 billion in 2019 (89 percent of its revenues)—comes from the contributions of workers and employers. As long as there are workers, Social Security will continue to collect billions of dollars in income, week in and week out, for the next seventy-five years and beyond.

Starting back in 1941, the year after monthly benefits began, Social Security's board of trustees has reported to Congress on the long-range financial health of the program, each and every year. The Trustees Report projects out seventy-five years so that Congress always has plenty of time to act when necessary to address a projected imbalance, to ensure that promised benefits will always be paid.

This careful and transparent monitoring should provide the American people with a sense of confidence. Instead, the annual reports have been the occasion for scare stories—false claims the program is going bankrupt every time there is a projected deficit, no matter how manageable in size or how far out in the future.

Bankruptcy is a meaningless concept when applied to the federal government or any of its programs. No one says that the Pentagon or Department of Agriculture are going bankrupt. Ironically, their funding is far less secure than Social Security's because they do not have dedicated revenue streams and because estimates of those agencies' costs are not projected out more than five or ten years.

Even if Congress were to take no action for a decade, Social Security is projected to have sufficient dedicated revenue to pay 100 percent of promised benefits for more than a decade. After that, it is projected to have enough income to pay around 75¢ on the dollar for the foreseeable future.[10] Obviously, in addition to expanding benefits, enough revenue should be brought in to cover that manageable shortfall, as the All Generations Plan does.

Congress has never failed to act to secure Social Security's funding. It never will. As long as there are politicians who want to keep their jobs it will continue to pay out all benefits earned by working Americans, just as it has for more than eighty years. The issue is one of political will, not economics, demographics, or mathematics.

**CLAIM:** *Social Security's trust funds are simply an accounting gimmick. The $2.9 trillion in bonds that Social Security holds are just a bunch of* *paper, worthless IOUs. The federal government has already spent the money, so it will have to raise everyone's taxes or cut earned benefits to pay promised benefits.*

**TRUTH:** These charges have been around for a long time, beginning in 1936, when the Republican nominee for president, Alf Landon, and his allies claimed that the Social Security trust fund was filled with worthless "IOUs."[11] They were not true then, and they are not today. Here's why.

Since 1935, the money that workers and their employers entrust to Social Security has been invested prudently and conservatively. The trustees are required by law to invest Social Security's trust funds in interest-bearing treasury obligations or in entities whose principal and interest are guaranteed by the United States, the safest investment in the world.

These are not casual promises to pay. They are legal instruments backed by the full faith and credit of the United States, just like those green paper things you have in your wallet that also have value because they too are similarly backed. The treasury bonds held by Social Security have the same legal status as bonds bought by you, a bank, a foreign government, or any other person or entity that invests in U.S. treasuries.

The charge that the money has already been spent indicates either a misunderstanding of bonds or a desire to deceive. All those who issue bonds, whether they are corporations or government entities, do so to raise funds to be spent. The fact that the funds are spent, and what they are spent on, does not alter the legal obligation to repay.

The U.S. government has not robbed the American people's trust fund. We do not believe it ever will. But we would be remiss to not acknowledge a danger. Should earned benefits be cut one day as an alternative to paying back borrowed funds, then this indeed would be a raid on the American people's earned benefits. It is highly unlikely that the United States would ever overtly renege on its debts. It would be outrageous if U.S. Treasury obligations held by China, Russia, or private pension funds would be honored but not those held in trust for America's workers. But, more fundamentally, why should the wealthiest nation in the world[12] default on any of its obligations? And why would anyone claim that our nation would ever do so?

**CLAIM:** *Social Security is unsustainable. Just look at the numbers. Once, sixteen workers supported each Social Security beneficiary. Today, less than three workers support each person receiving these benefits. With 10,000 Baby Boomers turning sixty-five every day from 2011 to 2029, there just will not be enough working-age people to support them.*

**TRUTH:** This is a scary claim. The truth is that the worker-to-beneficiary ratio, which compares the number of workers contributing to Social Security to the number of people drawing Social Security benefits, reveals very little about the affordability of Social Security. In fact, the logic behind this claim falls apart with a little analysis.

The sixteen-to-one ratio is a meaningless factoid, plucked from 1950, when Social Security was still in its start-up phase. Not unexpected, only five years later, the worker-to-beneficiary ratio was just about halved, dropping to 8.6-to-1 in 1955, and then to 3.2-to-1 by 1975. Neither is it surprising that in 2013, as increasing numbers of Baby Boomers began receiving their benefits, the ratio was down to about 2.8-to-1, where it has remained until today.[13] (Social Security's actuaries project further decline to 2.3-to-1 in 2035 when all Baby Boomers are at least age sixty-five.)

There's nothing remarkable here. Very high worker to beneficiary ratios have been experienced by all pension plans, public and private, at the start, when few workers have yet qualified for benefits. Moreover, Social Security was expanded in 1950 to cover millions of new workers in agriculture and other parts of the economy. All of these new workers were paying into Social Security, but none of them had worked long enough to become insured and start collecting benefits.

By itself, the worker-to-beneficiary ratio tells us very little. It sheds no light on how productive those workers are, on whether other burdens on those workers are increasing or decreasing, on how the gains from increased productivity will be distributed, or on the increase in the labor force participation of persons sixty-five and over since the early 1990s.[14] The worker-to-beneficiary ratio does not reveal the burdens imposed on workers from support of all dependents, just of those receiving Social Security benefits. All of these points are elaborated in response to the next, related charge.

**CLAIM:** *A demographic tsunami is on its way, threatening to drown our children and grandchildren. It's not just the growing cost of Social Security we have to worry about; it's all those programs directed at supporting a largely unproductive group, especially Baby Boomers as they continue to age.*[15]

**TRUTH:** This is another iteration of scare tactics, based on half-truths, misinformation, and harmful stereotypes used to create a sense of crisis where none exists and to pave the way for cuts that will fall most heavily on today's young.

The quality of life of the old, while still problematic for many, is much better than it was before Social Security, Medicare, and Medicaid, and a whole host of other investments made, some early in the twentieth century—in sanitation, improved public health, control of life-threatening diseases, education, the economy, and the like.

The United States, like virtually every other advanced industrial society, has reached a point in its social development where there is far less infant and childhood mortality than in the past, reduced fertility, and a growing older population relative to its younger populations. More people are reaching old age, and once getting there are, on average, living somewhat longer than in the past.

Indeed, the numbers of people sixty-five and older are projected to grow from 56 million in 2020 to 73 million in 2030 to 95 million in 2060, when all surviving Baby Boomers will be at least age ninety-five. The very old, persons eighty-five and older, will nearly triple from 6.7 million in 2020 to 19 million in 2060. There are challenges that come with this, including questions of how to engage the productive capacity of older people, how we should make meaning of the gift of longer lives, and how to approach the frailties and significant disabilities that often accompany aging. But paying for Social Security's modest benefits, as discussed in chapter 9, can be easily handled.

Nevertheless, the opponents of Social Security continue to focus on the so-called old-age dependency ratio as irrefutable evidence to further support their argument that a growing aged population cannot be supported by tomorrow's workforce. Again, there is no question that the estimates of the old-age dependency ratio show an increasing number of persons age sixty-five and older (all assumed to be financially dependent by this measure) to every hundred persons age twenty to sixty-four (all assumed to be productive workers). For example, it is projected to grow from twenty-eight per hundred in 2020 to forty-one per hundred in 2065 when all surviving Baby Boomers will be at least one hundred years old. But the old-age dependency ratio presents a one-sided, distorted picture of "dependency," leaving out children under age twenty, the vast majority of whom (no surprise!) do not work.

That's why a very different story emerges when children are counted as part of the dependent population, that is, when the "overall dependency ratio" is estimated, including children under twenty as well as seniors sixty-five and older. As figure 11.1 plainly shows, the ratio of the number of children and seniors to every hundred persons ages twenty to sixty-four will not be greater than it was in 1965, not even in 2065 when all surviving Baby Boomers are age one hundred and older!

But the overall dependency ratio figure tells only part of the story. It does not show that many people age sixty-five and older work and that more may do so in the future. Or that some adults ages twenty to sixty-four do not work and that some children under age twenty do work. Most fundamentally, it does not reflect the productivity of the economy or of how the benefits of this productivity will be distributed across various groups. It does not show how immigration may change the equation, how investments in education and technological advances may result in a more productive workforce, how political decisions to promote—or not promote—investment in green energy, environmental protection, and the nation's infrastructure may alter the equation. In other

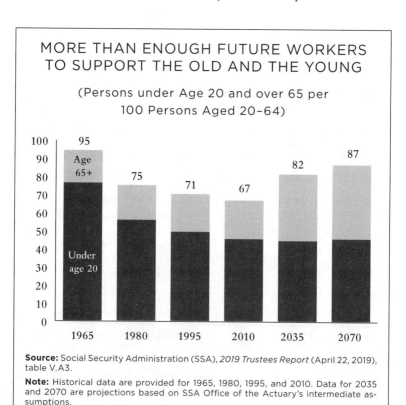

**MORE THAN ENOUGH FUTURE WORKERS TO SUPPORT THE OLD AND THE YOUNG**

(Persons under Age 20 and over 65 per 100 Persons Aged 20-64)

**Source:** Social Security Administration (SSA), *2019 Trustees Report* (April 22, 2019), table V.A3.

**Note:** Historical data are provided for 1965, 1980, 1995, and 2010. Data for 2035 and 2070 are projections based on SSA Office of the Actuary's intermediate assumptions.

Figure 11.1

words, the ability of our nation to support people of all ages is not a simple matter of demographics.

In short, once again, the conventional wisdom is wrong.

**CLAIM:** *Spending on entitlements—Social Security, Medicare, and Medicaid—is by far the major cause of federal deficits and debt. Left unchecked, this spending will bankrupt the nation.*[16]

**TRUTH:** Social Security, Medicare, and Medicaid are very different programs, with different structures and purposes. Moreover, as discussed in chapter 10, "entitlement" sounds to typical Americans like a government handout. Social Security and Medicare are earned through hard work and premiums, generally deducted from pay. Medicaid ensures that the very sick and poorest among us can obtain medical care, sometimes lifesaving medical care. Lumping these three programs together confuses clear analysis.

When one treats these three programs as distinct, several points become clear. First, Social Security does not add a penny to the public debt. By law, it cannot pay its benefits without sufficient income to cover the cost of doing so. It simply has no borrowing authority.[17] Moreover, the drivers of our current, short-term budget deficits and billowing federal debt were two wars fought on a credit card, tax cuts for the wealthy, and the Great Recession and the economic crash it caused.

As we write in August 2020, there is also a new and totally unexpected driver of deficits and debt—large unanticipated declines in federal revenues and unprecedented emergency spending to stabilize the economy during the first few months of economic crisis precipitated by the COVID-19 pandemic. Four bills were passed with bipartisan support in March and April 2020 and signed by President Trump, the largest a $2 trillion package that mainly went to large corporations and some small businesses.[18] More large investments in stabilizing the economy are virtually certain.

In the long term, large projected deficits and growing national

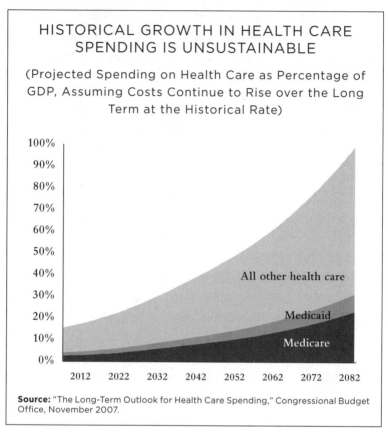

## HISTORICAL GROWTH IN HEALTH CARE SPENDING IS UNSUSTAINABLE

(Projected Spending on Health Care as Percentage of GDP, Assuming Costs Continue to Rise over the Long Term at the Historical Rate)

All other health care

Medicaid

Medicare

**Source:** "The Long-Term Outlook for Health Care Spending," Congressional Budget Office, November 2007.

Figure 11.2

debt are caused by unsustainable health-care costs, private as well as public. In chapter 9, figure 9.1 shows that Social Security's costs are essentially a straight, horizontal line, at around 6 percent of GDP. In contrast, figure 11.2, produced in 2007 by the CBO, illustrates that, if health-care costs—private and public—were to continue to rise as they did from 1975 through 2005, these costs would consume a whopping 99 percent of GDP in seventy-five years.

Obviously, not even a country as wealthy as ours can spend 99 percent of its GDP on health care. Figure 11.3 uses somewhat more recent data and does not project out as far. The basic trend is the same and is, of course, impossible to sustain.

Figures 11.2 and 11.3 reveal the rising costs of Medicare and

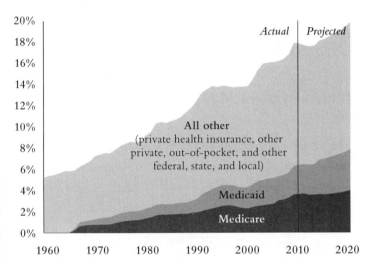

Figure 11.3

Medicaid are a symptom of and outpaced by the growth of our overly expensive private health-care system. Indeed, Medicare's per capita administrative costs are lower than those in the private sector—around 2 percent of program expenditures[19] versus 11 to 17 percent in private plans[20]—despite covering seniors and people with disabilities, groups that, on average, need more medical care. Even more striking, Medicaid, which has the complicated administrative burden of means-testing those it covers, also has much lower administrative costs than private insurance—less than 5 percent in 2019.[21]

If the United States had the same per capita health-care cost as any other industrialized country, our nation would project long-term federal budget surpluses for the next seventy-five years and beyond. (The highly respected Center for Economic Policy Research has an online calculator that allows you to pick any of those other countries and see the effect on the U.S. budget.[22])

When one stops looking simplistically at "entitlements" but instead analyzes with greater sophistication the three programs separately, the blinders come off, and what is affordable and what is not come sharply into focus.

**CLAIM:** *Everyone's living longer; it only makes sense to raise the retirement age.*

**TRUTH:** Those who make this charge use figures that show average life expectancies from birth before medicine had conquered many of the diseases that killed many infants and children. Back in 1935, when Social Security was enacted, infant mortality was extremely high. Nearly fifty-three (52.8) infants under the age of one died out of every thousand births. In 1940, when monthly benefits began, the infant mortality rate was 47 per thousand.[23] In contrast, in 2019, the rate was 5.69 per thousand.[24]

Consider how different and less sensational the story is when we look at changes in life expectancies at age sixty-five, not at birth. To be clear, most people who lived—and live—to twenty generally live to sixty-five. Life expectancies at age sixty-five have increased over the years but much, much less than life expectancies at birth. Men who made it to age sixty-five in 1940 lived, on average, an additional 11.9 years, to age 76.9, and women lived on average an additional 13.4 years, to age 78.4. How does that compare to today? In 2019—the most recent historical data available in the annual Social Security Trustees Report—men are living, on average, 6.2 years longer than they were in 1940; women are living, on average, 7.2 years longer.[25]

Moreover, changes in average life expectancies are not unidirectional and life expectancies differ considerably across race, ethnicity, gender, education, and income class. For example, an article in the *Journal of the American Medical Association* reveals that life expectancy at age twenty-five actually declined in the United States from 2010 to 2017, especially among those whose educations did not extend beyond high school. Life expectancy increased for college graduates. Life expectancy for non-Hispanic white men aged twenty-five was three and a half years longer than for non-Hispanic Black men. It was two years longer for white women relative to Black women.[26] But facts such as these do not slow down the rhetoric of people whose goal is to undermine confidence in the future of Social Security by making it sound unaffordable in the future.

Indeed, Social Security's most vociferous opponents emphasize changing life expectancies simply as a rationalization for cutting benefits. As chapter 5 explains, raising Social Security's defined "retirement age" by a year is mathematically indistinguishable from about a 6 to 7 percent cut in retirement benefits, whether one retires at sixty-two, sixty-seven, seventy, or any age in between. It is easy to think that if the retirement age is increased and you work longer, you will catch up—and that sounds reasonable, but it is wrong. To really, deeply understand why, one must be thoroughly immersed in how benefits are calculated. Figure 11.4 presents a picture that is better, we hope, than the proverbial thousand words. As that figure shows, if the retirement age is increased, you always get less than you would have without the change.

Moreover, this manner of cutting benefits—by raising the statutory retirement age—is especially hard on low-wage workers. Low-wage workers are disproportionately people of color, who are more likely to work in physically demanding jobs, and caregivers—disproportionately women—who often leave or reduce employment to care for aged parents or other family members, as we discuss in chapter 6. And some are older workers who, like many of their peers, have a much harder time finding new work after being laid off. With no job prospects, they may find themselves with no choice but to claim permanently reduced retired worker benefits at age sixty-two.

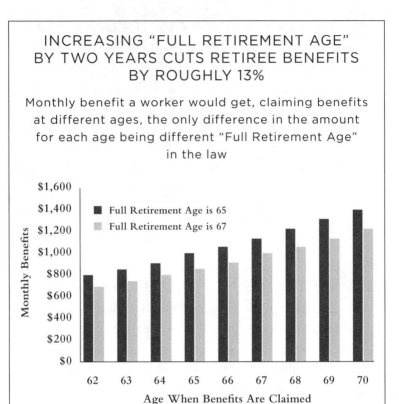

## INCREASING "FULL RETIREMENT AGE" BY TWO YEARS CUTS RETIREE BENEFITS BY ROUGHLY 13%

Monthly benefit a worker would get, claiming benefits at different ages, the only difference in the amount for each age being different "Full Retirement Age" in the law

**Note:** The Full Retirement Age is currently rising from 65 to 67, beginning with those born in 1938. The full retirement age for those born in 1960 or later is 67. Monthly benefits reflect the 8 percent delayed retirement credit after Full Retirement Age.

**Source:** Virginia P. Reno and Elisa A. Walker, "Social Security Benefits, Finances, and Policy Options: A Primer," National Academy of Social Insurance, April 2012.

Figure 11.4

We are right now in the middle of seeing the full retirement age rise to sixty-seven—a 13 percent across-the-board benefit cut. We think the current increase is poor policy, which will produce unanticipated hardship. Let's not compound it with further increases.

**CLAIM:** *Social Security is unfair to younger Americans. Too much is going to seniors, and not enough to children.*[27]

**TRUTH:** This claim has a veneer of reasonableness and even some academic respectability. Old versus young is catchy, sells newspapers, and gets online clicks. But it is a flawed concept, best understood as a political theme and strategy for undermining public investments in health, education, income supports, and other policies and programs serving all generations. It is based on a very narrow measure of what's fair, one that implicitly raises a virtually unmeasurable notion of fairness between generations over more measurable and visible matters of fairness, such as between the top 1 percent and the other 99 percent or between Black and white Americans.

Today's most important social justice issues include such matters as addressing institutional racism, eliminating poverty and moving those who are lower-income into the middle class, ending mass incarceration, and providing access to quality health care for all—not a poorly conceptualized notion of fairness between generations."

Elevating competition and fairness between generations as the primary basis for making public policy also ignores that there is far more inequality within any given age group than there is between age groups. There is little "inequality" between rich old people and rich children. But there is much to be concerned about when it comes to inequalities of income, wealth, and political power and health disparities that structure and scar the lives of generations, and when it comes to tax giveaways, deregulation of the banking industry, and decisions about war and peace.[28]

Further, the elevation of fairness between generations as one of the most, if not the most, important basis for making policy builds on a distorted view of who benefits from public policies. The federal government spends money on many important concerns, including military, environment, agriculture, health care, and much more. State and local governments fund public schools, higher education, criminal justice systems, public health, and more. That some

186	SOCIAL SECURITY WORKS FOR EVERYONE!

funding appears to do more for one age group than another does not mean it is right or wrong. It could be that too much or too little is being directed at the needs of both age groups. Or that tax and spending policies shower too much benefit on rich and shortchange low- and middle-income persons, regardless of age.

Those making claims of unfairness between generations either fail to understand or purposely overlook the many benefits of public spending flowing across all generations. For example, spending on Alzheimer's research sounds like spending on the old. Yet it is not today's old but today's children who will benefit most. And spending on early childhood education is an investment in the citizens and workers who will one day support the old.

Similarly, Social Security is not simply a program for today's old. As we discuss in chapter 3, it is also our largest children's program and the most important source of life and disability insurance that most families have. The anti–Social Security warriors also fail to mention that young workers and their families are accruing valuable lifelong protections against lost wages and that the children of today will be the seniors of tomorrow, relying heavily on their own Social Security.

In other words, taking a snapshot at one point in time obfuscates an inconvenient truth about those wanting to dismantle Social Security and, parenthetically, Medicare and Medicaid: in reality, it is today's young workers and today's children who will experience the largest cuts if the "generational equity" crowd has its way.

We should, as a society, spend more on children, especially those at greatest risk. And more on seniors and other groups as well. As the wealthiest nation in the world,[29] we can certainly do so, if we so choose.

**CLAIM:** *Social Security is unfair to African Americans because, on average, African Americans have shorter life expectancies.*[30]

**TRUTH:** This is a particularly misguided charge. It is true that African Americans have shorter life expectancies, on average, than European Americans, although, upon reaching sixty-five, the life expectancies of white and Black Americans are much closer than at younger ages, and, indeed, cross over around age 85.[31] The Census Bureau estimates that a sixty-five-year-old African American woman has a life expectancy of 84.8 in 2017, compared to 86.2 for white non-Hispanic women, and a sixty-five-year-old African American man has a life expectancy of 81.7, compared to 83.7 for white non-Hispanic men.[32] Because of these shorter average life expectancies, African Americans collect Social Security's retirement benefits, on average, for a shorter period of time than their white counterparts.

We believe that the government should be investing aggressively to eliminate the causes of social, health, and economic disparities. But Social Security is certainly not the cause and does much to protect the incomes of Black Americans. Moreover, more than any other government program, it offsets financial inequities. African Americans are more likely to become disabled or die prematurely than their white counterparts. While approximately 13 percent of the population is Black, 17 percent of those receiving disability insurance benefits are.[33] African American children constitute 23 percent of the children receiving Social Security survivor benefits.[34] Social Security's benefits are progressively structured. Due to lower median earnings than the population as a whole, and higher rates of unemployment, on average, African Americans receive benefits that are proportionately higher, as a percentage of wages, than those with higher wages and fewer years of unemployment. More fundamentally, the charge fails to acknowledge Social Security's vital importance to African Americans. In 2017, it was virtually the only source of retirement income for 35 percent of African American elderly married couples receiving Social Security and 58 percent of unmarried elderly African American beneficiaries.[35]

It should come as no surprise that without Social Security, the poverty rate among African American seniors would have increased from roughly 19 percent to 50 percent in 2018.[36]

But again, the explanation so far doesn't really get to the heart of the matter. At base, those making this charge are doing so in a particularly cold-blooded and calculated way. They rarely, if ever, focus on the root causes of these disparities or propose to address the factors that lead to the shorter average life expectancy, including disproportionately high rates of poverty, environmental hazards, discrimination, unaffordability of health care among others. These and other factors are what causes these discrepancies in the first place. Asserting the claim that Social Security is unfair to African Americans in order to undermine support for a program, so essential to African American families, is simply adding insult to a terribly unjust injury.

Parenthetically, many of these same arguments have been made to make the case that Social Security is unfair to Latinx populations. There is one big difference, though. Despite having, on average, lower incomes and less education than white non-Hispanics, the life expectancies of Hispanics are longer at ages sixty-five and seventy-five than the general population.[37] Other than this, the explanations about why this claim is flawed for Latinx populations are very similar to the type we just presented with respect to African Americans.

**CLAIM:** *You could do better investing on your own.*

**TRUTH:** As chapter 1 and 3 explain, Social Security is insurance, not savings. It provides joint and survivor old-age annuities, life insurance, and disability insurance. Plus, it provides inflation protection and protection in the case of divorce. Everyone should save, but for secure, guaranteed income to replace wages lost in the event of death, disability, and old age, what is needed is wage insurance. Everyone who has a home should have fire insurance, not just savings. Everyone who has a car should have car insurance, not just savings. And everyone who works must—and should—have wage insurance in the form of Social Security. Savings on top of that valuable foundation of insurance are to be applauded, but savings are not a replacement for Social Security. It is time to expand that foundation.

The near collapse of the economy following the subprime mortgage crisis of 2007–8 and the massive unemployment and economic instability generated by the COVID-19 crisis show that financial fortunes—even for those who have saved diligently—can change in a heartbeat. Such crises are another reason why wage insurance is so important. And even if the highly affluent can self-insure against crises, they benefit from living in a country that provides all working families with basic economic security when wages are lost. They benefit economically because the more income working families have, the more economic activity there is. They benefit because when low- and middle income families have more income, the nation is more stable. They also benefit simply as a matter of decency and morality, by living in a country that treats everyone with compassion and respect.

**CLAIM:** *People should be able to take money from Social Security just as they can from their 401(k)s.*

**TRUTH:** Again, Social Security is insurance. It is not savings. It most certainly should not be treated as a piggy bank. As the next chapter explains, this is the latest ploy of those who seek to end Social Security as we know it. In recent years, a number of plans have been floated that would allow people the ability to trade away a part of their future security by giving up some Social Security benefits in exchange for paid family leave, cancellation of student debt, or, most despicable, cash to survive the pandemic. All of us should have paid family leave, paid sick leave, debt-free educations, and sufficient income to survive the pandemic and other natural disasters. But the price shouldn't be our future security.

**CLAIM:** *We should target Social Security benefits to those who truly need them. Rich people should not get Social Security.*

**TRUTH:** Chapter 8 explains in more detail why everyone, including the wealthiest among us, should receive the benefits they have earned. In addition to that basic point of fairness, a very small portion of Social Security benefits go to the wealthy, so taking away their benefits would save a miniscule amount. It is unlikely to change a single number in the annual Trustees Report. It would, though—again, as chapter 8 explains—fundamentally change the nature of Social Security, cause the administrative costs to skyrocket, and fracture support for this institution that connects all of us as Americans. (Of every dollar spent, the Social Security Administration spends less than a penny on administrative costs.) Right now, workers applying for Social Security retirement benefits have to present only their Social Security number, proof of age, most recent W-2, and, if not born in this country, proof of legal status. If there were a means test, even one set at $10 million, everyone applying for benefits would likely have to disclose tax returns, bank accounts, valuations on homes, and other personal information to prove that they were poor enough to qualify. Social Security is insurance, not welfare. Benefits are not based on need, only on working long enough to be insured. That is a design the American people like. And it is a design that works well. And here's the kicker: means testing would penalize those who save!

**CLAIM:** *Cutting payroll taxes is an important government tool for stimulating the economy and quickly putting money into the hands of people whose finances are hard-hit by a major recession. It should be in the president's and Congress's arsenal.*

**TRUTH:** Throughout his presidency, Donald Trump has been obsessed with cutting or, in his words, "terminating," the "payroll tax." As explained throughout this book, those payments are premiums, not general taxes like the income tax. They are dedicated to Social Security, which means that they can only be used for Social Security.

Social Security is not a slush fund, to be used to stimulate the economy in bad economic times.

If the goal is to put money in the hands of the people who are in greatest need, cutting Social Security contributions is slow and poorly targeted. There is absolutely no benefit to the unemployed because they are not making payroll contributions. Neither would it benefit those who work for state and local governments and do not participate in Social Security. Those earning the most—including the president and Congress—would receive the largest benefit, as would employers, while low-wage workers would receive the least. For instance, if FICA payroll contributions had been eliminated in 2020 for employers and employees, someone who earned at or above the Social Security annual earnings threshold of $137,700 would save $8,537.40 as would the employer. In stark contrast, someone who earned $30,000 would save $1,860—about one-fourth as much!

Other proposals to stimulate the economy, such as restoring the Making Work Pay Tax Credit, expanding the existing Earned Income Tax Credit, or issuing additional emergency payments are more targeted and provide more fiscal stimulus. They place no administrative burdens on employers.

The main reason to support cutting Social Security contributions above those better-targeted approaches is to undermine Social Security. This is true even if borrowed federal funds are substituted for Social Security's dedicated revenue. Under the guise of stimulating the economy, reducing Social Security contributions would either undermine Social Security's financing or require general revenue, both of which would set the stage for future demands to cut Social Security.

In fact, for many of those advocating cutting these revenues, undermining Social Security is not the bug; it's the design. As the next chapter details, that appears to be part of the long game being played by Social Security's determined foes.

**CLAIM:** *Social Security is a Ponzi scheme.*

**TRUTH:** A Ponzi scheme is a criminal endeavor, a swindler's deceptive promise that investors will reap huge returns. Like a chain letter, it collapses, usually after a short period of time, leaving many investors holding the bag. Social Security has been around for more than eighty-five years, and there is absolutely no reason that it can't continue as long as the United States is here. It is completely transparent and aboveboard—the opposite of a Ponzi scheme.

Social Security is, in pension jargon, primarily current-funded. That means that most current benefits are paid out of current premiums from today's workers. Private pensions are required to be advance-funded because employers can go out of business, so they might not be around to pay future pensions. Because the government is permanent, that safeguard is unnecessary.

To call Social Security a Ponzi scheme is a slur on every president and every Congress since the program's creation, as well as every contributor and every beneficiary. The future of Social Security is too important to the well-being of future generations of workers to be shaped by such slanderous comparisons and name-calling.

**CLAIM:** *Senators and members of Congress make us pay into Social Security, but they don't. They should be forced to participate in Social Security, like everyone else.[38]*

**TRUTH:** They already do. All federal employees, including senators, members of Congress, and the president of the United States, have been covered by Social Security since January 1, 1984.[39]

**CLAIM:** *Undocumented persons get benefits without paying in. They should not get Social Security.*

**TRUTH:** They don't. Undocumented workers are prohibited by law from receiving Social Security benefits.[40] As an aside, Social Security's financing is strengthened by the contributions of immigrants and new Americans because they tend to be younger and also have more children.

## PULLING BACK THE CURTAIN AND REVEALING THE TRICK

In taking on the conventional "wisdom," this chapter corrects myths, misunderstandings, misinformation, and, in some cases, outright lies.

Now let's again pull back the curtain and see what's really going on. All of the charges, when analyzed, look like solutions in search of a problem. The solution is to cut Social Security or even dismantle it completely. The problem changes. Sometimes the problem is young people not getting their fair share. Sometimes, it's that African Americans don't live as long as whites. Sometimes, it's the cost of an aging population. Sometimes, it's that seniors have lower poverty rates than children.

The problem changes, but the solution is always the same: cut or dismantle Social Security and related institutions. The intergenerational theft charge—that spending on seniors is crowding out spending on children—is particularly deplorable. It is targeted at young people and designed to get them not just to oppose Social Security, but to be angry at seniors who are, supposedly, acting selfishly by opposing benefit cuts. Deplorable as the charge is, it is also, perhaps, the most revealing.

One giveaway that this is a solution in search of a problem is that the solution doesn't fit. The solutions proposed to address this concern would fall most heavily, or even entirely, on the supposed victims—today's young people and children. Indeed, most politicians proclaim that the benefits of those fifty-five or older won't be touched, perhaps unwittingly taking a play from the Leninist strategy playbook. So what gives?

In magic acts, this is called misdirection—focusing attention on one thing over here in order to distract from the real action over there. Linking the fact that the federal government should do more for children and young adults to the fact that seniors are benefited by Social Security is classic misdirection. The problem is not intergenerational; the problem is income and wealth inequality—which exists within every generation and, as chapter 7 details, is growing.

All of the charges discussed in this chapter are efforts of misdirection. Each one takes attention away from the fact that the wealthy are not being required to contribute their fair share toward the common good. Franklin Roosevelt understood this tactic extremely well. He laid it bare on the eve of the 1936 election, when the Republicans were trying to convince workers that the just-enacted Social Security was a hoax that would hurt them, rather than an important benefit to them, a benefit that the wealthy opposed.

Roosevelt called the misdirection for what it was, famously charging, "It is an old strategy of tyrants to delude their victims into fighting their battles for them."[41] That is what is going on today. The tyrant is the same. Moneyed interests behind the Peterson Foundation, Fix the Debt, The Can Kicks Back (the supposed Millennial group), and other groups seeking to undermine confidence, undermine support, and get natural allies to fight with one another. These are zombie charges. We have been responding to them over and over again since the late 1970s, and those who came before us did the same. But the charges never die; they always come back, because they are not really about seeking truth.

Everyone who wants an expanded Social Security and a more just society must be vigilant against these charges. The opponents of Social Security are clever and well-funded. And, as the next chapter explains, they are with us still.

PART FIVE

# WHERE WE GO FROM HERE

# 12

## THERE THEY GO AGAIN: WHY SUPPORTERS OF SOCIAL SECURITY MUST REMAIN VIGILANT

> *"If you know the enemy and know yourself, you need not fear the result of a hundred battles. If you know yourself but not the enemy, for every victory gained you will also suffer a defeat. If you know neither the enemy nor yourself, you will succumb in every battle."*
>
> —Sun Tzu, *The Art of War*[1]

FOR MORE THAN THREE DECADES, MUCH OF THE CONVERSA-tion about Social Security in Washington and across the mainstream media was disconnected from the facts and the preferences of the American people. It became conventional "wisdom" that Social Security is unaffordable, that it is headed for bankruptcy, and that it will not be around for younger workers.

Everyone "knew" that people are not saving enough or working long enough. Everyone "knew" that spending on the old is crowding out spending on the young and burdening them with crippling debt. And everyone "knew" that, with the aging of the population resulting in more beneficiaries receiving Social Security and relatively fewer workers paying into the system, Social Security is unsustainable.

Until recently, Social Security policy discussion was dominated by the twin questions: how much should we cut Social Security's modest benefits, and how do we do it through closed-door negotiations so as not to be voted out of office? Democratic and Republican politicians, alike, spoke of their strong and unflinching support for the American people's Social Security (perhaps they "doth protested too much"?) and their desire to "save" it through "bipartisan action." At times, it was difficult for the casual observer to discern much difference between the two parties when it came to Social Security.

However, as discussed in chapter 10, Social Security discussions began to shift after 2012, with some Democrats arguing that, in light of the nation's retirement income crisis, the program should be expanded. By 2016, candidate Donald Trump was pledging that he would not cut Social Security (more about this below), and candidate Hillary Clinton joined the large majority of Democrats in calling for expansion.

Fortunately, Democratic politicians today have shaken off most of the conventional thinking as detailed in the previous chapter. Most appreciate the reality that we remain the wealthiest nation in the world,[2] capable of investing in the development of all our families and communities. Most are concerned about the impacts of rising income and wealth inequality, stagnant wages, growing health-care costs (private as well as public), and a tax system riddled with rules extremely favorable to large corporations and the rich.

Today's Democratic Party supports expanding, not cutting, Social Security. That is also what the overwhelming majority of voters support—Republicans, Independents, and Democrats alike. But that doesn't mean that any of us who want to see Social Security expanded, not cut, can let down our guard. Quite the opposite.

In order to expand Social Security and protect against future efforts to undermine the program, advocates need to appreciate that the campaign against Social Security remains well-funded, well-organized, active, and strategic. The campaign will draw on variations of tactics used in the past. Consequently, it is important to be aware of what those tactics are.

## ANTISOCIAL SECURITY CAMPAIGNS ARE HERE TO STAY

Unrelenting foes of Social Security have always been, in the words of President Eisenhower, "a tiny splinter group" whose "number is negligible."[3] The hundreds of millions of dollars behind them and their organizational infrastructure, however, make them formidable.

Largely due to their efforts, much of the conversation about Social Security in Washington and across the mainstream media has been disconnected from both the facts and the preferences of the American people. Their campaign convinced many influential people, including many among the mainstream media, to falsely believe that Social Security is not affordable, headed for bankruptcy, and will not be around for younger workers. As a result of their work, today, relatively few younger Americans believe that Social Security will even be there for them. Indeed, the American people, unwavering in their support of Social Security, do not realize just how closely opponents came to succeeding, in large measure because of the tactics they employ.

The anti–Social Security campaigners know how to adjust their tactics to changing situations, how to fade away, how to blend in, and how and when to attack. If we are to be successful, we must understand their moves, as well as how and when they will likely strike again. So let's review some of the broad tactics of those seeking to radically cut or dismantle Social Security. No doubt, in one form or another, we'll see them again.

# THE REVOLVING DOOR TACTICS TO UNDERMINE SOCIAL SECURITY

Social Security's opponents rely on a small number of tactics. Understanding how popular Social Security is, they claim "crisis" where none exists, link the program to the deficit despite the facts, seek to cut the program behind closed doors, and play various groups against each other (young versus old, seniors versus persons with disabilities)—all while keeping in their back pockets various privatization schemes, innocuous-sounding large benefit cut proposals, reductions to the program's revenue streams, and proposals to undermine the program's administration. So far, their efforts have failed, but not for want of trying. The following are a few examples.

## MESSAGING THAT OBFUSCATES AND DISTORTS THE POLICY DEBATE

One messaging narrative has tried to convince Americans that all of a sudden our nation can no longer afford Social Security. Their strategy was and remains to convince politicians and the media that "hard choices" (i.e., unpopular ones) had to be made, and that the "system" was "broke." Strategic use of such sound bites as "Social Security has become unaffordable because everyone is living longer" dominated the facts outlined in the previous chapter.

Along with the unaffordability argument, foes of the program linked the highly affordable Social Security to rising health-care costs, private as well as public. "Entitlements," a word that combined Social Security with Medicare and Medicaid—two very different programs that are victims of uncontrolled health-care costs, private as well as public—was just what was needed. Now, Social Security could be attacked as unaffordable, as part of an entitlement crisis, irresponsibly saddling our children and grandchildren with mountains of debt. The first term of the Obama presidency shows that tactic in action.

## USING FEDERAL DEFICITS TO PROMOTE
## RADICAL SOCIAL SECURITY CHANGES

There's a curious ebb and flow to declarations of putative "deficit crises." Like tides, they seem to come in when a Democrat occupies the White House (think Clinton and Obama) and recede as Republican presidents (think G.W. Bush and Trump) dramatically drive up the deficit with large tax cuts for the rich and large expansions of military spending.

The enemies of Social Security use federal deficits and debt as bludgeons, one of their most important strategies. Understanding how popular Social Security is, they try to stampede change in the name of saving Social Security and cutting deficits and debt.

The Wall Street–caused crash of the economy in 2008 coincided with the election of Barack Obama, a man who values compromise among those who disagree with him. The most serious and immediate problem facing the nation as he prepared to take office was the Great Recession, which had destabilized banking and many large corporations and caused many Americans to lose their jobs and homes. Upon taking office, President Obama proposed a stimulus package, which became law on February 17, 2009, less than a month after his inauguration. Along with the need for short-term spending to stimulate the economy and stem the recession's impact on banks, corporations, and citizens, Obama adopted long-range deficit reduction, including reform of "entitlements," as a primary goal. That was the opening those who were itching to undo Social Security needed. They made good use of this opportunity, focusing on building public and lawmaker support for change by framing deficits and debt as the nation's most important economic problems and supporting political strategies to advance their agenda.

The efforts of the anti–Social Security warriors helped kick off a series of deficit reduction efforts, all directed at an elusive "Grand Bargain"—a comprehensive package that dealt with all federal spending, including Social Security.[4] The first, the National Commission on Fiscal Responsibility and Reform (a.k.a. the

Bowles–Simpson Commission, discussed in chapter 10), was established by President Obama's executive order on February 18, 2010. It was unable to achieve a supermajority (at least fourteen of its eighteen members voting yes) on a legislative package. Had it done so, it would have triggered a single up or down vote without amendments in the House and Senate. It closed its doors in December shortly after issuing its final report, *Moment of Truth*.[5]

Congressional leaders and the White House reached an informal agreement in 2011 that led to the second effort, the U.S. Congress Joint Select Committee on Deficit Reduction, established by legislation on August 2, 2011. Generally known as the "Supercommittee," it was composed of six senators and six members of the House with equal numbers of Democrats and Republicans. Shockingly, the members were reportedly prepared to support large Social Security cuts and structural change.[6] According to the *New York Times*, "The only reason the committee failed was because Republicans refused to raise taxes on the rich, and, in fact, wanted to cut them even below their current bargain-basement level."[7] If the supercommittee had been successful, it would have been difficult for members to vote against a bipartisan proposal because it would have been framed as voting for or against the deficit. If enacted, Social Security as we know it would have disappeared.

There is much more to tell about negotiations and efforts to change Social Security through 2014, and we tell it in much greater detail in the 2015 edition of this book, *Social Security Works! Why Social Security Isn't Going Broke and How Expanding It Will Help Us All*.[8]

Here, what's most important to know is that the multiyear quest for a Grand Bargain ended with a whimper. Harmful sequestration went into effect. As a related strategy, Republicans shut down the federal government over so-called Obamacare. That proved to be extremely unpopular with the American public, and Republicans' popularity suffered as a result. Struggles over federal spending and the debt limit continued, but pundits declared the death of the Grand Bargain.

For the moment, explicit Social Security cuts were off the table. Spoiler alert: the deficit tactic will come roaring back toward the end of the chapter.

## BLACKMAIL BY HOLDING BACK
## NECESSARY INCREASES IN THE U.S. DEBT CEILING

Action-forcing events—deadlines that, if unmet, force grave changes—are an important part of the legislative process. During the Obama years, congressional enemies of Social Security elevated the tactic of holding hostage the necessity of periodically increasing the national debt ceiling to an art form. This is a tactic that is too good not to be used again in the future–when the debt ceiling needs to be raised and a Democrat is in the White House. It is tied to the prior strategy because those refusing to raise the limit can present themselves as serious about the deficit.

In fact, the debt limit has nothing to do with the amount of debt the United States carries. Neither does it affect spending. Rather, the level of debt increases whenever Congress supports spending and appropriations. The federal debt is simply a function of the difference between how much the government spends and how much it taxes. Voting against raising the debt ceiling would not reduce spending at all; rather it limits borrowing. Nevertheless, the limit has to be raised from time to time, or else the United States would be forced to default on its obligations, something it has never done.

Politicians hate taking that highly visible vote because, in our sound-bite world, those voting to do so can be made to look like they are in favor of incurring more debt. During the Obama years, Republicans used the necessity of raising the debt limit to force the supercommittee and other efforts to cut Social Security described in the prior and next sections.

## HIDING POLICYMAKING FOR SOCIAL SECURITY FROM THE AMERICAN PEOPLE

A chief impediment to dismantling Social Security is the overwhelming unpopularity of the idea. Understanding how wide and deep the support for Social Security is, anti–Social Security forces seek to have politicians vote for their unpopular measures in a manner that helps avoid accountability. The way to shield politicians from their angry constituents is to enact changes to Social Security behind closed doors, through expedited procedures and comprehensive pieces of legislation. That was the impetus behind both the Bowles-Simpson Commission and the Supercommittee, as well as other efforts to form a Grand Bargain. This is another tactic we are likely to see again. And, of course, the anti–Social Security forces always have other tricks up their sleeves.

## DEMONIZING DISABILITY

As the effort to force action through a Grand Bargain failed, at least temporarily, Social Security's determined foes began focusing on another avenue to get their way: the part of Social Security that insures workers and their families against the loss of wages as the result of serious and permanent disability.

Just as the Grand Bargain efforts were disappearing from the agenda, the media started reporting sensationalist stories about those receiving Social Security disability benefits. In March 2013, for example, National Public Radio ran several broadcasts on the program *All Things Considered*. NPR's online story begins, "In the past three decades, the number of Americans who are on disability has skyrocketed."[9]

The next three paragraphs of its report paint a picture of something seriously amiss. It talks about the growth in the rolls despite "medical advances" and "new laws" against "workplace discrimination of the disabled." It mentions the alarmist but unremarkable fact that the government spends more on "disabled former workers" than on "food stamps and welfare," failing to point out that the latter are means-tested because they are welfare, while disability insurance is not, because it is insurance and so has been earned and purchased with premiums.[10]

Similarly, a December 2012 *Bloomberg News* opinion piece on the same subject confides, "There are now 8.8 million workers receiving disability payments from Social Security. I find this number haunting."[11] Perhaps NPR would have been less startled and *Bloomberg* less haunted if they had talked to the chief actuary of the Social Security Administration.

Just as the aging of the population has not been a surprise to Social Security's actuaries, they also had long projected that the numbers of workers receiving disability insurance benefits would increase as the Baby Boom generation aged. This is because disabilities predictably increase as people age. Social Security's actuaries knew that the Baby Boomers, those born between 1946 and 1964, would reach age fifty between 1996 and 2014. They also knew that the Baby Boom generation had larger numbers of women in the paid workforce for full-length careers, adding to the number of persons eligible to receive disabled worker benefits.[12]

They also understood that a technicality accompanying the legislative increase to Social Security's statutorily defined retirement age would cause the Disability Insurance (DI) Trust Fund to have to pay more money. That is, disability benefits are paid from the DI Trust Fund until the workers, on whose record the benefits are being paid, reach their full retirement ages. From that point on, the benefits are paid from the Old-Age and Survivors Insurance (OASI) Trust Fund. Consequently, when the full retirement age is increased, benefits are paid for a longer time from the DI Trust Fund and for a shorter time from the OASI Trust Fund. Moreover, as the statutorily defined retirement age is increased, it becomes more difficult for people with disabilities who had hoped to hang on in the workforce until that age to actually do so. Of necessity, some apply for disability benefits.

Not only was this perfectly predictable, but Social Security's actuaries also understood that the rates of disability would slow down once these workers were old enough to receive retirement benefits. Those simple facts did not temper the scary headlines about the out-of-control growth in the disability rolls.

Not only has Social Security's chief actuary explained in detail what has caused these increased numbers, but he wrote that "all of these trends have stabilized or are expected to do so in the future." Consequently, he projected that "the number of DI beneficiaries will continue to increase in the future, but only at about the rate of increase in workers."[13] None of this appeared in either story.

Even worse, many of the stories used anecdotes, without national data, to give the impression that the rolls had been growing as a result of fraud. What failed to get reported is that the levels of fraud under Social Security disability insurance are extremely low, especially when compared to private insurance.[14]

Roughly 10 percent of the losses paid out by the property/casualty insurance industry are fraudulent.[15] In contrast, less than 1 percent of all Social Security payments—that is, all payments of old age, survivors, and disability benefits—are more than should be paid. In fiscal year 2017, the overpayment rate was just 0.64 percent of all program payments.[16] And, by definition, fraudulent payments had to be only a small fraction of that.

What also failed to get reported is that the Social Security Administration has zero tolerance for fraud. It vigilantly ferrets it out. Two thirds of fraud investigations and successful prosecutions come from reports by the frontline workers of the Social Security Administration,[17] and the agency has a hotline for reporting suspected fraudulent claims. Indeed, this misinformation forced the Social Security Administration to undertake an initiative to set the record straight.

Actually, what we were seeing in this reporting was the recycling and faulty amplification of an old charge that fraud, waste, and dishonesty are supposedly endemic in Social Security's disability programs, a drumbeat that, as the *New York Times* reports, led to "an attempt by the Reagan administration to reduce federal spending by way of a purge of the disability rolls."[18] In the early 1980s, the Reagan administration instituted new continuing disability review processes and standards, resulting in over 485,000 people, most of whom were later deemed eligible, receiving notices that their benefits would be removed. Bipartisan revulsion to the new procedures and standards led to eighteen states refusing to follow the Social Security Administration's new directives, class action lawsuits, and ultimately unanimous votes in the House and Senate for the Social Security Reform Act of 1984. That act undid much of the damage but not before much harm was inflicted on beneficiaries, especially those with severe mental health disabilities.[19]

Just as anti–Social Security forces had an action-forcing event with the debt limit, they had an action-forcing event for this tactic, as well: Congress had to enact a technical change to Social Security by 2016 to maintain the uninterrupted flow of benefits to disabled workers and their families. To understand this, it is necessary to take a brief digression.

When the Social Security Disability Insurance program was enacted in 1956, a new trust fund, the Disability Insurance Trust Fund, was established for the revenue dedicated specifically to it.[20] The annual Trustees Report projects both trust funds independently, but also projects them on a combined basis, since they are so intertwined. The same formula is used for calculating old age, disability, and survivors benefits. The revenues for the two funds have always come from the same sources. Indeed, workers have a combined 6.2 percent of their salaries withheld, up to the maximum, without knowing how much goes to each trust.[21] Over the years, the exact percentage allocated to one fund or the other has been changed by law many times, but from the worker's perspective nothing noticeable changed. Indeed, sometimes the amounts going to one fund have decreased and the amounts going to the other have increased, and sometimes the reverse. In 1994, the percentage of the Social Security contribution going to the DI Trust Fund was increased and that going to the OASI Trust Fund was reduced. (The All Generations Plan combines the two trust funds into one.)

The need for simple legislation to rebalance the two funds provided new opportunity for those wanting to cut Social Security. First, they would start with a drumbeat vilifying the disability insurance program in order to set the stage to demand changes affecting not just disability benefits but, since all parts of the program are intertwined, retirement and survivors benefits as well.

But then, Social Security was saved by Pope Francis! Then Speaker of the House John Boehner, a devout Catholic, had tried for twenty years to get the pope to come before Congress.[22] On September 24, 2015, he succeeded. Pope Francis addressed Congress; Boehner was moved to tears. Having met the pope, who blessed his grandchild, and having survived a fractious speakership, Boehner announced the very next day that he was resigning. Before he resigned, though, he negotiated a closed-door budget deal with Obama and the rest of the congressional leadership just days before yet another debt limit deadline. Insiders who supported Social Security managed to negotiate a reallocation between the trust funds. Given the actuaries' projections the expectation was that the deal bought supporters of Social Security only a few years, until 2022. But that is not how it worked out. Inexplicably, with each new annual trustees report, the news got worse for Social Security opponents. First, the Disability Insurance Trust Fund would be depleted in 2023, then 2028, then 2032, then 2052, and, in the 2020 report, 2065!

With the action-forcing event disappearing in the sunset, the public attacks on people with disabilities quieted—but they haven't disappeared. Another spoiler alert: this effort to undermine our Social Security has gone underground, along with what seems to be never-ending tactics employed by anti–Social Security forces.

## DEATH BY A THOUSAND CUTS

Though the legislative efforts to cut Social Security temporarily stalled, administrative cuts that make it hard for people to access their earned benefits continued unabated. The theory seems to be that if people's experience in claiming benefits and getting information is a frustrating one, their general support for the program, and indeed for government, may be subtly compromised. Social Security is the face of the federal government for many Americans. Virtually all workers contribute directly to Social Security from every paycheck. Nearly one in five Americans receives a monthly Social Security check.

People contact the Social Security Administration at times of transition, ones often involving sadness, vulnerability, and stress. Americans claim benefits when a loved one of the person contacting Social Security has died, when the person contacting Social Security or a family member has become so seriously and permanently disabled that work is impossible, or when the person contacting Social Security or a family member has attained old age and generally is retiring from work.[23]

Determined that Americans who had earned Social Security receive the world-class service they deserve, the first commissioner of Social Security wrote:

> Employees who would come in direct contact with the public were impressed with the importance of making certain that people were given necessary assistance in understanding their rights and duties. This included assisting claimants in the preparation of their applications for benefits under the federal old age insurance system and ensuring that those who had valid claims received the benefits to which they were entitled.[24]

That emphasis on first-class customer service has been a hallmark of the Social Security Administration. Distressingly, at the same

time that the anti–Social Security forces were seeking to undermine the program legislatively, there were starve-the-beast stealth
attacks on the program's administration, including large cuts in its
budget. Moreover, some people appointed during the administration of President George W. Bush were at odds with core Social
Security principles.

Some of the effects of budget cuts and decisions made within
the agency can be easily seen. Since 1996, 107 Social Security field
offices have been closed. Public hours in the remaining offices were
reduced by the equivalent of one full day a week. Altogether, staff
in field offices has been reduced by nearly 14 percent. More callers to the agency's 800 number experienced busy signals—about
14 percent of all callers—and those who did get through had to
wait an increasing amount of time to get assistance.[25]

All of those reductions occurred as the numbers of older Americans were rapidly increasing. Not surprisingly, those applying for
disability benefits often experienced excessively long waits before
hearing whether their claims were accepted. With large backlogs of
disability claims and not enough funding for sufficient numbers of
trained workers to process those claims, those applying for benefits
had to wait, on average, increasingly long times before receiving
an initial determination; and for those appealing a denial, the wait
was sometimes years.[26]

The erosion of service could be seen in other ways as well. Until
2011, annual earnings statements, listing workers' wages and earned
benefits, were automatically mailed, each and every year, from the
Social Security Administration directly into the homes of each
of those workers aged twenty-five and older. People valued the
statements. Moreover, a Gallup Poll commissioned by the Social
Security Administration found that Americans who received the
statement had a better understanding of the program.[27]

Notwithstanding the value of these statements, their modest cost,
and the legal requirement that they be mailed, the commissioner

whom President Bush appointed ordered the mailings stopped on budget grounds, with only a website notice.

Another troubling development during this same period, the government began to aggressively go after overpayments, often decades in the past—even when the mistake was the government's.[28] And adding insult to injury, those who, through no fault of their own, had been overpaid, were labeled debtors. Letters from the government, out of the blue, claiming that a beneficiary owes tens of thousands of dollars, when the mistake was the government's, is wrong. In one case that came to the authors' attention, the anxiety caused by that government letter resulted in a temporary hospital stay.

The insensitive administration and death by a thousand cuts were harmful to all of us, but the degree of harm was not distributed evenly. Imagine the difficulty for those for whom English is not their primary language, who are developmentally disabled or physically challenged, or who do not have a high school education.

The deterioration in service to the American people is especially outrageous because the Social Security trust funds, out of which Social Security's administrative costs are paid, have an accumulated surplus of $2.9 trillion. The problem is that Congress wouldn't allow the agency to spend just a small amount more of this surplus on administration to restore the first-class service the American people have paid for.[29]

But here's a spoiler alert, this time surprisingly happy: though not all of these cuts have been reversed, and though some new ones have been added (more about that below), there have been some improvements. The acting commissioner during the last few years of the Obama administration, who served after the Bush-named commissioner's term expired, resumed mailing the earnings statements to workers every five years beginning at age twenty-five (though not every year as the law requires). In addition, Democrats, now fully on board with expansion, have forced increases to the Social Security Administration's budget in recent years. And so far, the current commissioner, named by Donald Trump, has put an emphasis on customer service. He restored the field office hours before the pandemic forced all offices to close. Also, he hired more people to answer the phones in a determined effort to cut wait times.

Notwithstanding that good news, there are new dangers on the horizon as the result of the worldwide pandemic and the economic crisis it has brought. But before we get to that let's get caught up to date.

## THE LULL BEFORE
## THE GATHERING STORM

With the Democrats once more the true champions of Social Security, the momentum to expand, not cut, Social Security gathered impetus. Senator Bernie Sanders's decision to run in the 2016 race for president gave the fledgling movement to expand Social Security nationwide exposure. Though he did not win the nomination, he was able to influence the party to embrace his position.

On the Republican side, reality host Donald Trump distinguished himself from the large Republican field by promising not to cut Social Security. While it was a welcome position from a leading Republican, there was good reason not to trust that promise.

In 2000, well before Trump ran for president, he released a book with a chapter on Social Security that displayed his utter contempt for the program and its beneficiaries.[30] Trump referred to Social Security as "a Ponzi scheme"—an outrageous slander, since a Ponzi scheme is a criminal ploy to defraud.

Trump called for raising the retirement age to seventy because, as he phrased it, "How many times will you really want to take that trailer to the Grand Canyon?" Trump said that he "plan[s] to work forever," implying that everyone else should as well—even if they have jobs like nursing or construction that involve hard physical labor. He added that destroying Social Security by privatizing it "would be good for all of us." The "all of us" to whom he referred were presumably his fellow plutocrats with inherited wealth.[31]

But Trump demonstrated, well before running for office, that he understood the politics of Social Security. In a 2011 interview with Sean Hannity, Trump said that Republicans should be very careful "not to fall into a Democratic trap" of advocating Social Security cuts without bipartisan cover, or they would pay the price politically.[32]

As a presidential candidate, Trump exploited that knowledge. He realized that even voters who tend to support Republicans overwhelmingly oppose cutting Social Security. With the media distracted by Hillary Clinton's emails, Trump was never questioned hard, and little attention was paid to Social Security. Nevertheless, on the surface, the debate had shifted. Democratic nominee Hillary Clinton called for expansion; Republican nominee Donald Trump called for no cuts.

Notwithstanding Trump's rhetoric, his selection of Mike Pence as a running mate foreshadowed how he would govern. Pence has a long history of opposing Social Security and favoring raising the retirement age and other measures that would weaken its protections. Indeed, he criticized George W. Bush's Social Security privatization plan because he thought it didn't go far enough![33] Once in office, Trump doubled down by choosing a staunch opponent of Social Security, Mick Mulvaney, as his budget director and another staunch opponent, Tom Price, as secretary of health and human services (one of Social Security's trustees, by law).

Price was forced to resign after just ten months due to a scandal over his use of private planes, but Mulvaney remained hard at work targeting Social Security until March 2020. Signaling where the administration was going, Mulvaney appeared on the Sunday morning talk show *Face the Nation* on March 19, 2017, just two months after Trump was inaugurated. In response to host

John Dickerson's question about whether Trump might in the future go after Social Security and Medicare, which he labeled, "entitlements," Mulvaney responded with a question of his own: "Let me ask you a question, do you really think that Social Security disability insurance is part of what people think of when they think of Social Security? I don't think so."[34]

Sure enough, every year, his budget included cuts to Social Security.[35] As the 2018 midterm election approached, the storm clouds grew darker. Shortly before the 2018 midterm election, Trump and his Republican allies in Congress enacted an enormous tax cut, overwhelmingly benefiting the wealthy and substantially expanding the federal deficit. Powerful Majority Leader Mitch McConnell (R–KY) revealed step two of the game plan.

> An October 16, 2018 Newsweek article summed what was going on as follows:
>
> After instituting a $1.5 trillion tax cut and signing off on a $675 billion budget for the Department of Defense, Senate Majority Leader Mitch McConnell said Tuesday that the only way to lower the record-high federal deficit would be to cut entitlement programs like Medicare, Medicaid and Social Security.[36]

Sound familiar? There they go again.

Fortunately, the Democrats took control of the House of Representatives that November, so the plan had to be postponed. Moreover, an indefatigable champion of expanding Social Security, Congressman John Larson (D–CT), became chairman of the Social Security Subcommittee of the House Ways and Means Committee. On Franklin Roosevelt's birthday, January 30, 2019, Larson introduced the Social Security 2100 Act with 208 cosponsors. That is about 90 percent of the Democratic caucus and only ten fewer than a majority of the House of Representatives! The bill expands benefits across-the-board, as well as other targeted improvements described in chapter 8. It is called the Social Security 2100 Act because it ensures that all benefits can be paid in full and on time through the year 2100 and beyond.

Under Larson's leadership, his subcommittee and the full committee had a number of hearings. It is ready to go after the 2020 election, if Democrats retake the Senate and the White House. (The 2020 presidential election has not occurred at the time of this writing.) But, never quiet, the opponents are dusting off the old playbook and coming up with some new tactics. Unfortunately, the coronavirus pandemic and the resulting economic crash have given them new opportunities.

## THE PANDEMIC AND RESULTING ECONOMIC CRASH GIVE COVER

The worldwide pandemic gave cover for Trump and his allies in Congress to wage new, stealth attacks on Social Security. In the spring of 2020, in the midst of the crisis, after the Trump administration and his Republican allies in Congress had secured a $4.5 trillion bailout primarily for the largest corporations in the nation,[37] and when the death count from COVID-19 had just passed 80,000, the *Washington Post* reported that "senior Trump administration officials are growing increasingly wary of the massive federal spending to combat the economic downturn and . . . considering ways to limit the impact of future stimulus efforts on the national debt."[38] What was one of those ways? Radically transforming Social Security, of course.

Exploiting the pandemic, Trump's son-in-law Jared Kushner rolled out yet another way to undermine Social Security: the oddly named "Eagle Plan," which would give people upfront cash in exchange for relinquishing some of their earned Social Security benefits. This plan asked desperate families, terrified of going without food or being thrown out of their homes, to sacrifice their retirements.

Chairman Larson wasted no time responding to Kushner's "Eagle Plan." Together with his colleague Congressman Joaquin Castro (D-TX), chairman of the Subcommittee on Oversight and Investigations of the Committee on Foreign Affairs, he fired off a letter to Kushner's State Department crony, which minced no words:

> In this moment of crisis, when millions of Americans are struggling to make ends meet and fear for their retirement, we should be enhancing Social Security, not developing policies to reduce benefits. The idea that you would ask individual Americans to sell out their hard-earned retirement security as the price of desperately-needed help during a crisis is unacceptable. . . . We will never force people to choose between putting food on the table now, and ensuring that they will receive the full, earned Social Security benefits they'll need when they retire or if they become severely disabled or die prematurely.[39]

In response to where the plan was apparently "birthed," the letter charged, "Moreover, if these reports are accurate, this input into domestic policy is entirely outside the mandate of the State Department, and is a wholly inappropriate use of its resources."[40]

But, of course, laundering the plan through the State Department and having the White House issue a lame disavowal were simply a way to float an anti–Social Security plan, in an election year, in the middle of a pandemic, without Trump having to admit that his promise to not cut Social Security was a lie.

The Kushner plan betrayed a willful misunderstanding of Social Security, which, as explained throughout this book, is insurance, not a piggy bank. But turning Social Security from guaranteed insurance into a private account has been, as we have seen, a long-standing goal of the far right, as a step to eventually ending Social Security once and for all.

Kushner's plan is cruel in the choice it would foist upon people in the middle of a pandemic, when families across the country found themselves in desperate need of income. Thanks to the Trump administration's utter failure to manage the pandemic by implementing a widespread testing and tracing program, that desperation wasn't going away any time soon, when the sinister anti–Social Security plan was floated.

Nor was the plan truly in response to the pandemic. Another variation on this scheme came years before the pandemic, from former Rep. Tom Garrett (R-VA) who sponsored the so-called Student Security Act of 2017. The sneaky assault on Social Security would have provided young Americans some relief from crippling student debt—if they forfeited some of their future Social Security benefits.

Like Garrett's bill, another plan, the Ivanka Trump–Marco Rubio plan, is an attack on young people and their Social Security, as mentioned in chapter 8. Our country faces a looming retirement crisis caused by the decline of traditional pensions, the inadequacy of 401(k)s, and decades of stagnant wages. The younger you are, the more serious the crisis. Rubio and Trump would force workers to either forfeit some of those benefits or forfeit spending time with their newborn children. Garrett would force young people to enter adulthood with massive student debt or forfeit part of their earned Social Security. Kushner's approach is even crueler: starve during the pandemic or starve in old age. This is just the latest battle in the war against Social Security.

One of Social Security's many strengths is that its benefits are guaranteed and, unlike savings, cannot be outlived. Republican politicians have a long-standing goal to convert Social Security's wage insurance into inadequate savings accounts that would force workers to pay enormous management fees to Wall Street. They tried directly in 2005, but the American people overwhelmingly rejected their plan. With these current proposals, they are seeking to seed the ground to make their plan more acceptable.

In fact, a leading privatization proponent, Carrie Lukas of the Independent Women's Forum, admitted as much in an article in *The Federalist*. She stated that the goal of these types of plans is to change how "Americans think about Social Security, which has long been considered the untouchable third rail of politics." Lukas candidly makes clear their goal that, through proposals like those of Garrett, Trump, and Kushner, "public opinion will undergo a sea change to embrace personal accounts or other substantial Social Security reforms"—code for ending Social Security as we know it.[41]

Our message for those who support Social Security is, in short, stay vigilant and don't be fooled. Beware of Trojan Horse proposals that provide some economic security today in exchange for less economic security tomorrow. There is yet another Trojan Horse that Trump and his colleagues have pushed hard, supposedly in response to the crisis of the pandemic and the resulting economic crash.

As the pandemic spread unabated throughout the United States, Donald Trump's favorite policy had nothing to do with ramping up testing, getting protective equipment to workers, or protecting people in nursing homes. Instead, he was obsessed with cutting payroll "taxes"—Social Security's dedicated premiums. He even went so far as to threaten to veto any relief legislation that did not have a cut to Social Security's dedicated funding.

As a response to the coronavirus crisis, cutting Social Security contributions makes no sense. It's slow, inefficient, and fails to get money into the pockets of those who need it most. The far superior approach is to make direct cash payments to the American people—as the Coronavirus Aid, Relief, and Economic Security (CARES) Act did.

Indeed, Trump's obsession with cutting Social Security's dedicated revenue preceded the economic collapse caused by the worldwide pandemic. It started with his first year in office. As Pulitzer

Prize–winning business columnist Michael Hiltzik for the *Los Angeles Times* reported at the time (and accurately characterized):

> According to the Associated Press, [the Trump administration is] toying with the idea of eliminating the payroll tax, which funds Social Security and part of Medicare, or cutting it drastically. This is an absolutely terrible idea, partially because it smells like a back-door way of cutting Social Security benefits. It needs to be nipped in the bud.[42]

The idea of starving Social Security of its dedicated revenue did not start with Trump. The "absolutely terrible idea" is what opponents of Social Security have wanted from the beginning. Eliminating Social Security's dedicated revenue has been a long-standing goal of those who oppose Social Security but have failed in their frontal attacks.

Trump and his allies knew that they could not succeed by attacking Social Security directly. It is too popular. Indeed, Trump professes his support for Social Security, all while undermining the program's funding, presumably so he can demand cuts down the road. Indeed, in a candid moment, Trump admitted his desire to cut Social Security's dedicated revenue was never about the pandemic at all. He said he would support a "permanent" reduction in payroll contributions "regardless" of the pandemic and resulting economic collapse.[43]

To be clear, what Trump called payroll taxes—a subtly destructive phrase, like the word "entitlement," that became part of the everyday language of policymakers—are federal insurance contributions. They are premiums that workers pay every month in return for insurance against loss of wages due to old age, disability, or death of a breadwinner. Social Security's dedicated revenue is the reason, conservative President Ronald Reagan understood and explained, that Social Security does not add a penny to the deficit.[44]

Most alarming, when even Republicans in Congress seemed unwilling to cut Social Security's dedicated revenue, Trump took the unprecedented, unilateral step of deferring the collection of the contributions until the end of 2020 and promised that, once reelected, he would "terminate" the contributions permanently. At the time of this writing, before the 2020 election, this is a serious threat. Unilaterally delaying the collection of Social Security's dedicated revenue is the ultimate "starve the beast" tactic.

At a moment when the government is running unprecedented deficits, keeping Social Security self-financing is more important than ever. President Franklin D. Roosevelt understood this, famously remarking,

> We put those payroll contributions there so as to give the contributors a legal, moral, and political right to collect their pensions and their unemployment benefits. With those taxes in there, no damn politician can ever scrap my social security program.[45]

The "damn politicians" that Roosevelt foresaw have tried privatizing Social Security. They've tried cutting benefits behind closed doors. Each time, they failed. This tactic to "starve the beast" by cutting the program's funding may be the most dangerous attack of all. It is especially dangerous because few Democrats are sensitive to the danger. In the height of the Great Recession, when Republicans blocked extending the more targeted relief of the Making Work Pay tax credit, the Obama administration and Democrats in Congress agreed to a temporary "payroll tax holiday," despite the objections of Social Security advocates.

In the economic crisis caused by the pandemic, Democratic leadership in Congress similarly appeared comfortable in voting for temporary credits against Social Security contributions, as were contained in the various bipartisan packages enacted in the spring of 2020. Once again, they seemed unaware of, or at least unconcerned about, the danger of the approach.

The game plan of the Social Security opponents is obvious. The pandemic and resulting economic upheaval required sharp increases in expenditures, which in turn have resulted in massive, unprecedented deficits. At some point, they presumably will be addressed. Social Security has generally been protected because it does not add to the deficit. If policymakers have temporarily substituted borrowed funds for Social Security's dedicated revenue, even temporarily, would that protected status disappear?

While seeking to starve Social Security on the road to cutting its modest benefits may be the most serious threat on the horizon, the pandemic gave cover for more of the revolving-door set of anti–Social Security tactics. Before the pandemic, the Trump-selected commissioner of Social Security, Andrew Saul, had a mixed track record on Social Security. On the one hand, he restored the hours of the field offices and also hired more people to answer the 800 hotline to cut down on busy signals and wait times. [46] Unfortunately, he also engaged in union-busting,[47] which harms not only Social Security employees but the public. In an attack on the employees, he precipitously ended, without much warning, the ability to telework, claiming he did so to improve customer service.[48] Ironically, then came COVID-19. Every field office was closed for public health reasons and virtually every employee switched to full-time telework!

Closing Social Security field offices, like closing post offices, is one of the long-standing goals of those who want to "shrink [government] down to the size where we can drown it in the bathtub," in the words of Grover Norquist, whose antitax crusade was aimed at "starving" the "beast."[49]

Unfortunately, while the commissioner made customer service a priority, the pandemic provided a cynical cover for other attacks on our Social Security system. The agency began changing the regulations to make successful claims for disability benefits harder.[50] Whether those are reversed in a Democratic administration, only time will tell.

## PREPARING FOR VICTORY

It is important to understand that the campaign to undermine Social Security is ongoing. Although the moneyed interests and conservative ideologues have hated Social Security and battled against it since before it was enacted, the will of the people has always ultimately prevailed. The intensity of the battle and fields of engagement may ebb and flow, but the battle lines are always drawn. The efforts to undermine and chip away at Social Security are part of a war that has been ongoing from its inception.

What is new, today, compared to the past four decades, a window of opportunity is opening, thanks to the return of the Democratic Party to its roots of support for Social Security. That return can lead to significant expansion of Social Security—the program and the vision.

Giving the devil its due, the billionaire campaign against Social Security has put a serious dent in public understanding of and confidence in Social Security. But like previous efforts to undo Social Security and notwithstanding the hundreds of millions of dollars invested in undermining this institution, their campaign failed to enact anti–Social Security legislation. Standing in the way, resolute, are, as they have always been, the American people. And today, there is a growing movement to expand, not cut, Social Security.

It is time to prevail. The anti–Social Security campaign can be defeated, but it will take vigilance. The campaign is well-funded, and its members are smart and determined. We must all resist cuts to Social Security—all cuts, but emphaticallythose being attempted behind closed doors.

But a strong defense against those who want to tear Social Security apart is only part of the solution. We must work to expand Social Security benefits and to restore the world-class service that Americans have paid for and deserve.

The good news is that the Democratic Party is on the side of expansion with no cuts. The better news is so are the American people.

There is the key. As the concluding chapter discusses, the American people will carry the day, as ultimately they always have, if—and this is crucial—they are informed, get involved, and insist on reminding politicians that those in Washington work for the American people, not the other way around.

# 13

## PASSING SOCIAL SECURITY FORWARD: A LEGACY FOR ALL GENERATIONS

SOCIAL SECURITY DIDN'T JUST HAPPEN. PAST GENERATIONS worked tirelessly to create, improve, and defend our Social Security system. They fought for it, protected it, safeguarded it, expanded it, and passed it forward, stronger than before, as a legacy to all of us, young and old alike. Now it is our turn.

All of us who care about the economic security of our families have a stake in this cause. Everyone who cares about what kind of nation we leave for our children and grandchildren has a stake.

How do we successfully build on the legacy that has been bequeathed to us, leaving it even better for the generations that follow? In short, how do we get our elected officials—who, after all, work for us—to vote to expand Social Security?

We already have some very dedicated leaders championing the cause of expansion, but we need more of them. Getting those now in office who disagree with us to change their minds and getting people elected who already do agree is tricky. All politicians these days claim to support Social Security. All say that their goal is to strengthen or save it. We cannot be satisfied with platitudes. We must demand more.

Electing more champions and convincing others to change their minds won't be done without hard work. It won't be done without knowledge, commitment, perseverance, and action. It won't be done without vision backed by values that we all share. It won't be done without politics and policies that involve the American people and put us first.

And, it won't be done without a fight. Nor will the fight be an easy one. There is too much money on the side of those who want to dismantle our Social Security system. But we have growing numbers of champions calling for expansion. They cannot win on their own, however. They need our help, just as past champions did.

We can expand Social Security, even in the face of distortions, misunderstandings, and outright lies promoted by moneyed interests. But we must all educate ourselves and those we know. We must get involved, and we must work together.

## EXPANDING SOCIAL SECURITY IS ABOUT VALUES

As we began this book, so we conclude it. We must understand that today's debate over the future of Social Security is most fundamentally a debate about decency and fairness. It is a debate about our values. In the words of President Franklin Roosevelt, it's not about "the creation of new and strange values," but, as he explained more than eighty-five years ago: "It is rather the finding of the way once more to known, but to some degree forgotten, ideals and values. If the means and details are in some instances new, the objectives are as permanent as human nature. Among our objectives I place the security of the men, women and children of the Nation first."[1]

All the talk about Social Security going broke—talk that opponents of Social Security have exploited the pandemic and economic crisis to double down on—has robbed us of that security.[2] As its name suggests, Social Security is intended to provide not only tangible cash benefits, but also the intangible benefit of peace of mind. For Social Security to accomplish its goal of providing peace of mind and security, people must feel confident that it will be there for them. Otherwise, the program ceases to function as intended;

it provides income replacement only, not true security. Many no longer have that sense of security and peace of mind that they and their families are assured of financial security in the event of disability, death, or old age. That sense of security has been lost as the result of the extremely effective forty-year campaign against Social Security. It is now time to restore that intangible benefit of peace of mind. That is one value we all should be fighting for.

Americans appropriately have a sense of contributing toward their own retirement and feel good about receiving Social Security benefits. They understand the importance of providing disability protections for themselves and their families and the importance of protecting children and other family members with life insurance if they die. The benefits are not based on need but rather have been earned through labor and contributions from salaries and wages.

Yet some have lost the sense that Social Security benefits are earned compensation, thanks to the use of words and phrases like "entitlement," "makers versus takers," and "safety net." The language subtly implies that Social Security is a government handout, not insurance that we have earned and paid for. A safety net, after all, is something you fall into if you make a mistake on the high wire or trapeze. One is glad the safety net is there, but falling into it is to be avoided, if possible. Insurance, in contrast, is what prudent people buy because they are aware of life's risks and are planning ahead. People who are prudent do not need or want safety nets. It is why they purchase insurance (and accumulate savings).

The phrase "social safety net" in connection with Social Security was introduced into the political lexicon and popularized by President Reagan.[3] Revealingly, Reagan rejected the idea that Social Security is insurance. He asserted, in a stump speech he gave in 1964 in support of the election of Republican presidential nominee Barry Goldwater, that supporters of Social Security "only use the term 'insurance' to sell it to the people."[4]

The phrase "safety net" has become embedded in the language in the same way that the word "entitlement" has in relation to

Social Security. The next step by Social Security's opponents seems to be to redefine the image of a "safety net" into a "hammock," lulling able-bodied people to sleep.[5]

The false claim that Social Security is a government giveaway has become a standard talking point of those who would dismantle the program. They try to make us believe it is simply a transfer program supported by taxes, rather than insurance purchased with our work and contributions.

The recognition that Social Security is part of our compensation for our hard work and contributions is another value this fight over Social Security is about. People who receive the Social Security benefits they have earned are not "takers." They are not feckless souls who have fallen into a safety net. They are not spoiled, over-entitled adults taking advantage of working Americans. They are not dependent on government any more than our elected politicians whose salaries we pay.

Social Security beneficiaries are our parents, our grandparents, our children, our friends, and our neighbors who have earned these benefits. They are all of us, who see mandatory contributions to Social Security deducted from every paycheck. None of us deserves to be assaulted by language that diminishes our accomplishments and undermines our dignity. We have earned our benefits, and we should claim our benefits with pride.

Yet another value that underlies the fight over Social Security is compassion for our neighbors. After the tragic events of September 11, 2001, millions of Americans reached into their pockets to contribute to the Red Cross and other charitable organizations assisting the families of the 9/11 victims. What most Americans do not know is that the most immediate, sustained, and generous support came from Social Security. The money withheld from every worker's paycheck for Social Security goes into the program's Old-Age and Survivors Insurance and Disability Insurance Trust Funds, out of which those so tragically affected by the terrorist attacks that day received benefits. And, unfortunately, once again, and without politics, our Social Security is responding—quickly, automatically, and respectfully—to a national crisis: the deep losses caused by the COVID-19 pandemic. This is the type of emergency response a nation that values the care and dignity of all must have.

Still another value the fight is about is recognition of Social Security's conservative, prudent management of our money. Of all federal programs, Social Security and Medicare are the most closely monitored. Social Security is extremely conservatively financed and must balance its budget without any borrowing whatsoever. Yet this important value is disregarded by our politicians, who tend to lump it together with all other federal spending.

This is not a time for compromising the economic well-being of the middle class and poor, not when income inequality[6] and wealth inequality[7] are higher than they have been in the past fifty years. Not when the worldwide pandemic has exacerbated income and wealth inequality.

This is not a time to accept cuts to our Social Security as "reasonable compromise," as little "tweaks" that will do no lasting harm. Rather, this is the time for our elected leaders to expand Social Security, as the overwhelming majority of Americans who elected them want.

At base, this is about what kind of nation we want to live in and leave for those who follow. Although couched largely in terms of economics, the debate over the future of Social Security is most fundamentally a debate about the role of government, about all of us working together, and about the societal values the nation seeks to achieve through Social Security.

## EXPANDING SOCIAL SECURITY REQUIRES YOUR INVOLVEMENT

As important as facts and values are, they alone are not enough. Those of us who want to expand Social Security must work for it.

We know we can expand Social Security because working

together and bringing the voices of the American people into the policy debate has always won in the past struggles for the creation and expansion of our Social Security.

These victories didn't happen by themselves. Indeed, woven throughout the history of Social Security is the story of how coalitions of organizations, citizen advocates, and politicians—with the support of the American people—successfully blunted the four-decade-long, billionaire-funded campaign to pull Social Security apart and of how the coalitions are now positioned to further momentum for a historic expansion of Social Security.

Expanding the current program is vitally important. Moreover, the nation can, should, and we believe will draw on the broader vision of Social Security, achieving the long-sought goal of universal, guaranteed quality health care, debt-free four-year college and advanced trade education, employment and housing, paid sick leave and family leave, as well as an adequate basic income as fundamental human rights, befitting a compassionate and rich nation.

Over the past decade, our elected officials came closer than most people realize to cutting and, worse, beginning the dismantling of our Social Security system, as chapters 10 and 12 describe. When the president of the United States and the leadership of the opposition party all supported cutting Social Security, when hundreds of millions of dollars were directed at making the case for cutting Social Security, when so many in the mainstream media seemed so supportive of such cuts, it is truly inspiring that they were stymied by the coordinated efforts of public interest organizations and the American people. It is truly gratifying that one of the two major political parties now supports expanding, not cutting, Social Security.

But now is not the time to let up. The fight continues. Now is the time to redouble our efforts and fight harder. If you are not yet involved, we urge you to become so, in ways we explain below. The goal is clear: block destructive cuts and enact wise, responsible, and bold Social Security expansions.

# EXPANDING SOCIAL SECURITY REQUIRES AN AMERICAN STRATEGY

We who want to protect and expand Social Security must join together and develop a winning strategy, an American strategy. In deploying that American strategy, we must be persistent, prepared for a long campaign. Unlike the anti–Social Security ideologues, the Leninist strategists, our strategy doesn't require deception or division. Quite the opposite. The American strategy involves truth-telling and joining forces, all of us together—young, old, and those in between; rich, poor, and those in the middle; Republicans, Democrats, and Independents alike; and all races, all religions, all genders.

Combating the billionaire-funded campaign, with us still, and achieving greater economic security for all of America's working families will require all of us to become actively involved. A crucial goal in the American strategy is reversing the lack of confidence in the future of Social Security, felt most widely by young Americans but infecting even those who are old. It is, in short, restoring confidence.

Because the misinformation is so deeply embedded in the minds of the general public, and especially the elites, a multipronged approach is necessary. This book is but one source of information. Other sources of accurate information are discussed in appendix D. Indeed, the Social Security Administration itself has an excellent website with much useful information, available at www.ssa.gov.

Social Security experts who are supportive of the program must educate students, teachers, professors, media, and elected officials. In addition to appearing on panels and at symposia, these experts should be increasingly drawn upon to hold Washington briefings for policymakers and influencers. All of their work should be backed by solid information.

But that is not enough. Citizen organizations, religious communities, and everyone whose life is touched by Social Security (that's all of us) should get involved in the effort to restore confidence in this sound institution. Everyone should become informed and work to dispel the myths highlighted in chapter 11. But that is only one step.

We know that Social Security works for everyone. Now we need to fight to make it work even better—to understand how expanding this institution is part of the solution to the economic insecurities facing many of today's old; to the retirement income crisis confronting today's workers; to the pressures—financial, time, and stress-related—experienced by those caring for children or disabled and ill family members of all ages; and to unacceptable inequality threatening the American Dream, ours, our children's, and our grandchildren's.

Building on the broad vision of Social Security is the path to greater equality, fairness, and justice. The pandemic exposed both the fault lines and the shortcomings of our United States. Fighting for the expansive vision of Social Security means fighting for a more perfect union, in the words of the preamble to the Constitution. It means fighting for a fairer, more just, more decent, more prosperous—a prosperity that is more equitably shared—United States.

The American people are sometimes called a "sleeping giant." Despair can feed inaction. But we cannot let ourselves be discouraged.

It is time for the sleeping giant to awaken. Poll after poll shows that the overwhelming majority of Americans support expanding Social Security. And we are, after all, a democracy, where the majority is supposed to rule. But we must make sure our voices are heard. We must get involved.

It is time for those of us who have a stake in the fight—and that is everyone—to take action. Educate your friends, coworkers, children, grandchildren, parents, and grandparents. Go to town hall meetings when your representative holds them. And ask hard questions. Don't let them off the hook with platitudes. And make clear that you and your allies will hold them accountable. Seek pledges, circulate petitions, write and call elected officials. Write letters-to-the-editor and make calls to radio shows, especially when they spout the tired charges found in chapter 11. Support candidates not just with contributions, but with time. If you want to be involved with others, we have listed in appendix D our organization and its website. We would love to have your energy and talent. The bottom line: get involved however you can.

Social Security has transformed the United States. It has reshaped America, providing wage insurance for virtually all of today's working families. These benefits matter greatly to workers and families who are protected against the economic devastation that death, disability, and retirement might otherwise pose. But Social Security is more than dollars and cents. It is a cherished institution, embodying the noblest of American values and ideals.

As we have emphasized throughout this book, Social Security builds on, reinforces, and reflects what is best about our nation.

Prior generations have created and improved our Social Security system. Now it is our turn.

# APPENDIX A

## ADDITIONAL EXPLANATION
## ABOUT HOW SOCIAL SECURITY WORKS

This appendix provides more detail about how Social Security works. More comprehensive explanations of the intricacies of Social Security can be found on the Social Security Administration website (www.ssa.gov).

Social Security provides cash benefits based on a worker's earnings record. Those benefits may be paid to workers, as well as to family members, including spouses, divorced spouses, dependent children (including adult children disabled before age twenty-two), and occasionally to financially dependent grandchildren and parents. Monthly benefits vary according to such factors as type of benefit, prior contributions, age when benefits begin, and the number of people receiving benefits in a household. The maximum monthly benefit for workers retiring in 2020 at full retirement age is $3,011 in 2020.[1]

Workers covered by Social Security (virtually all workers other than about 25 percent of state and local government employees and some federal employees hired before 1984) contribute 6.2 percent of their earnings (with an equal employer match) up to a maximum taxable ceiling ($137,700 in 2020) into two trust funds: the Old-Age and Survivors Insurance Trust Fund and the Disability Insurance Trust Fund, or what is more conveniently called the combined

OASDI Trust Fund.[2] Self-employed workers make contributions equivalent to those made by regular employees and their employers. The employer portion is deductible as a business expense; the employee portion is paid out of after-tax earnings.

The maximum taxable ceiling is adjusted each year by the percentage that wages have increased, on average, nationwide. Although it did not work out as intended, the goal of indexing the maximum amount to average wages was for Social Security to receive a constant share, 90 percent, of national earnings.[3] Because wages at the top of the income scale have grown so much faster than the wages of everyone else over the past few decades, the percentage has dropped. In 1982, 90 percent of wages were covered by Social Security, as Congress intended. Through the inadvertent impact of the way wages have grown, that percentage was 83.1 percent in 2019.[4] Another 1.45 percent contribution, paid by employees and matched by their employers, and assessed on all wages (with no maximum amount), goes to Medicare's Hospital Insurance (HI) Trust Fund.[5]

To qualify for benefits, workers must have contributed on large enough wages for a sufficient amount of time to become insured. There are several categories of insured status. To be "fully" or "permanently" insured, workers must have contributed to Social Security for forty "quarters of coverage."[6] In 2020, one credit is given for contributions made on each $1,410 of earnings anytime in the calendar year, up to a maximum of four quarters or credits in a single calendar year.[7] Because workers can become disabled or die at any time, workers under age thirty-one may become insured for those benefits with fewer than forty quarters, as few as six quarters out of the preceding three years for the youngest workers. Disability Insurance applicants must meet an additional requirement of recency of work, usually twenty out of the preceding forty quarters, except that in the case of workers under age thirty-one, it may be as little as six quarters out of the preceding three years.

The vast majority of retirement, disability, survivor, spousal, widow(er), divorced, and children's benefits make use of the same benefit formula. The benefit formula produces what is called the "primary insurance amount" (PIA). Think of the PIA as the basis of nearly all Social Security benefits. Is that clear? Probably not. So try this. Think of it as equivalent to the amount you are eligible for if you claim retired worker benefits in the first month you reach the full retirement age. For example, if you were born after 1959 and retire at age sixty-seven, your initial monthly benefit would be 100 percent of your PIA. If, on the other hand, you first take this benefit when you reach age sixty-two, the monthly benefit would be 70 percent of your PIA; 124 percent if you wait until age seventy. Benefits available to certain family members are also based on a percent of the PIA (e.g., 100 percent for a disabled worker and up to 75 percent of the PIA for a surviving child).

Social Security's benefit formula is progressive, a recognition that lower-wage workers have less discretionary income and less ability to save, and so need a larger percentage of their preretirement wages replaced to maintain their standard of living during their working years. The formula uses career earnings, so workers who have periods of unemployment may receive larger proportionate benefits as well.

To calculate benefits, a worker's career earnings are indexed to adjust for real wage growth, averaged to determine a monthly amount (the average indexed monthly earnings, or AIME). inserted in Social Security's progressive formula, and then adjusted, based on the age at which the worker first retires and other factors. The formula for 2020 is:

> [T]he sum of:
> (a) 90 percent of the first $960 of average indexed monthly earnings, plus
> (b) 32 percent of average indexed monthly earnings over $960 and through $5,785, plus

(c) 15 percent of average indexed monthly earnings over $5,785.[9]

The percentage factors are fixed by law while the dollar amounts (known as bend points) are adjusted annually by the percentage increase of average wages nationwide.

Workers who have earned higher salaries over their careers receive benefits that are larger in absolute dollars, but are smaller in proportionate terms, than those received by lower-paid workers. For workers retiring at the full retirement age in 2018, Social Security benefits replace about 56.4 percent of the preretirement earnings of workers with "very low" earnings, defined by the Social Security actuaries as a hypothetical worker with average income monthly earnings (AIMEs) of $12,916 in 2018. It replaces 40.9 percent for "low" earners (AIME $23,249); 30.9 percent for "medium" earners (AIME $51,665); 25.2 percent for "high" earners (AIME $82,664) and 19.9 percent for "maximum" earners (AIME $127,061).[10] In addition to Social Security's main benefit formula, other benefit formulas apply in specific circumstances, such as the special minimum benefit, which, as discussed in chapter 8, is payable to certain persons who have worked in covered employment or self-employment for many years at low earnings levels. (This formula is used only if it results in higher than the regularly computed benefit.[11])

**Retired worker benefits.** Retired worker benefit amounts are affected by a worker's prior contributions and earnings, and by the age when benefits are first claimed. Although the Social Security Act defines the full retirement age as a single defined age (age sixty-seven for individuals born after 1959).[12] Social Security provides what really amounts to a continuum of retirement ages, ranging from sixty-two to seventy. Workers are eligible to claim benefits as early as age sixty-two. For every month after age sixty-two up to age seventy that benefits are claimed, the initial benefit amount is increased in recognition that benefits will be received for a shorter time.[13]

The age of eligibility for full retirement benefits has been gradually increasing since 2000. In 2022, it will be age sixty-seven for those born after 1959. When age sixty-seven is fully phased in, this amounts to a roughly 12 to 13 percent cut regardless of when a worker accepts these benefits—age sixty-two, seventy, or any age in between.[14]

Covered workers may accept retired worker benefits beginning with the first month that they turn sixty-two, but if they do, their monthly benefits are permanently reduced (for example, by 30 percent when age sixty-seven is fully phased in as the full retirement age for workers born after 1959). Alternatively, those workers in a position to postpone receipt of benefits past the full retirement age get credits that permanently increase the value of their monthly benefits for each month benefit receipt is postponed past their full retirement age, up to age seventy.[15]

As must be apparent by now, Social Security's terminology and rules sometimes defy "hard and fast" explanation. Here's another example. People who receive retired worker benefits can hold a paid job and, in many cases, receive some or all of their earned benefits. Retired worker benefits are not affected by any earnings received after reaching the full retirement age, but retired workers under full retirement age generally lose $1 in benefits for every $2 earned in excess of an earnings exempt amount—$18,240 in 2020. A more liberal exempt amount ($48,600 in 2020) and benefit reduction offset ($1 for every $3 of earnings above the exempt amount) are applied in the year a worker obtains the full retirement age.[16]

**Disabled worker benefits.** When covered workers become severely disabled, they may be eligible, after a five-month waiting period, to receive monthly Disability Insurance (DI) benefits. After an additional twenty-four months, disabled workers (as well as disabled widow[er]s age fifty through sixty-four), and disabled adult children (of retired, disabled, or deceased workers) are eligible for all Medicare benefits.[17]

Roughly 8.4 million workers with disabilities, 112,0000 of their spouses, and 1.4 million of their children receive DI benefits each month.[18] The disability criteria are strict. To be considered disabled, in 2020 a person must be unable to engage in substantial gainful activity (SGA), defined as earning $1,260 a month ($2,110 for the blind) in 2020, because of a physical or mental impairment that is expected to last at least a year or result in death.[19] A worker does not actually have to earn this amount, just be able to earn it. A worker must be unable to do any kind of job that exists in significant numbers in the national economy. The local or regional availability of jobs is not taken into consideration, although age, education, and previous work experience are.[20]

**Surviving spouse benefits.** Three types of benefits exist for widows and widowers of a covered spouse or, in some cases, of a divorced spouse whose marriage had lasted for at least ten years. Reduced benefits are available at age sixty (or age fifty if severely disabled) to the surviving spouses of deceased workers; full benefits are available at full retirement age or later.[21] Among the 4.0 million widow(er)s receiving benefits in 2013, the large majority, 3.6 million, are aged widow(er)s, sixty and older. About 110,000 widowed parents caring for a child under age sixteen also receive monthly benefits.[22] As with many Social Security matters, there are some complexities. Aged widow(er)s with earnings histories essentially receive a benefit equivalent to their spouse's, or what they have earned through their own work histories, whichever is higher. The benefit will also be affected by other factors, such as the age it is first accepted and decisions made to maximize household benefits when both spouses are eligible.[23]

**Disabled widow(er)s benefits.** Widow(er)s ages fifty to sixty who are not caring for young children may be eligible for monthly benefits if they meet disability eligibility standards that are somewhat more strict than those applied to workers with disabilities. About 245,000 people receive these benefits in 2020.[24]

**Benefits for spouses of disabled and retired workers.** About 2.4 million spouses of retired workers and 112,000 spouses of persons receiving DI benefits receive monthly benefits based on Social Security contributions made by their married or, in some cases, divorced spouses.[25] There are a number of complexities for spouses of retired worker beneficiaries. Those who have worked receive their own earned benefit. In addition, if that benefit is less than one-half of their spouse's benefit, they may receive an additional benefit based on their spouse's work history.[26]

**Young children's and grandchildren's benefits.** Young children, and in some cases grandchildren, of deceased, retired, and disabled workers are eligible to receive benefits. Nearly all are under age eighteen, but some who are full-time elementary or secondary school students may receive benefits until age nineteen and two months.[27] At one time, as discussed in chapter 8, these benefits were continued until age twenty-two if a child was a full-time college student or in an advanced vocational education program.[28]

**Disabled adult children's benefits.** A little-known Social Security benefit provides vital support for some people with very significant, lifelong disabilities. Social Security's disabled adult children (DAC) benefits essentially protect everyone who is, or hopes to be, a parent; every young child; those yet to be born; and 1.1 million adults whose severe disabilities began prior to age twenty-two.[29] A DAC is usually the child of a parent who is deceased or receiving retirement or disability benefits. In some cases, a DAC may be a stepchild, grandchild, or stepgrandchild.[30]

**Cost of living adjustment (COLA).** The cost of living adjustment is one of Social Security's most important features. Its purpose is to ensure that Social Security benefits, once received, maintain their purchasing power no matter how long someone lives. Although many, including ourselves, believe that it falls short of its goal, one thing is clear: virtually no other occupational pension provides inflation protection that compares favorably to Social Security's. Without the cost of living adjustment, inflation would halve the value of benefits after roughly twenty years with normal inflation rates (3 percent a year).[31]

# APPENDIX B

## ADDITIONAL INFORMATION ABOUT THE SOCIAL SECURITY WORKS ALL GENERATIONS PLAN AND OTHER PROPOSALS, INCLUDING COST AND REVENUE ESTIMATES

This appendix provides a more detailed discussion of the proposals highlighted in chapters 8 and 9, together with costs and savings.

As explained in chapter 9, absolute dollar amounts over long periods of time are hard, if not impossible, to comprehend and compare. Consequently, Social Security's actuaries express their projections as a percent of taxable payroll—that is, as a percent of all covered earnings. In 2020, covered earnings are all earnings of employees covered by Social Security up to a maximum of $137,700.

Expressing costs and savings as a percent of taxable payroll over Social Security's seventy-five-year estimating period is much more useful than dollar amounts, because over seventy-five years the value of the dollar will change considerably, and even so-called constant dollars involve extremely large numbers. Because the main source of Social Security's financing is from Social Security contributions assessed against covered earnings, expressing the projected deficit/surplus, the cost/savings of proposals in that form permits an easy comparison of costs. In addition, we also express these large numbers as a percent of Gross Domestic Product (GDP).

In 2020, Social Security's Board of Trustees reported that under the most widely accepted set of assumptions, the program had an unfunded obligation of 1.0 percent of GDP, which also equals 3.03 percent of taxable payroll. The actuarial deficit, which is closely related but also includes the cost of having a reserve at the end of the valuation period equal to at least one year's outgo, is 3.21 percent of taxable payroll. In other words, the entire shortfall could be eliminated totally if the FICA rates on employers and employees, each, were increased immediately from 6.2 percent to 7.81 percent.[1] That provides a sense of scale but, as the All Generations Plan details, we believe that there are better ways to eliminate the projected shortfall and finance the projected costs of the improvements advocated here. All estimates of costs or savings, unless otherwise noted, are for the traditional seventy-five-year valuation period and were derived by Social Security Administration's Office of the Chief Actuary, unless otherwise noted. Most of the numbers can be found on that office's website at ssa.gov/oact/.

# INCREASING ECONOMIC SECURITY OF CURRENT AND FUTURE SENIORS

### Increase Benefits for All Current and Future Beneficiaries

The Social Security Works All Generations Plan's most significant provision enables the large majority of working persons and their families to maintain their standards of living when earnings are lost due to retirement, disability, or death of a worker. Retirement experts generally suggest that individuals should replace 70 to 85 percent of preretirement wages to maintain living standards once wages are gone. Higher percentages are needed for low-paid workers, somewhat lower for the highest paid. Less than 100 percent is needed because people no longer have work expenses, generally pay less in taxes, and, instead of saving, start to spend their savings. Similar income replacement goals apply for insuring against economic shocks related to disability and death.

The All Generations Plan substantially increases the monthly benefits of all current and future beneficiaries, especially important in addressing much of the personal impacts of our developing retirement crisis. Social Security currently appropriately replaces a higher percentage of the average earnings of lower-income workers than higher-income workers, but the percentages of everyone's wages that are replaced are too low. Consequently, we keep the same basic design of the current formula but simply increase the so-called percentage factors and bend points. That is, for those turning sixty-two, or becoming disabled or dying before age sixty-two in 2020, their so-called primary insurance amount (PIA), or essentially the benefit they would receive on their statutorily specified retirement age of sixty-six and eight months, is substantially increased.

A little background here for nonexperts. Think of the so-called primary insurance amount (PIA) as the benefit you are entitled to if you accept retired worker benefits at your full retirement age (for example, sixty-seven for persons born after 1959)—in Social Security parlance 100 percent of the PIA. The PIA is the basis of all other benefits. A worker's monthly disability benefits are 100 percent of a worker's PIA. The benefits of a deceased worker's child are up to 75 percent of the deceased worker's PIA.

All right, that's clear (sort of) but, you might ask, how does the Social Security Administration (SSA) figure out a worker's PIA?

To compute a worker's PIA, the SSA first calculates a worker's average wages in jobs in which they contributed into Social Security, not just any average earnings, but the Average Indexed Monthly Earnings (AIME). "Fine," you might say, "but what's the AIME?"

The AIME compensates for changes in average earnings over many years of work. Without it, nominal dollars earned early in one's career, when salaries and standards of living were much lower, would be averaged with dollars earned near retirement, resulting in a lower retirement benefit. Maybe clearer, but again, nonexperts might ask, "What's the AIME have to do with the PIA?" The PIA is derived from a worker's AIME. Under current law, the Social Security Administration explains:

> For an individual who first becomes eligible for old-age insurance benefits or disability insurance benefits in

2020, or who dies in 2020 before becoming eligible for benefits, his/her PIA will be the sum of:

(a) 90 percent of the first $960 of his/her average indexed monthly earnings, plus

(b) 32 percent of his/her average indexed monthly earnings over $960 and through $5,785, plus

(c) 15 percent of his/her average indexed monthly earnings over $5,785.[2]

The All Generations Plan increases the 90, 32, and 15 percentage factors in the formula to 95, 65, and 45 percentage factors. It also increases the so-called dollar-amount bend points in the formula to $1,000, $4000, and $5,000, up to a maximum benefit of $8,200. That is, the new formula, if in effect in 2020, would have been:

(a) 95 percent of the first $1,000 of worker's average indexed monthly earnings, plus

(b) 65 percent of worker's average indexed monthly earnings over $1,000 and through $5,000, plus

(c) 45 percent of worker's average indexed monthly earnings over $5,000 up to a maximum PIA of $8,200.

Current and future beneficiaries will receive substantial monthly benefits under the All Generations Plan. A low-income worker who had an AIME of $24,112 in 2019, turned sixty-two in 2020, and claimed benefits would receive a Social Security benefit of $10,171 in 2020, equal to 42.2 percent of preretirement wages. In contrast, under the All Generations Plan, that worker would receive a benefit of $19,272, equal to 79.9 percent of preretirement pay.

A medium-earnings worker who had an AIME of $53,582 in 2019, turned sixty-two in 2020, and claimed benefits would receive a Social Security benefit of $16,736 in 2020, equal to 31.2 percent of preretirement wages. In contrast, under the All Generations Plan, that worker would receive a benefit of $8,428, equal to 71.7 percent of preretirement pay.

A high-earnings worker who had an AIME of $85,732 in 2019, turned sixty-two in 2020, and claimed benefits would receive a Social Security benefit of $22,230 in 2020, equal to 25.9 percent of preretirement wages. In contrast, under the All Generations Plan, that worker would receive a benefit of $54,779, or 63.9 percent of preretirement pay.[3]

This provision of the All Generations Plan costs 7.0 percent of taxable payroll, or 2.52 percent of GDP.[4]

# IMPROVED ECONOMIC SECURITY FOR WORKERS CLAIMING BENEFITS EARLY

Social Security benefits are reduced for every month that they are claimed prior to "normal" retirement. Workers accepting retired worker benefits before their full retirement age experience two types of permanent reductions in benefits. The most well known are the actuarial reductions in monthly retired workers benefits, which will be reduced by as much as 30 percentage points, once the "full" retirement age is completely phased in. Independent of the actuarial adjustment, time out of the labor force before the age of eligibility for full benefits can lower a worker's AIME, ultimately translating into a smaller monthly benefit, especially for those who leave work in their early- and mid-fifties. The reductions for claiming benefits early can be especially undermining for those with health, employment, and financial exigencies limiting their control over when they leave the workforce and whether they must accept permanently reduced retired worker benefits.

## Reduce Actuarial Reduction for Early Receipt of Benefits

Because early retirement reductions are too large, and lower benefits too much, the Social Security Works All Generations Plan reduces the actuarial reductions for early claimants. It reduces retirement reductions to one third of 1 percent for every month benefits are claimed before one's statutorily defined retirement age. When age sixty-seven is fully phased in as the full retirement age for persons born after 1959, the maximum reduction will be to 80 percent of a full benefit for someone who claims benefits as soon as they are age sixty-two, as opposed to 70 percent under current law. The proposal costs 0.60 percent of taxable payroll, or 0.21 percent of GDP.

## Change Disability Insurance
## Eligibility Criteria for Older Workers

Recognizing that many low- and modest-income workers face work-limiting health- and employment-related circumstances that often result in early claiming of benefits, the All Generations Plan calls for changing disability insurance eligibility criteria to give greater weight to age-related health limitations, partial disabilities, and vocational and educational factors for applicants aged fifty and older. The proposal costs 0.50 percent of taxable payroll, or 0.18 percent of GDP.

## Adopt CPI-E to Ensure That Benefits
## Maintain Purchasing Power over Time

As chapter 8 explains and appendix C illustrates, virtually every expansion plan proposes basing cost-of-living adjustments on the more accurate Consumer Price Index for the Elderly, especially beneficial to seniors and people with disabilities. (Technically, this change is not an increase, but it is an improvement because it will do a better job of maintaining the purchasing power of benefits no matter how long someone lives.) This proposal would cost 0.41 percent of taxable payroll, or 0.15 percent of GDP.

## A More Adequate Special Minimum Benefit

As chapter 8 explains, a number of expansion plans update the special minimum benefit, which is targeted toward low-income workers. There are many ways to structure this expansion. The Social Security Works All Generations Plan would update the special minimum benefit to equal 125 percent of the federal poverty line when benefits are claimed at full retirement age by workers who have at least thirty years of credited work (that is, 120 quarters of coverage), inclusive of up to eight years for caring for children under age five. Specifically, beginning in 2022, the proposal reconfigures the special minimum benefit: for those with less than thirty years of coverage, the benefit is proportionately lower. This improvement costs 0.24 percent of taxable payroll, or 0.09 percent of GDP.

# STRENGTHENING FAMILY PROTECTIONS FOR ALL GENERATIONS

## Provide Paid Family Leave and Paid Sick Leave

The Social Security Works All Generations Plan would provide those workers who are insured for Social Security disability benefits with up to twelve weeks of paid family leave in the event of the birth or adoption of a child, the illness or disability of a family member, or the illness of the covered worker. The benefit would be two-thirds of gross salary, capped to a monthly ceiling that would be inflation-indexed. For the first year after the enactment of the law, the maximum benefit would be $4,000. This proposal costs 0.62 percent of taxable payroll or 0.22 percent of GDP.

## Provide Caregiving Credits

Some have proposed giving credit for unpaid child care to improve the benefits of those who have taken the time out from the paid workforce to undertake this important work. The proposals can be structured in a variety of ways. The Social Security Works All Generations Plan would give credits toward future Social Security benefits for up to five years of caring for a child under age six or for caring for family members over age six with serious health or functional limitations requiring significant care assistance with activities of daily living. The earnings credited for a caregiving year would equal one half ($27,821 in 2020) of the Social Security Administration average wage index (about $55,642 in 2020). The credits would be available for all past years to newly eligible retired-worker and disabled-worker beneficiaries starting in 2021. The proposal costs 0.40 percent of taxable payroll, or 0.14 percent of GDP.

### Eliminate Five-Month and Twenty-Four-Month Waiting Periods for Persons with Disabilities

This provision eliminates requirements that newly eligible persons with disabilities wait five months after being determined eligible to receive their first monthly cash benefit and twenty-four months after that before they are eligible to begin receiving Medicare benefits. Removal of these barriers to benefits costs 0.12 percent of taxable payroll, or 0.04 percent of GDP. Costs would also accrue to the Medicare program.

### Increase Benefits for Families of Disabled, Deceased, or Retired Workers

Because the benefits of children and other qualified family members are derived from the same single benefit formula, expanding benefits across the board will increase the benefits of all current and future family members who themselves are beneficiaries.

### Provide New Child Benefit of $2,000 at Birth or Adoption of a Child

The Social Security Works All Generations Plan would provide a $2,000 benefit at the birth or adoption of a child. The payment could be accompanied by information about the other Social Security protections earned on behalf of the child by the covered parent(s). This proposal would cost 0.14 percent of taxable payroll, or 0.05 percent of GDP.

## Expand Student Benefits

This provision restores student benefits through age twenty-two and extends these benefits through age twenty-six for children enrolled in a college, university, or advanced vocational educational program and whose insured parent(s) are deceased, disabled, or retired. This proposal would cost 0.11 percent of taxable payroll, or 0.04 percent of GDP.

## Enhance Independence, Marriage, and Family Support for Disabled Adult Children

Social Security imposes a maximum family benefit, which limits the amount that can be paid based on a worker's earnings record. Children disabled prior to age twenty-two may receive disabled adult child (DAC) benefits if a parent (or in a few cases a grandparent or other relative providing the principal financial support and care) is retired, disabled, or deceased. These benefits are counted toward the family maximum, regardless of whether that disabled adult child lives at home. This can have the unfortunate side effect of reducing monthly benefits for the parent's household. While this adjustment may make sense when a DAC beneficiary lives in the family home and shares household expenses, it makes little sense for those DAC beneficiaries who do not live with their parents, and it poses a significant barrier for DAC beneficiaries who wish to live more independently.

Another problem is that DAC beneficiaries lose their entire benefit if they get married, unless their spouse is also a Social Security DAC beneficiary. In addition, an individual cannot requalify for the DAC benefit should the marriage end in divorce or death of their spouse. These constraints on the DAC benefit are unduly restrictive, run counter to our long-held American value of supporting marriage and families, and demonstrate the persistent bias that people with disabilities are somehow unable or unsuited to marry. Congress should end the DAC benefit marriage penalty and allow people to continue to receive the DAC benefit after marriage, regardless of whom they marry.

Excluding the coverage of the family maximum for DAC beneficiaries who live independently would cost 0.01 percent of taxable payroll, or 0.004 percent of GDP.

### Provide Equity for Disabled Widow(er)s Both by Eliminating the Age-Fifty Requirement and Seven-Year Rule and by Providing Unreduced Benefits

Under current law, disabled widow(er)s may collect widow(er) benefits, reduced in amount if they are at least age fifty, and the disability began within seven years of the worker's death or seven years after the last month the widow(er) was eligible to receive a benefit as a surviving spouse with child in care. The Social Security Works All Generations Plan would extend protection to persons under age fifty, eliminate the seven-year rule, and increase the level of benefits, aligning the treatment of disabled widow(er)s more closely to that of other disability beneficiaries. This proposal would cost 0.04 percent of taxable payroll, or 0.01 percent of GDP.

## SECURING SOCIAL SECURITY'S FINANCING

With the following revenue proposals, the All Generations Plan eliminates Social Security's projected long-range shortfall, pays for all benefits, and leaves the program in surplus at the end of the century.

### Gradually Eliminate the Maximum Taxable Wage Base, Giving Credit for Contributions

As chapter 9 explains, Social Security contributions are assessed up to a maximum amount of wages, which in 2020 is $137,700. Earnings above that amount are exempt. The Social Security Works All Generations Plan would gradually eliminate that maximum, over ten years, for both employers and employees. When fully phased in, this would result in the roughly 6 percent of workers with earnings above the maximum paying into Social Security all year, as other workers do.

Those paying the increased contributions would qualify for higher benefits, but just as Social Security has a minimum benefit and a maximum family benefit, the All Generations Plan would specify a maximum benefit of $8,200/month, indexed to the average wage index. This proposal would generate 2.3 percent of taxable payroll or 0.83 percent of GDP.

### Gradually Increase Social Security Contribution Rate from 6.2 Percent on Both Employees and Employers to 7.7 Percent by 2054

Social Security's contribution rate has not been increased since 1990. As chapter 9 explains, the rate could be increased a small or large amount, quickly or slowly. The Social Security Works All Generations Plan would increase the rate gradually. It would increase the Social Security contribution rate by 1/20th of a percentage point per year from 2025 to 2054 until the rate reaches 7.7 percent on both employers and employees. Its impact each year from 2025 to 2054 would be to require a worker earning an average income to contribute about 50¢ more a week to our Social Security system.

If needed as a fail-safe in sixty years, the Plan includes a contingent contribution rate of an additional 0.50 percent on employers and employees. This contingent rate increase could be accelerated, postponed, or eliminated, as needed. Because it is contingent, we are not claiming any revenue for it.

The proposal would increase Social Security's revenue 2.30 percent of taxable payroll, or 0.83 percent of GDP.

## Treat All Salary Reduction Plans the Same as 401(k) Plans with Respect to the Definition of Wages under Social Security

By treating all salary reduction plans the same as 401(k)s, the Social Security Works All Generations Plan would generate modest revenues while also correcting an inconsistency in the law. This proposal would increase Social Security's revenue 0.25 percent of taxable payroll, or 0.09 percent of GDP.

## Increase Social Security's Investment Income

Social Security currently has an accumulated reserve of $2.9 trillion, which by law is invested solely in interest-bearing obligations of the United States.[5] Standard investment advice is to diversify one's portfolio, investing in both equities and bond instruments. This proposal would achieve that diversification. The more that is invested in equities, the higher the return, generally. The Social Security Works All Generations Plan directs that 40 percent of trust fund assets be gradually, over fifteen years, invested in a broadly diversified, indexed equity fund or funds. A variety of safeguards would be introduced to ensure no interference with the market or the entities in which the trust funds are invested. Assuming a 6.4 percent real rate of return, this proposal would increase Social Security's revenue 0.59 percent of taxable income, or 0.21 percent of GDP.

## Double Immigration

The nation is aging as a result of declining fertility rates. Consequently, we may face a labor force shortage unless we increase immigration. The Social Security Works All Generations Plan calls for a compassionate and wise immigration policy that provides a path to citizenship for undocumented workers living in the shadows and calls for doubling the rate of immigration for the next seventy-five years and beyond. After all, most Americans are descendants of immigrants, if not immigrants themselves. Immigration and diversity adds to the nation's strength. This proposal would generate 1.0 percent of taxable payroll, or 0.36 percent of GDP.

## Eliminate the Tax Expenditure on Fossil Fuels and Repeal Expenditures for Other Activities Destructive to the Environment and Civil Society

The authors have written repeatedly that the question is one of values, of what kind of society we want to inhabit. The All Generations Plan invests in the well-being of future generations by repealing tax expenditures enjoyed by the fossil fuel industry and for activities destructive to the environment. After all, climate change is an existential threat to all of us. The Plan also eliminates private prisons and private management that undermine our society. The Plan dedicates those savings to Social Security so that everyone benefits from both sides of the equation—the damaging activities that are stopped and the increase in all of our economic insecurity.

## Tax Financial Speculation

The Plan includes a financial transactions tax on Wall Street speculation, the proceeds of which are dedicated to Social Security. The Plan places a tax of 0.5 percent on stock transfers—0.25 percent on the seller and buyer, each—on the sale and purchase of stocks, credit swaps, and other exotic financial instruments. This raises 2.8 percent of taxable payroll, or one percent of GDP.

## Treat Capital Gains as Ordinary Income, Reported and Taxed Annually with Proceeds Dedicated to Social Security Trust Funds.

The Social Security Works All Generations Plan would create a new dedicated source of revenue from reforming the treatment of capital gains under the federal income tax code and dedicating the funds to Social Security. People work harder for their earned income than they do for passive income on their investments. Yet capital gains are taxed at a fraction of earned income. Moreover, tax lawyers spend much of their time seeking to convert ordinary income to capital gains, adding enormous complexity to the federal income tax system.

Senator Ron Wyden (D-OR) has introduced legislation to end this special advantage for just the wealthiest 1 percent of Americans.[6] The proposal is estimated to bring in between $1.5 trillion and $2 trillion in the next ten years alone. Wyden dedicates the revenue to Social Security. Eliminating the tax expenditures and dedicating revenue of the amount of the savings to Social Security will both make the nation's income tax system fairer and allow Social Security benefits to be raised, while restoring Social Security to long-range actuarial balance.

It seems unlikely that this reform could pass if the funds went into general revenue. But, under the All Generations Plan, the American people have a fighting chance. Instead of these trillions of dollars staying in the pockets of billionaires, they would go to Social Security to ensure everyone a secure and adequate retirement income. This proposal would generate 2.00 percent of taxable payroll, or 0.72 percent of GDP.

## Restore Federal Estate Tax to Year 2000 Level

Inherited wealth is antithetical to our principles of a meritocracy. Of course, some are born into privilege and so have many advantages from birth. They, of course, will inherit wealth, but it is completely fitting that some of that wealth be spent for the public good. Since 2000, antigovernment, anti–Social Security forces that decided to "starve the beast"—that is, to eliminate federal taxation—have had a campaign against this most American of taxes. To offset those efforts, the authors believe the tax should be dedicated to Social Security so the American people can see the gain from the imposition of the tax. In 2000, when the campaign against the tax started to succeed, it taxed only estates over $675,000 ($1.35 million for a couple) only after the second spouse died, and then at a tax rate of 55 percent. This proposal would generate 0.80 percent of taxable payroll, or 0.29 percent of GDP.

## Dedicate the Peace Dividend to Social Security

Like the prior few proposals, this one is about our values. There is no reason the United States has to spend more on its military and defense than China, India, Russia, Saudi Arabia, France, Germany, the United Kingdom, Japan, South Korea, and Brazil combined. Nor should more than half the federal discretionary budget be spent on militarization. When the Soviet Union collapsed, there was much talk of a peace dividend. The authors believe the American people must claim it. Therefore, the proposal dedicates 10 percent of the monies currently spent on military and defense to Social Security. This proposal reflects the nation's values as a peacekeeper, not a conqueror. Dedicating it to Social Security provides a clear counterforce to what President Eisenhower labeled the military-industrial complex. This proposal would generate 1.7 percent of taxable payroll, or 0.61 percent of GDP.

## Simplify and Streamline Accounting

Social Security's disability, survivors, and retirement benefits are all intertwined, generated from the same benefit formula. For this reason, the Social Security annual trustees report often treats the separate trust funds as a single entity. The Social Security Works All Generations Plan simply makes that change a reality by combining the OASI Trust Fund with DI Trust Fund. This change has no cost. It simplifies and streamlines accounting.

Figure B.1 shows the costs of the benefit expansions and the increased revenue of the financing proposals contained in the All Generations Plan. As the table reveals, the Plan leaves Social Security in long-range actuarial surplus for the next three-quarters of a century and beyond.

# SOCIAL SECURITY WORKS ALL GENERATIONS PLAN

|  | As percent of taxable payroll | As percent of GDP |
|---|---|---|
| *Current projected 75-year shortfall (present value)* | *–3.21* | *–1.16* |
| **Addressing the Retirement Income Crisis** | Cost/ Savings as percent of taxable payroll | Cost/ Savings as percent of GDP |
| Increase monthly benefits for all current and future beneficiaries by changing benefit formula so that Social Security benefits replace 80% of preretirement income of Low-Earner (increasing monthly benefit from $795 to $1,559), 72% for Medium Earner (increasing monthly benefits from $1,309 to $3,098), and 64% for High Earner (increasing monthly benefits from $1,734 to $4,400), with maximum benefit of $8,200 a month | –7.00 | –2.52 |
| Reduce early retirement reductions to 1/3th of one percent for every month retired worker benefits claimed before statutorily-defined full retirement age | –0.60 | –0.22 |
| Change disability insurance eligibility criteria to give greater weight to age-related health limitations, partial disabilities, vocational, and educational factors for applicants, aged 50 and older | –0.50 | –0.18 |
| Ensure benefits do not erode over time by using more accurate Consumer Price Index for the Elderly (CPI-E) | –0.41 | –0.15 |
| Provide minimum benefit, at full benefit age, of 125 percent of poverty for covered workers, who have 30 years of work experience (inclusive of up to eight years for caring for children under age 5) | –0.24 | –0.09 |

| Strengthening Family Protections for All Generations | | |
|---|---|---|
| Provide up to 12 weeks of paid family leave and paid sick leave | -0.62 | -0.22 |
| In recognition of the value of caregiving, give credits toward future Social Security benefits for up to five years of caring for a child under age 6 or family member over age 6 with serious health or functional limitations requiring significant care | -0.40 | -0.14 |
| Eliminate 5-month waiting period | -0.12 | -0.04 |
| Provide $2,000 new child benefit at birth or adoption of a child | -0.14 | -0.05 |
| Facilitate higher education by restoring student benefits for children from 19 to 22 and extending up to age 26 whose covered parents have died, retired, or become disabled | -0.11 | -0.04 |
| Provide equity for disabled widow(er)s by eliminating both the age 50 requirement and 7-year rule, and by providing unreduced benefits | -0.04 | -0.01 |
| Encourage work and support family caregiving by not applying the Family Maximum when Disabled Adult Children do not live at home and by eliminating the marriage penalty | -0.01 | -0.004 |
| *Current projected shortfall plus cost of improvements* | *-13.40* | *-4.824* |
| Securing Social Security's Financing for Generations to Come | | |
| Increase Social Security contribution rate by 1/20th of a percentage point per year, on employers and employees each, from 2025-2054, until rate reaches 7.7 percent on both employers and employees in 2054; and, if needed as a fail-safe in sixty years, increase the contribution rate by an additional 0.50 percent on both employer and employee | +2.30 | +0.83 |

| | | |
|---|---|---|
| Starting in 2021, gradually eliminate the maximum taxable wage base, giving credit for these contributions up to a maximum monthly benefit of $8,200 | +2.30 | +0.83 |
| Treat capital gains as ordinary income, reported and taxed annually with proceeds dedicated to Social Security trust funds | +2.00 | +0.72 |
| Tax financial speculation | +2.80 | +1.00 |
| Peace Dividend | +1.70 | +0.61 |
| Double immigration | +1.0 | +0.36 |
| Restore federal estate tax to year 2000 level ($675 with tax rate of 55%) | +.80 | +0.29 |
| Invest 40% of Trust Funds in equities, phased in from 2021-2035 | +.59 | +0.21 |
| Treat all salary reduction plans the same as 401(k) plans with respect to the definition of wages under Social Security | +.25 | +0.09 |
| Invest in well-being of future generations by repealing tax expenditures enjoyed by fossil fuel industry, and activities destructive to the environment and civil society (e.g., private criminal justice facilities) | +.25 | +0.09 |
| Combine the OASI Trust Fund with DI Trust Fund | 0 | 0 |
| *Increased revenues* | *+13.99* | *5.03* |
| *Long-range surplus* | *+0.59* | *+0.21* |

**Source:** Based on Social Security Office of the Chief Actuary estimates, 2020, supplemented by authors' estimates and extrapolations.

**Note:** These estimates do not include interaction effects. "Percent of taxable payroll" is the customary way of showing the projected deficit/surplus of the Social Security Trust Fund—and the cost/savings generated by various proposals—over 75 years.

# APPENDIX C

## DESCRIPTION OF VARIOUS SOCIAL SECURITY EXPANSION PROPOSALS THAT WERE INTRODUCED IN THE 116TH CONGRESS (2019–2020)

Prepared by Jasmine Jefferson Wigfall, Legislative Director, Social Security Works.

| Bill Name | Changes to Social Security | Lifts the cap | CPI-E | Extends Solvency | Other Benefits Increases |
|---|---|---|---|---|---|
| Social Security 2100 Act S. 269 \| H.R. 860<br><br>Sen. Richard Blumenthal (CT) Rep. John Larson (CT-1) | Subjects earning above $400k to payroll tax. Switches to the more accurate CPI-E. Changes the benefit formula in a way that boosts benefits for all Social Security beneficiaries by approximately $65 per month. Raises the minimum benefit to 125% of poverty line. Combines the OASI and SSDI trust funds. Raises the threshold on the taxation of benefits. | ✓ | ✓ | ✓ | ✓ |
| Surviving Widow(er) Income Fair Treatment Act of 2019 (SWIFT Act) S. 345<br><br>Sen. Bob Casey (PA) | Allows widows and surviving divorced spouses to (1) receive 100% of survivors benefits regardless of age during disability; (2) receive survivor benefit with value increased beyond current caps; (3) receive child-in-care benefits through child's time in school (age 18 or 19); (4) receive eligibility, claiming information, and deadlines from the federal government. | | | | ✓ |

| Bill Name | Changes to Social Security | Lifts the cap | CPI-E | Extends Solvency | Other Benefits Increases |
|---|---|:---:|:---:|:---:|:---:|
| Social Security Expansion Act S. 478 \| H.R. 1170<br><br>Sen. Bernie Sanders (VT) Rep. Peter DeFazio (OR-04) | Subjects earned and unearned income above $250k to payroll tax. Switches to the more accurate CPI-E. Changes the benefit formula in a way that boosts benefits for all Social Security beneficiaries by approximately $65 per month. Raises the minimum benefit to 125% of the poverty line. Combines the OASI and SSDI trust funds. | ✓ | ✓ | ✓ | ✓ |
| Protect Our Widow(er) Retirement (POWR) Act H.R. 1540<br><br>Rep. Linda Sanchez (CA-38) | Allows widows who previously lived in a two-beneficiary household to choose a new option for benefit calculation that equals 75 percent of the combined household benefit. | | | | ✓ |
| Fair COLA for Seniors Act of 2019 H.R. 1553<br><br>Rep. John Garamendi (CA-3) | Switches to the more accurate CPI-E. | | ✓ | | |
| Protecting and Preserving Social Security Act S. 1132 \| H.R. 2302<br><br>Sen. Mazie Hirono (HI) Rep. Ted Deutch (FL-22) | Lifts the cap on high-income contributions gradually over seven years. Switches to the more accurate CPI-E. | ✓ | ✓ | ✓ | |
| ALJ Competitive Service Restoration Act H.R. 2429 \| S. 2348<br><br>Sen. Maria Cantwell (WA) Rep. Elijah Cummings (MD-7) | Reverts the ALJ hiring process back to competitive service, rather than to political appointment, as outlined in a Trump Administration Executive Order. | | | | ✓ |

| Bill Name | Changes to Social Security | Lifts the cap | CPI-E | Extends Solvency | Other Benefits Increases |
|-----------|---------------------------|---------------|-------|------------------|--------------------------|
| **Strengthening Social Security Act** H.R. 2654 Rep. Linda Sanchez (CA-38) Rep. Mark Pocan (WI-02) | Increases monthly benefits for current and future retirees. Replaces CPI-W with CPI-E for the purpose of calculating COLAs. Phases out the taxable cap of $132,700. Increases widow(er) benefits to the greater of 75% of combined benefits or the Primary Insurance Amount. | ✓ | ✓ | ✓ | ✓ |
| **Maintain Access to Vital Social Security Services Act** S. 1616 \| H.R. 2901 Sen. Tammy Baldwin (WI) Rep. Gwen Moore (WI-04) | Requires SSA to operate a sufficient number of field offices and employ an adequate number of personnel at each field office to provide convenient and accessible services to the public while minimizing wait times. Additionally, requires new reporting to Congress on these matters. | | | | ✓ |
| **Protection of Social Security Benefits Restoration Act** S. 1649 \| H.R. 2991 Sen. Ron Wyden (OR) Rep. Raul Grijalva (AZ-3) | Repeals the 1996 Social Security garnishment rules for Social Security. The legislation would prevent Social Security from being garnished for federal student debt, home loans owed to the Veterans Administration, and food stamp overpayments. | | | | ✓ |
| **Grandfamilies Act of 2019** S. 1660 \| H.R. 2967 Sen. Bob Casey (PA) Rep. Danny Davis (IL-7) | Alleviates restrictions on Social Security benefits so that relative children can receive benefits if they are under legal custody of a relative who already receives benefits. Additionally, extends TANF program. | | | | ✓ |
| **Social Security Administration Accountability Act** H.R. 3905 Rep. Brian Higgins (NY-26) | Requires SSA to submit to Congress an annual report with yearly statistics for hearing office backlogs. Prohibits the SSA from closing or limiting hours at field offices until six months after providing justification to Congress. Requires the SSA to hold public hearings in the impacted community. | | | | ✓ |

| Bill Name | Changes to Social Security | Lifts the cap | CPI-E | Extends Solvency | Other Benefits Increases |
|---|---|---|---|---|---|
| Social Security Fairness Act H.R. 141 \| S. 521<br><br>Sen. Sherrod Brown (OH)<br>Rep. Rodney Davis (IL–13) | Eliminates the Windfall Elimination Provision (WEP) and the Government Pension Offset (GPO), which unfairly reduce or eliminate Social Security benefits for millions of public service workers and their families. | | | | ✓ |
| Social Security for Future Generations Act H.R. 4121<br><br>Rep. Al Lawson (FL–5) | Subjects earned and unearned income above $250k to payroll tax. Switches to the more accurate CPI-E. Extends student benefit to age 22. Increases special minimum benefit. Updated benefit formula for widow(er)s. | ✓ | ✓ | | ✓ |
| Strengthen Social Security by Taxing Dynastic Wealth Act S. 1950<br><br>Sen. Chris Van Hollen (MD) | Returns the estate tax to 2009 levels—rolling back the most recent boon for wealthy estates in the 2017 Republican tax law—and deposits all of the revenues from this tax into the Social Security Trust Fund. | | | | ✓ |
| Supplemental Security Income Restoration Act H.R. 4280 \| S. 2753<br><br>Rep. Raul Grijalva (AZ–3)<br>Sen. Sherrod Brown (OH) | Modernizes and improves SSI by streamlining and simplifying the claiming process, expanding the resources and income limits, and eliminating punitive reductions in benefits. | | | | ✓ |
| Stop the Wait Act H.R. 4386 \| S. 2496<br><br>Sen. Bob Casey (PA)<br>Rep. Lloyd Doggett (TX–35) | Eliminates 5-month SSDI and 24-month Medicare waiting periods for disabled Americans. Directs the National Academy of Medicine to conduct a study of whether the elimination of the waiting periods are resulting in better health and community living outcomes for eligible SSDI recipients and their families. | | | | ✓ |

| Bill Name | Changes to Social Security | Lifts the cap | CPI-E | Extends Solvency | Other Benefits Increases |
|---|---|---|---|---|---|
| **Public Servants Protection and Fairness Act** H.R. 4540 <br><br> Rep. Richard Neal (MA-01) | Fixes the Windfall Elimination Provision (WEP) by introducing a new proportional formula. Provides meaningful WEP relief to current retirees. Includes a benefit guarantee so that no current or future retirees can be worse off. | | | | ✓ |
| **Know Your Social Security Act** H.R. 5306 \| S. 2989 <br><br> Rep. John Larson (CT-1) Sen. Ron Wyden (OR) | Clarifies the requirement for the Social Security Administration (SSA) to mail an annual Social Security Statement to all workers ages 25 and older with covered earnings, who are not receiving Social Security benefits. | | | | ✓ |
| **Social Security Enhancement and Protection Act** H.R. 5392 <br><br> Rep. Gwen Moore (WI-4) | Increases special minimum benefit. Increases benefits for seniors later in life by 5%. Extends student benefit. Eliminates cap on payroll contribution rate. | ✓ | | | ✓ |
| **The Gig Is Up Act** H.R. 5419 <br><br><br><br><br><br> Rep. Deb Haaland (NM-1) | Requires companies that gross at least $100 million and employ at least 10,000 independent contractors to pay the full cost of both the employer contribution and the worker contribution to Social Security and Medicare, which will serve as an incentive to classify employees appropriately. | | | | ✓ |
| **Improving Social Security Service to Victims of Identity Theft Act** H.R. 5446 <br><br> Rep. John Larson (CT-1) | Requires the Social Security Administration (SSA) to provide identity theft victims with a single point of contact within SSA when the misuse of their Social Security number (SSN) results in the need to resolve one or more issue(s) with SSA. | | | | ✓ |

| Bill Name | Changes to Social Security | Lifts the cap | CPI-E | Extends Solvency | Other Benefits Increases |
|---|---|---|---|---|---|
| **Emergency Social Security Benefits Improvement Act** H.R. 6356<br><br><br><br><br><br><br>Rep. John Larson (CT-1) | Increases benefits by an average of 2% across the board to all 64 million Americans receiving Social Security benefits. Increases threshold for Special Minimum Benefit to 125% of poverty. Reduces tax on benefits for lower- and middle-income taxpayers. Ensures grandparents are entitled to benefits to care for their grandchildren.<br>Improves the widow(er)s' benefits for lower- and middle-income beneficiaries. Ensures dependent students are qualified for benefits through age 21. | ✓ | ✓ | ✓ | ✓ |

# APPENDIX D

## LEADING ORGANIZATIONS WORKING TO EXPAND SOCIAL SECURITY

The victories described in chapter 12 were the work of many. In 2010, the authors cofounded Social Security Works, which staffs the Strengthen Social Security Coalition (SSSC), a broad-based diverse coalition of more than 350 national and state organizations, representing over 50 million Americans, including seniors, women, people with disabilities, workers, people of color, and veterans. (A list of all members of the coalition can be found at https://strengthensocialsecurity.org/about/coalition/.)

Many members of the coalition continue to work tirelessly to educate their members, the public, media, and our representatives in Congress. They are the force behind the movement to protect and expand Social Security.

We urge those who want to get involved to check out the website of Social Security Works (www.socialsecurityworks.org), a nonprofit organization founded by the coauthors, and sign up for alerts. Social Security Works annually publishes fifty state reports—including eleven in Spanish and reports for the District of Columbia, Puerto Rico, American Samoa, Guam, the Northern Mariana Islands, and the U.S. Virgin Islands—highlighting the protections afforded to each state's citizens—children, seniors, veterans, persons with disabilities, persons of color, and women—

and providing data about the numbers of people served and benefits provided across all congressional districts and in every county (socialsecurityworks.org/category/resources/state-reports).

To keep informed about the latest developments in the battle for Social Security and to join the fight, please visit our website at socialsecurityworks.org.

# ACKNOWLEDGMENTS

We have dedicated this book to the late Robert M. Ball, our mentor, role model, adviser, teacher, colleague, and friend. Without his wisdom, insight, and inspiration, this book would never have been written.

There are others without whom this book would never have come to be. Primary among them is David Cay Johnston—Pulitzer Prize–winning journalist, bestselling author, and Distinguished Visiting Lecturer at Syracuse University, whose book *Divided: The Perils of Our Growing Inequality*, is also published by The New Press. David, also the author of our book's foreword, provided a generous introduction to Ellen Adler, publisher of The New Press from which this book's predecessor, *Social Security Works!: Why Social Security Isn't Going Broke and How Expanding It Will Help Us All*, resulted.

That introduction began an outstanding, productive relationship not only with Ellen, but also with assistant editor Jay Gupta. Both Ellen and Jay provided careful, thoughtful editing of our manuscript, as well as guidance through the process. Everyone at The New Press has been both very extremely able and helpful: Maury Botton, senior managing editor; Brian Ulicky, associate publisher and director of marketing and publicity; Josh Itkin, sales and inventory manager; Derek Warker, publicity manager; and Emily Janakiram, publicist, all of whom lent their collective creative genius to the book's design, marketing, and distribution; and Sharon Swados, director of sales and subsidiary rights; and James

Phelan, director of development, who ably and efficiently helped with the technical business aspects of the relationship, including promotion of the book. Also, thanks to Terry Buck for copyediting and to Bookbright Media for typesetting. We are privileged to be published by The New Press, a nonprofit trade publisher and unionized press with national reach and a social justice mission.

We especially want to thank Kelly Olsen, formerly an analyst with both the Social Security Administration and the Employment Benefit Research Institute and now a clinical social worker. We benefited from her expertise, thoughtful critiques, thorough editing, and humor. We also thank Alexandra Kerr, then a graduate assistant at the Syracuse University School of Social Work, for her able assistance double-checking, inserting, and proofing endnotes

Several members of the Social Security Works staff also deserve special mention. Alex Abbott, policy and research specialist at Social Security Works, worked tirelessly on updating and confirming the data included in this new edition. Jasmine Wigfall, Social Security Works legislative director, did the background research for and drafted appendix C. Michael Phelan, deputy director, provided, as he always does, invaluable technical assistance. And Alex Lawson, the creative and tireless executive director of Social Security Works, who first suggested we write a book about Social Security, lent his talent to facilitating and disseminating the book. Linda Benesch, communications director, was extremely helpful with outreach and publicity. We also want to acknowledge, with gratitude, Ben Veghte, who was the policy director of Social Security Works in 2015 and worked tirelessly on the predecessor volume of this book. We acknowledge Ben and his work with gratitude.

Eric would like to acknowledge his colleagues at the Syracuse University School of Social Work, especially professor emeritus Alejandro Garcia, for their considerate support, as well as Syracuse University, which generously allowed him to take leaves of absence that facilitated his work with Social Security Works and the Strengthen Social Security Coalition, leading in turn to the writing of this book.

On a substantive note, we want to alert readers that, while some of the stories related in the book are drawn from real people, some, as mentioned in the pertinent endnotes, were created as illustrative. We also want to acknowledge that some material that appears in this book builds on and was drawn from earlier publications of the authors, as listed in the first endnote to chapter 1.

This book came out of our work as the founding co-directors of Social Security Works and founding co-chairs of the Strengthen Social Security Coalition, which involves many organizations and wonderful people. We do not thank by name the many dedicated people engaged with the Coalition, though we owe a debt of gratitude to each and every one of them and the organizations they represent.

We want to give an enormous thank-you to the thousands of individual grassroots donors who collectively give Social Security Works the freedom to fight for an agenda that puts people first, along with the institutions with the foresight to join that agenda. Without those 76,000 contributors of small dollar amounts, our work, and the book that is a product of that work, would not have been possible.

We would be remiss if we did not also highlight the special role the Atlantic Philanthropies, its board of directors, and its staff played in helping us to launch, shape, and sustain Social Security Works and the Strengthen Social Security Coalition. In 2009, the Atlantic Philanthropies had the foresight to recognize that the future of our Social Security system would soon emerge on the national agenda. Concerned that policymaking might proceed without adequate input from those most directly affected, the Atlantic Philanthropies asked us to develop a plan and then proceeded to generously fund Social Security Works and the coalition's work, which grew from that plan. Atlantic's staff, especially Stephen R. McConnell, then director of United States programs, as well as Laura Robbins and

Stacey Easterling, our grant officers, provided advice, guidance, enthusiastic support, and friendship as our work proceeded.

We also thank, with tremendous appreciation, the other funders of Social Security Works: the Open Society Foundation, CREDO, and the Retirement Research Foundation, along with, again, the individual donors who have generously supported and advanced Social Security Works.

Finally, but most importantly, we want to thank our families, without whose love and support our work would be impossible. Eric lovingly thanks his wife, Nancy, and his children, Aaron, Johanna, and Sarah. Nancy lovingly thanks her husband, Chip, and her children, Toni, Adam, Jennifer, and Michael. We both thank our grandchildren—Ezekiel, Kylie, Beatrice, and Sadie on Nancy's side, and Sammy, Maggie, and Jameson on Eric's—whose love enriches our lives and whose very presence provides a window into the future. It is for them and all generations, now and in the future, for whom we and many others work to expand Social Security.

# NOTES

## Chapter 1

1. Franklin D. Roosevelt, Presidential Statement Signing the Social Security Act, August 14, 1935, at Social Security Administration History website: https://www.ssa.gov/history/fdrstmts.html#signing.

2. See Christopher Ingraham, "Wealth concentration returning to 'levels last seen during the Roaring Twenties,' according to new research," *Washington Post* (February 18, 2019), washingtonpost.com/us-policy/2019/02/08/wealth-concentration-returning-levels-last-seen-during-roaring-twenties-according-new-research/.

3. Arthur J. Altmeyer, "Social Security—Yesterday and Tomorrow," December 9, 1965, on Social Security Administration History website: https://www.ssa.gov/history/aja1265.html.

4. J. Douglas Brown, *Essays on Social Security* (Princeton, NJ: Princeton University Press, 1977): 31–32.

5. Franklin D. Roosevelt, "Message to Congress Reviewing the Broad Objectives and Accomplishments of the Administration," June 8, 1934, at Social Security Administration History website: https://www.ssa.gov/history/fdrstmts.html#message1.

6. Martin Luther King Jr., "The King Philosophy," The King Center, Atlanta, Georgia, thekingcenter.org/king-philosophy/.

7. Eric Kingson, "Framing Social Security for the Twenty-First Century," in *A Promise to All Generations*, ed. Christopher Breiseth and Kirstin Downey (Newcastle, ME: The Frances Perkins Center, 2011): 146–160.

8. Dwight Eisenhower, "Special Message to the Congress Transmitting Proposed Changes in the Social Security Program," Social Security Administration, August 1, 1953, www.ssa.gov/history/ikestmts.html#special.

9. Franklin D. Roosevelt, "Fireside Chat 5: On Addressing the Critics," June 28, 1934, Miller Center, millercenter.org/the-presidency/presidential-speeches/june-28-1934-fireside-chat-5-addressing-critics.

10. Frances Perkins, *The Roosevelt I Knew* (New York: Viking Press, 1946): 299.

11. Jasmine Tucker, Virginia Reno, and Thomas Bethell, "Strengthening Social Security: What Do Americans Want?" National Academy of Social Insurance, January 31, 2013, www.nasi.org/sites/default/files/research/What_Do_Americans_Want.pdf.

12. Social Security Works, "Polling Memo, Americans' Views on Social Security," March 29, 2019, https://socialsecurityworks.org/2019/03/26/social-security-polling/.

13. Kim Parker, Rich Morin, and Juliana Menasce Horowitz, Pew Research Center, "Political Polarization in the American Public," June 2014, pewresearch.org/politics/2014/06/12/political-polarization-in-the-american-public/. See also AARP, Social Security Opinions and Attitudes on Its 85th Anniversary, August 13, 2020, https://www.aarp.org/content/dam/aarp/research/surveys _statistics/econ/2020/social-security-anniversary-survey.doi.10.26419-2Fres .00400.001.pdf.

## Chapter 2

1. Franklin Roosevelt, "Statement of the President Upon Signing the Social Security Bill," August 14, 1935, fdrlibrary.marist.edu/_resources/images/sign /fdr_14.pdf#search=social%20security.

2. "I Will Not Promise the Moon," Alf Landon Opposes the Social Security Act, History Matters, The U.S. Survey Course on the Web, http://historymatters .gmu.edu/d/8128/ See generally Nancy J. Altman, *The Battle for Social Security: From FDR's Vision to Bush's Gamble* (Hoboken, NJ: John Wiley & Sons, 2005): 101–103.

3. Social Security Administration, "Research Note #16: Summary of Major Benefits Under The Social Security Program," Research Notes and Special Studies by the Historian's Office, available at https://www.ssa.gov/history/benefittypes .html. *Weinberger v. Wiesenfeld*, 420 U.S. 636 (1975), available at https://supreme .justia.com/cases/federal/us/420/636/.

4. U.S. Bureau of Labor Statistics, "The So-Called 'Core' Index: History and Uses of the Index for All Items Less Food and Energy," *Focus on Prices and Spending* 1, no. 15 (February 2011), bls.gov/opub/btn/archive/the-so-called-core-index-history -and-uses-of-the-index-for-all-items-less-food-and-energy.pdf .

5. U.S. Bureau of Labor Statistics, "Labor Force Statistics from the Current Population Survey," 2014, data.bls.gov/timeseries/LNU04000000?years_option=all _years &periods_option=specific_periods &per iods=Annual+Data.

6. John Haaga, "Just How Many Baby Boomers Are There?" Population Reference Bureau, December 2002, prb.org/Publications/Articles/2002 /JustHowManyBabyBoomersAreThere.aspx.

7. Larry W. DeWitt, Daniel Béland, and Edward D. Berkowitz, *Social Security: A Documentary History* (Washington, DC: Congressional Quarterly Press, 2007): 318.

8. Ronald Reagan, "Second 1980 Presidential Debate," October 28, 1980, debates.org/index.php?page=october-28-1980-debate-transcript.

9. William Safire, "Third Rail," *New York Times* (February 18, 2007), nytimes .com/2007/02/18/magazine/18wwlnsafire.t.html?_r= 0.

10. Ronald Reagan, "Remarks on Signing the Social Security Amendments of 1983," April 20, 1983, ssa.gov/history/reaganstmts.html.

11. Stuart Butler and Peter Germanis, "Achieving Social Security Reform: A 'Leninist' Strategy," *Cato Journal* 3, no. 2 (Fall 1983), cato.org/cato-journal/fall-1983.

12. George W. Bush, "Address Before a Joint Session of the Congress on the State of the Union," February 2, 2005, The American Presidency Project, presidency.ucsb .edu/ws/index.php?pid=58746.

13. Robert F. Kennedy, Remarks at the University of Kansas, March 18, 1968 (quoting George Bernard Shaw), https://www.jfklibrary.org/learn/about-jfk/the

-kennedy-family/robert-f-kennedy/robert-f-kennedy-speeches/remarks-at-the
-university-of-kansas-march-18-1968.

## Chapter 3

1. Social Security Trustees, *2020 Annual Report of the Board of Trustees of the Federal Old-Age and Survivors Insurance and Federal Disability Insurance Trust Funds*, April 22, 2020, tables IV.B3 and IV.A3., ssa.gov/OACT/TR/2020/tr2020.pdf.

2. Johanna Maleh and Tiffany Bosley, "Disability and Death Probability Tables for Insured Workers Born in 1999," Actuarial Note, no. 2019, Social Security Administration, August 2019, ssa.gov/oact/NOTES/ran6/an2019-6.pdf.

3. Michael Clingman, Kyle Burkhalter, and Chris Chapman to Karen P. Glenn, memorandum, "The Present Value of Expected Lifetime Benefits for a Hypothetical Worker Dying or Becoming Disabled at Age 30," Social Security Office of the Chief Actuary, Social Security Administration, November 8, 2016, available at socialsecurityworks.org/wp-content/uploads/2017/09/23_Illustrative_Survivor_and_Disability_Case_2016.pdf. The worker must have achieved insured status. See appendix 1 for details.

4. Clingman, Burkhalter, and Chapman to Glenn, "The Present Value of Expected Lifetime Benefits."

5. Andrew Achenbaum, personal communication with author (Eric R. Kingson), March 31, 2014.

6. A portion of the proceeds are credited to the Hospital Insurance Trust Fund of Medicare.

7. Barry F. Huston, Social Security Primer, Congressional Research Service. Updated May 7, 2019, and available at fas.org/sgp/crs/misc/R42035.pdf. Other benefit formulas apply in specific circumstances, such as for the special minimum benefit.

8. To the extent possible, we use the term "full retirement age" throughout this book.

9. There are some exceptions. For instance, if retired worker benefits are claimed after the full retirement age, then the aged widow(er) benefits of such workers will also be larger than a "full benefit."

10. Social Security Trustees, *2020 Annual Report.*

11. Social Security Administration, "Fact Sheet on the Old-Age, Survivors, and Disability Insurance Program," August 2019, figure D.1, ssa.gov/OACT/FACTS/fs2019_06.pdf.

12. Social Security Trustees, *2020 Annual Report.*

13. Social Security Trustees, *2020 Annual Report.*

14. U.S. Census Bureau, "2018: ACS 1-Year Estimates Data Profiles," 2018 American Community Survey 1-Year Estimates, 2019, data.census.gov/cedsci.

15. Social Security Administration, *Annual Statistical Supplement, 2019*, November 2019, table 5.A4 and table 5.A6, ssa.gov/policy/docs/statcomps/supplement/2019/5a.pdf.

16. Thomas Gabe, *Social Security's Effect on Child Poverty*, Congressional Research Service, December 22, 2011: 3–4, wlstorage.net/file/crs/RL33289.pdf.

17. Kathleen Romig, "Social Security Lifts More Americans Above Poverty Than Any Other Program," Center on Budget and Policy Priorities, updated July 19, 2019, cbpp.org/research/social-security/social-security-lifts-more-americans-above-poverty-than-any-other-program.

18. Generations United, *State of Grandfamilies 2019*, grandfamilies.org/Portals/0/19-Grandfamilies-Report-APlacetoCallHome.pdf.

19. Maya Rockeymoore and Meizhu Lui, *Plan for a New Future: The Impact of*

*Social Security Reform on People of Color, Commission to Modernize Social Security*, 2011, modernizesocialsecurity.files.wordpress.com/2013/04/new_future_social _security_10_24_11.pdf; see also, Benjamin W. Veghte, Elliot Schreur, and Mikki Waid, "Social Security and the Racial Gap in Retirement Wealth," National Academy of Social Insurance, December 2016, No. 48, nasi.org/sites/default/files/research /SS_Brief_48.pdf.

20. Veghte, Schreur, and Waid, "Social Security and the Racial Gap in Retirement Wealth."

21. Social Security Administration, "Income of the Population 55 or Older, 2014," April 2016, table 9.A3, ssa.gov/policy/docs/statcomps/income_pop55/2014 /sect09.pdf.

22. Tabulations by the Center on Budget and Policy Priorities (CBPP) for Social Security Works of data from its 2018 report, "Social Security Lifts More Americans Above Poverty Than Any Other Program."

23. Diane Oakley et al., "Shortchanged in Retirement: Continuing Challenges to Women's Financial Future National Institute of Retirement Security," March 2016, nirsonline.org/reports/shortchanged-in-retirement-continuing-challenges-to -womens-financial-future/.

24. Romig, "Social Security Lifts More Americans Above Poverty."

25. Social Security Administration, "Income of the Population 55 or Older, 2014."

26. Rockeymoore and Lui, *Plan for a New Future.*

27. Social Security Administration, Office of Retirement Policy, "Veteran Beneficiaries, 2018," February 2019, ssa.gov/policy/docs/population-profiles/veteran -beneficiaries.html; see also Nancy Altman, "Social Security Serves Those Who Serve Our Nation," *Forbes* (November 11, 2019), forbes.com/sites/nancyaltman /2019/11/11/social-security-serves-those-who-serve-our-nation/#4e8a03702291.

28. Social Security Works, "Social Security: Serving Those Who Serve Our Nation," March 2011, https://socialsecurityworks.org/wp-content/uploads/2020 /02/VeteransReportInHousePrintVersionFinal5-23-11.pdf.

29. As the United States has become more tolerant, the acronym used for those who are not exclusively heterosexual has expanded from LGBT to add Q for questioning or queer, I for intersex, A for ally or asexual, and often a plus sign for others, who may include gender nonconforming and others. In an effort to be inclusive, the authors have chosen to use LGBTQ+. See Michael Gold, "The ABCs of L.G.B.T.Q.I.A.+," *New York Times* (June 21, 2018, updated June 7, 2019), nytimes .com/2018/06/21/style/lgbtq-gender-language.html.

## Chapter 4

1. Jerry Flint, "The Old Folks," *Forbes* (February 18, 1980), 51–56.

2. Phillip Longman, "Justice Between Generations," *Atlantic Monthly* (June 1985), 256, 73–81, theatlantic.com/past/docs/issues/96may/aging/longm.htm.

3. Richard Lamm, *Megatraumas: America at the Year 2000* (Boston: Houghton Mifflin, 1985).

4. Henry Fairlie, "Greedy Geezers: Talkin' 'bout my generation," *New Republic*, March 28, 1988, 19–22.

5. U.S. Census Bureau, "Income of Families and Persons in The United States: 1960," Current Population Reports: Consumer Income, January 17, 1962, table 6, www2.census.gov/library/publications/1962/demographics/p60-37.pdf. In 1960,

income of families sixty-five or older was $2,900 in 1960 dollars. Inflation adjusted to 2018 dollars using Bureau of Labor Statistics, "CPI Inflation Calculator," data.bls .gov/cgi-bin/cpicalc.pl?cost1=2%2C900.00&year1=196006&year2=201806.

6. Illustrative vignette created by the authors for the purpose of this publication.

7. Statement of Rita Lewis on "The Multiemployer Pension Plan System: Recent Reforms and Current Challenges," before the U.S. Senate Committee on Finance, March 1, 2016, finance.senate.gov/imo/media/doc/03012016%20Rita%20 Lewis%20SFC%20Statement%20Multiemployer%20Pensions.pdf.

8. James Sterngold, "Madoff Victims Recount the Long Road Back," *Wall Street Journal*, December 9, 2013, online.wsj.com/news/articles/SB100014240527 02303560204579248221657387860. This vignette is the authors' paraphrase of the account given in Sterngold's article above. See "Bernie Madoff victims speak out," ABC 25 WPBF NEWS (February 5, 2016), wpbf.com/article/bernie-madoff -victims-speak-out/1402086.

9. Jessica Semega et al., U.S. Census Bureau, Current Population Reports, P60-266, Income and Poverty in the United States: 2018, U.S. Government Printing Office, Washington, DC, 2019, census.gov/content/dam/Census/library /publications/2019/demo/p60-266.pdf.

10. Carol Morello, "Census Releases Alternative Formulas for Gauging Poverty," *Washington Post* (January 5, 2011), washingtonpost.com/wp-dyn/content/article /2011/01/04/AR2011010405677.html.

11. Semega et al., Income and Poverty.

12. Liana Fox, "The Supplemental Poverty Index, 2018. U.S. Census Bureau, *Current Population Reports*, P60-268, September 2019, census.gov/content/dam /Census/library/publications/2019/demo/p60-268.pdf.

13. Fox, "The Supplemental Poverty Index, 2018."

14. Juliette Cubanski et al., "How Many Seniors Live in Poverty?" Kaiser Family Foundation, November 2018, files.kff.org/attachment/Issue-Brief-How-Many -Seniors-Live-in-Poverty.

15. Cubanski et al., "How Many Seniors Live in Poverty?"

16. Jan Mutchler, Yang Li, and Nidya Velasco Roldán, "Living Below the Line: Economic Insecurity and Older Americans, Insecurity in the States 2019," Center for Social and Demographic Research on Aging Publications, 2019, 40, scholarworks .umb.edu/demographyofaging/40.

17. Hank Lobel, Colleen Jaconetti, and Rebecca Cuff, "The replacement ratio: Making it personal," *Vanguard Research*, April 2019, personal.vanguard.com/pdf /ISGRR.pdf.

18. Lobel, Jaconetti, and Cuff, "The replacement ratio"; see also Vickie Bajtelsmit and Anna Rappaport, "Retirement Adequacy in the United States: Should We Be Concerned?" Society of Actuaries, 2018, soa.org/globalassets/assets/files/resources /research-report/2018/retire-adequacy-us-concern.pdf.

19. Note that the full retirement age (FRA) was age sixty-six and two months for persons born in 1955, sixty-six and four months for persons born in 1956, sixty-six and six months for persons born in 1957, sixty-six and eight months for persons born in 1958, sixty-six and ten months for persons born in 1959, and sixty-seven for persons born in 1960 or later.

20. Social Security Administration, "Annual Statistical Supplement, 2019," Table 6.A4—Number and average monthly benefit for retired and disabled workers, by age and sex, 2018, ssa.gov/policy/docs/statcomps/supplement/2019/6a.pdf.

21. Michael Clingman, Kyle Burkhalter, and Chris Chaplain, "Replacement

Rates for Hypothetical Retired Workers," Actuarial Note, no.2019.9, Social Security Administration, April 2019, ssa.gov/oact/NOTES/ran9/an2019-9.pdf.

22. U.S. Census Bureau, 2017 National Population Projections Tables, Table 2, Projected age and sex composition of the population, census.gov/data/tables/2017 /demo/popproj/2017-summary-tables.html.

23. U.S. Census Bureau, "Wealth, Asset Ownership, & Debt of Households Detailed Tables: 2016," table 1, Median Value of Assets for Households, by Type of Asset Owned and Selected Characteristics: 2016, census.gov/data/tables/2016/demo /wealth/wealth-asset-ownership.html.

24. U.S. Census Bureau, "Wealth, Asset Ownership, & Debt."

25. Social Security Administration, "Income of the Population 55 or Older, 2014," April 2016, table 9.A1, ssa.gov/policy/docs/statcomps/income_pop55/2014 /sect09.pdf.

26. Social Security Administration, "Income of the Population 55 or Older, 2014," Table 10.5.

27. Social Security Administration, "Income of the Population 55 or Older, 2014."

28. Social Security Administration, "Income of the Population 55 or Older, 2014."

29. Juliette Cubanski et al., "Medicare Beneficiaries' Out-of-Pocket Health Care Spending as a Share of Income Now and Projections for the Future," Kaiser Family Foundation, January 26, 2018, kff.org/report-section/medicare-beneficiaries-out-of -pocket-health-care-spending-as-a-share-of-income-now-and-projections-for-the -future-report/.

30. Cubanski et al., "Medicare Beneficiaries' Out-of-Pocket Health Care Spend-ing."

31. Fidelity Investments, "How to plan for rising health care costs," April 1, 2019, fidelity.com/viewpoints/personal-finance/plan-for-rising-health-care-costs.

32. Victoria Sackett, "Nursing Home Costs Top $100,000 a Year," AARP, Octo-ber 24, 2018, aarp.org/caregiving/financial-legal/info-2018/nursing-home-costs -rising.html.

33. Centers for Medicare and Medicaid Services, "National Health Expenditure Projections: 2018–2027," cms.gov/Research-Statistics-Data-and-Systems/Statistics -Trends-and-Reports/NationalHealthExpendData/Downloads/ForecastSummary .pdf.

## Chapter 5

1. Monique Morrissey, "These Social Security Plans Could Help Solve Amer-ica's Retirement Crisis," CNN Business (October 17, 2019), cnn.com/2019/10/17 /perspectives/social-security-proposals-retirement/index.html.

2. Alicia Munnell, Wenliang Hou, and Geoffrey Sanzenbacher, "National Retirement Risk Index Shows Modest Improvement in 2016," Center for Retire-ment Research at Boston College, 2018, crr.bc.edu/briefs/national-retirement-risk -index-shows-modest-improvement-in-2016/.

3. Alicia Munnell, Anthony Webb, Dan Muldoon, and Francesca Golub-Sass, "Long-Term Care Costs and the National Retirement Risk Index," *Center for Retire-ment Research at Boston College*, 2009, crr.bc.edu/briefs/long-term-care-costs-and-the -national-retirement-risk-index/.

4. Lydia Saad, "Paying for Medical Crises, Retirement Lead Financial Fears," Gallup

.com,September 4,2019,news.gallup.com/poll/233642/paying-medical-crises-retire ment-lead-financial-fears.aspx.

5. Diane Oakley and Kelly Kenneally, "Retirement Insecurity 2019: Americans' Views of the Retirement Crisis," National Institute on Retirement Security, 2019, nirson line.org/wp-content/uploads/2019/02/OpinionResearch_final-1.pdf.

6. Joanne (Femino) Jacobsen, "Testimony by Joanne Jacobsen," Senate Committee on Aging, September 25, 2013, aging.senate.gov/imo/media/doc /04_Jacobsen_9_25_13.pdf.

7. Retirement USA, "Faces of the Retirement Income Deficit," 2014, retire ment-usa.org/stories/story-145.

8. Retirement USA, "Faces of the Retirement Income Deficit."

9. Retirement USA, "Faces of the Retirement Income Deficit."

10. Alicia Munnell, Wenliang Hou, and Anthony Webb, "Will the Explosion of Student Debt Widen the Retirement Security Gap?" *Center for Retirement Research at Boston College*, 2016, crr.bc.edu/briefs/will-the-explosion-of-student-debt-widen -the-retirement-security-gap/.

11. Ephrat Livni, "The gig economy is quietly undermining a century of work-er protections," *Quartz*, February 26, 2019, available at qz.com/1556194/the-gig -economy-is-quietly-undermining-a-century-of-worker-protections/.

12. Larry DeWitt, "Research Note #1: Origins of the Three-Legged Stool Meta-phor for Social Security," Social Security Administration, May 1996, ssa.gov/history /stool.html.

13. Emily Brandon, "The Retirement Pogo Stick," *U.S. News & World Report*, February 5, 2009, money.usnews.com/money/blogs/planning-to-retire/2009/02 /05/the-retirement-pogo-stick.

14. Virginia Reno, "What's Next for Social Security? Essential Facts for Action," *National Academy of Social Insurance*, October 2013, nasi.org/sites/default/files /research/Whats_Next_for_Social_Security_Oct2013.pdf.

15. The "statutorily defined retirement age" is the age at which a worker is eligi-ble to receive full Social Security retired worker benefits, more commonly termed by the Social Security Administration as the "Normal Retirement Age (NRA)" or the "Full Retirement Age (FRA)." For further explanation, see discussion in chapter 2.

16. Reno, "What's Next for Social Security?"

17. Canyon Bosler and Nicolas Petrosky-Nadeau, "Job-to-Job Transitions in an Evolving Labor Market" (2016), Federal Reserve Bank of San Francisco, frbsf .org/economic-research/publications/economic-letter/2016/november/job-to-job -transitions-in-evolving-labor-market/; see also, Jess Scherman, "Employee Tenure Trends: Recent Retention, Millennials and More," Rasmussen Business Blog, Octo-ber 29, 2018, rasmussen.edu/degrees/business/blog/employee-tenure-trends/.

18. Bureau of Labor Statistics, U.S. Department of Labor, Job Openings and Labor Turnover, December 2019 and May 2020, bls.gov/news.release/archives /jolts_02112020.htm; bls.gov/news.release/jolts.nr0.htm.

19. Bureau of Labor Statistics, U.S. Department of Labor, The Economics Dai-ly; 51 percent of private industry workers had access to only defined contribution retirement plans, October 2, 2018, bls.gov/opub/ted/2018/51-percent-of-private -industry-workers-had-access-to-only-defined-contribution-retirement-plans -march-2018.htm.

20. Urban Institute, State and Local Government Pensions, undated website, urban.org/policy-centers/cross-center-initiatives/state-and-local-finance-initiative /projects/state-and-local-backgrounders/state-and-local-government-pensions.

21. Gordon Lafer, "The Legislative Attack on American Wages and Labor Standards, 2011–2012," Briefing Paper, no. 364, Economic Policy Institute, October 31, 2013, epi .org/files/2013/EPI-Legislative-Attack-on-American-Wages-Labor-Standards-10 -31-2013.pdf.

22. Mark Maremont, "Romney's Unorthodox IRA," *Wall Street Journal*, January 19, 2012, online.wsj.com/news/articles/SB10001424052970204468004577168972507188592.

23. Alexander Sammon, "100 CEOs Have the Retirement Savings of 116 Million Americans," *Mother Jones*, December 16, 2016, motherjones.com/politics/2016 /12/ceo-executives-retirement-income-inequality/; Institute for Policy Studies, "Report: A Tale of Two Retirements," *Institute for Policy Studies*, December 15, 2016, ips-dc.org/report-tale-two-retirements/.

24. Jennifer Erin Brown, Joelle Saad-Lessler, and Diane Oakley, "Retirement in America: Out of Reach for Working Americans?" 2018, nirsonline.org/wp-content /uploads/2018/09/FINAL-Report-.pdf.

25. Brown, Saad-Lessler, and Oakley, "Retirement in America."

26. Alicia H. Munnell, Wenliang Hou, and Geoffrey T. Sanzenbacher, "The National Retirement Risk Index Shows Modest Improvement in 2016," Issue Brief 18-1, *Center for Retirement Research at Boston College*, January 2018, crr.bc.edu/wp -content/uploads/2018/01/IB_18-1.pdf.

27. Alicia Munnell et al., "Health Care Costs Drive Up the National Retirement Risk Index," no. 8-3, *Center for Retirement Research at Boston College*, February 2008, crr.bc.edu/wp-content/uploads/2008/02/ib_8-3.pdf.

28. Alicia H. Munnell, Anthony Webb, and Francesca N. Golub-Sass, "The National Retirement Risk Index: An Update, Issue Brief 18-1, *Center for Retirement Research at Boston College*, November 2012, crr.bc.edu/briefs/the-national-retirement -risk-index-an-update/.

29. Munnell, Hou, and Sanzenbacher, "The NRRI Shows Modest Improvement."

30. In its 2016 at-risk estimates, the Center for Retirement Research did not include an estimate of the additional share of households that would be at risk if health and long-term care costs were taken into account. If in 2016 this additional share were equivalent to the 20 percent it amounted to in 2006, then more than seven in ten households would be at risk after taking into account health and long-term care costs.

31. Jack VanDerhei, "Retirement Savings Shortfalls: Evidence from EBRI's 2019 Retirement Security Projection Model," Employee Benefit Research Institute, Issue Brief, no. 410, March 7, 2019.

32. Jacobsen, Senate Committee Testimony.

33. Social Security Administration, "Annual Statistical Supplement, 2019," November 2019, table 6.B3, ssa.gov/policy/docs/statcomps/supplement/2019/6b .pdf.

34. Eric Kingson and Monique Morrissey, Briefing Paper, no. 343, Economic Policy Institute, May 30, 2013, epi.org/files/2012/bp343-social-security-retirement -age.pdf.

35. Richard W. Johnson, "Is It Time to Raise the Social Security Retirement Age?" Urban Institute, December 6, 2018, urban.org/research/publication/it-time -raise-social-security-retirement-age.

36. Government Accountability Office, "Social Security Reform: Raising the Retirement Ages Would Have Implications for Older Workers and SSA Disability Rolls," November 2010, gao.gov/new.items/d11125.pdf.

37. Social Security Administration, Fact Sheet, 2019, ssa.gov/news/press/factsheets/basicfact-alt.pdf.

38. Kingson and Morrissey, Briefing Paper.

39. "Long-Term Unemployment: A National Crisis for Older Workers," *Huffington Post* (September 9, 2012), huffingtonpost.com/2012/09/05/long-term-unemployment-a-_n_1857516.html.

40. Ben Casselman, "For Middle-Aged Job Seekers, a Long Road Back," *Wall Street Journal*, June 22, 2012, online.wsj.com/news/articles/SB10001424052702303506404577448751320412974.

## Chapter 6

1. Ai-jen Poo with Ariane Conrad, *The Age of Dignity: Preparing for the Elder Boom in a Changing America* (New York: The New Press, 2015).

2. U.S. Department of Health and Human Services, Health Resources and Services Administration, "HRSA releases new data on child health across the U.S.," October 1, 2018, hrsa.gov/about/news/press-releases/hrsa-releases-national-survey-child-health-data.

3. National Alliance for Caregiving and the AARP Public Policy Institute, "Caregiving in the U.S., 2015," June 2015, aarp.org/content/dam/aarp/ppi/2015/caregiving-in-the-united-states-2015-report-revised.pdf.

4. U.S. Census Bureau, "Annual Estimates of the Resident Population for Selected Age Groups by Sex for the United States, States, Counties, and Puerto Rico Commonwealth and Municipios," April 1, 2010, to July 1, 2020, Population Estimates, data.census.gov/cedsci/table?q=NUMBER%20OF%20CHILDREN%20UNDER%2018%20IN%202018&hidePreview=false&tid=ACSDT1Y2018.B09001&t=Children&y=2018&vintage=2018.

5. Susannah Fox, Maeve Duggan, and Kristen Purcell, "Family Caregivers Are Wired for Health," Pew Research Center, June 20, 2013, pewresearch.org/internet/2013/06/20/family-caregivers-are-wired-for-health/.

6. AARP Public Policy Institute and National Alliance for Caregiving, "Caregiving in the U.S."

7. Ibid, 33.

8. Richard Harris, "Heading Toward the Caregiving Cliff," *Washington Post* (March 4, 2013), washingtonpost.com/national/health-science/heading-toward-the-caregiving-cliff/2014/03/04/eb1661ec-9846-11e3-afce-3e7c922ef31e_story.html.

9. Tara Bahrampour and Nikki Kahn, "As Americans Age, Families Are Critical to Nation's Health-Care System," *Washington Post* (March 4, 2014), washingtonpost.com/local/as-americans-age-families-are-critical-to-nations-health-care-system/2014/03/04/d40ab934-9446-11e3-84e1-27626c5ef5fb_story.html.

10. Richard Harris, "Heading Toward the Caregiving Cliff."

11. Alzheimer's Association, "2019 Alzheimer's Disease Facts and Figures," alz.org/media/Documents/alzheimers-facts-and-figures-2019-r.pdf, p. 33.

12. U.S. Department of Health and Human Services, Health Resources and Services Administration, *The National Survey of Children with Special Health Care Needs Chartbook 2009–2010*, June 2013, mchb.hrsa.gov/cshcn0910/more/pdf/nscshcn0910.pdf.

13. Autism Society, "Keisha's Story," August 18, 2013.

14. Gail Hunt et al., "Young Caregivers in the U.S.," National Alliance for Caregiving, September 2005, caregiving.org/data/youngcaregivers.pdf.

15. Generations United, State of Grandfamilies 2019, grandfamilies.org/Portals/0/19-Grandfamilies-Report-APlacetoCallHome.pdf.

16. Raising Your Grandchildren, "Raising 4 Grandchildren at 60," 2014, raisingyourgrandchildren.com/More_Stories.htm.

17. Mark Lino et al., *Expenditures on Children by Families, 2015*, U.S. Department of Agriculture, Center for Nutrition Policy and Promotion, January 2017, Revised March 2017. Miscellaneous Report No. 1528-2015, fns-prod.azureedge.net/sites /default/files/crc2015_March2017.pdf.

18. Nancy Folbre, *Valuing Children: Rethinking the Economics of the Family* (Cambridge, MA: Harvard University Press, 2008).

19. Danit Kanal and Joseph Ted Kornegay, "Accounting for Household Production in the National Accounts: An Update, 1965–2017." *Survey of Current Business* [s. l.], 99, no. 6 (June 2019): 1, apps.bea.gov/scb/2019/06-june/pdf/0619-household -production.pdf.

20. Judy Feder, "Testimony Before the Senate Committee on Aging, on the Future of Long-Term Care Policy: Continuing the Conversation," December 18, 2013, aging.senate.gov/imo/media/doc/Feder_12_18_13.pdf.

21. Susan C. Reinhard et al., "Valuing the Invaluable: 2019 Update Charting a Path Forward," *Insight on the Issues* 146, AARP Public Policy Institute (November 2019), aarp.org/content/dam/aarp/ppi/2019/11/valuing-the-invaluable-2019 -update-charting-a-path-forward.doi.10.26419-2Fppi.00082.001.pdf.

22. Congressional Budget Office, "Rising Demand for Long Term Services and Supports for Elderly People," June 2013, cbo.gov/sites/default/files/cbofiles /attachments/44363-LTC.pdf.

23. Alzheimer's Association, *2019 Alzheimer's Disease Facts and Figures*, p. 33, alz .org/media/Documents/alzheimers-facts-and-figures-2019-r.pdf.

24. Generations United, "Grandparents," grandparentsday.org/activity-ideas /grandfamilies/.

25. E.R. Kingson et al., *Ties That Bind: The Interdependence of Generations* (Cabin John, MD: Seven Locks Press, 1986); Eric R. Kingson et al., *Supporting Care Across Generations: Perspectives for Assessing Social and Public Policy Issues* (unpublished paper, 2006).

26. Kim Parker and Wendy Wang, "Modern Parenthood: Roles of Moms and Dads Converge as They Balance Work and Family," Pew Research Center, March 14, 2013, fatherhood.gov/library-resource/modern-parenthood-roles-moms-and-dads -converge-they-balance-work-and-family.

27. National Alliance for Caregiving and AARP, "Caregiving in the U.S., 2020," May 2020, ssa.gov/policy/docs/ssb/v71n2/v71n2p1.html

28. Parker and Wang, "Modern Parenthood."

29. Parker and Wang, "Modern Parenthood."

30. Sarah Jane Glynn and Jane Farrell, "Caregiving in America," Center for American Progress, February 5, 2014, americanprogress.org/issues/labor/report /2014/02/05/83427/family-matters.

31. U.S. Department of Health and Human Services, Health Resources and Services Administration, *The National Survey of Children with Special Health Care Needs Chartbook 2009–2010*, June 2013, mchb.hrsa.gov/cshcn0910/more/pdf/nscshcn0910 .pdf.

32. Associated Press-NORC Center for Public Affairs Research, "Long-Term Care in America: Views on Who Should Bear the Responsibilities and Costs of Care," longtermcarepoll.org/long-term-care-in-america-views-on-who-should-bear-the -responsibilities-and-costs-of-care/.

33. Nancy Folbre, *Valuing Children: Rethinking the Economics of the Family* (Cambridge, MA: Harvard University Press, 2008): 5.

34. Susan C. Reinhard, *Valuing the Invaluable*.

35. AARP Public Policy Institute and National Alliance for Caregiving, "Caregiving in the U.S., 2015," June 2015, aarp.org/content/dam/aarp/ppi/2015 /caregiving-in-the-united-states-2015-report-revised.pdf.

36. Lynn Feinberg et al., "Valuing the Invaluable: 2011 Update, the Growing Contributions and Costs of Family Caregiving," assets.aarp.org/rgcenter/ppi/ltc/i51 -caregiving.pdf.

37. The MetLife Mature Market Institute, STUDY The MetLife Study of Caregiving Costs to Caregivers, "The MetLife Study of Caregiving Costs to Working Caregivers Double Jeopardy for Baby Boomers Caring for Their Parents," at 14 (June 2011), https://www.caregiving.org/wp-content/uploads/2011/06/mmi-caregiving -costs-working-caregivers.pdf

38. Stipica Mudrazija, "Work-Related Opportunity Costs of Providing Unpaid Family Care in 2013 and 2050," *Health Affairs* 38, No. 6, (Jun 2019): 1003–10, healthaffairs.org/doi/full/10.1377/hlthaff.2019.00008.

39. Susan C. Reinhard, *Valuing the Invaluable*, 8.

40. A Better Balance, Comparative Chart of Paid Family and Medical Leave Laws in the United States, abetterbalance.org/resources/paid-family-leave-laws-chart/.

41. Organisation for Economic Co-operation and Development, "PF2.1: Key Characteristics of Parental Leave Systems," August 2019, oecd.org/els/soc /PF2_1_Parental_leave_systems.pdf.

42. Organisation for Economic Co-operation and Development, *Long-term Care*, oecd.org/els/health-systems/long-term-care.htm.

43. Organisation for Economic Co-operation and Development, *Public Spending on Childcare and Early Education*, oecd.org/els/soc /PF3_1_Public_spending_on_childcare_and_early_education.pdf.

44. Jonathan Vespa, Lauren Medina, and David M. Armstrong, *Demographic Turning Points for the United States: Population Projections for 2020 to 2060*, U.S. Census Bureau, Population Estimates and Projections Current Population Reports P25-1144, Issued March 2018, Revised February 2020, census.gov/content/dam /Census/library/publications/2020/demo/p25-1144.pdf.

45. Vespa, Medina, and Armstrong, *Demographic Turning Points for the United States*.

46. Donald Redfoot, Lynn Feinberg, and Ari Houser, "The Aging of the Baby Boom and the Growing Care Gap: A Look at Future Declines in the Availability of Family Caregivers," *Insight on the Issues* 85, AARP Public Policy Institute (August 2013), aarp.org/content/dam/aarp/research/public_policy_institute/ltc/2013/baby -boom-and-the-growing-care-gap-insight-AARP-ppi-ltc.pdf.

47. PHI, *U.S. Home Care Workers: Key Facts (2019)*, September 3, 2019, phina tional.org/resource/u-s-home-care-workers-key-facts-2019/; see also, PHI, *U.S. Nursing Assistants Employed in Nursing Homes: Key Facts (2019)*, September 3, 2019, phinational.org/resource/u-s-nursing-assistants-employed-in-nursing-homes-key -facts-2019/.

48. PHI, *U.S. Home Care Workers*.

49. PHI, *U.S. Home Care Workers*.

50. Susan G. Pfefferle and Dana Beth Weinberg, "CNAs Making Meaning of Direct Care," *Quality Health Research*, July 2008, 18 (7): 952-961.

51. PHI, "Direct Care Worker Projected Job Openings, 2018 to 2028," phina tional.org/policy-research/workforce-data-center/#tab=National+Data.

52. PHI, Stephen Campbell, "New Research: 7.8 Million Direct Care Jobs Will Need to Be Filled by 2026," January 24, 2019, phinational.org/news/new-research -7-8-million-direct-care-jobs-will-need-to-be-filled-by-2026/.

53. C. Wright Mills, *Sociological Imagination* (London: Oxford University Press, 1959).

## Chapter 7

1. Chuck Collins, Omar Ocampo, and Sophia Paslaski, *Billionaire Bonanza 2020: Wealth Windfalls, Tumbling Taxes, and Pandemic Profiteers*, Institute for Policy Studies, 2020, ips-dc.org/wp-content/uploads/2020/04/Billionaire-Bonanza-2020.pdf.

2. Kevin Kelleher, "Gilded Age 2.0: U.S. Income Inequality Increases to Pre-Great Depression Levels," February 13, 2019, *Fortune*, fortune.com/2019/02/13/us-income-inequality-bad-greatdepression/?utm_campaign=fwd_economy. unpaid.engagement&utm_source=hs_email&utm_medium=email&_hsenc=p2ANqtz-9g2ggSkcktk3o-VP2AF5zEIgiJDLWjx8TOj_BF_dYbWe1La0XAn-RGEcko9Aw5BjnIDaAPG4ipi1TdIxTGROfte3y1sIlkjFwDGNrR8h0dxYYRGng.

3. Thomas Piketty, *Capital in the Twenty-First Century* (Cambridge, MA: The Belknap Press of Harvard University Press, 2014), table 8.5, 291; also see Thomas Piketty, Emmanuel Saez, and Gabriel Zucman, "Distributional National Accounts: Methods and Estimates for the United States," *Quarterly Journal of Economics* 133. no. 2 (May 2018): 553–607, gabriel-zucman.eu/files/PSZ2018QJE.pdf.

4. Chuck Collins and Josh Hoxie, "Billionaire Bonanza 2017: The Forbes 400 and the Rest of Us," Institute for Policy Studies, 2017, inequality.org/wp-content/uploads/2017/11/BILLIONAIRE-BONANZA-2017-Embargoed.pdf.

5. Chuck Collins and Josh Hoxie, "Billionaire Bonanza 2018," Institute for Policy Studies, October 2018, ips-dc.org/wp-content/uploads/2018/11/Billionaire-Bonanza-2018-Report-October-2018-1.pdf.

6. Collins and Hoxie, "Billionaire Bonanza 2018."

7. Chuck Collins, Omar Ocampo, and Sophia Paslaski, *Billionaire Bonanza 2020*.

8. Economic Policy Institute, "News from EPI," August 14, 2019, epi.org/press/ceo-compensation-kept-surging-in-2018-the-ratio-of-ceo-to-worker-compensation-was-278-to-1/.

9. Emmanuel Saez, "Striking It Richer: The Evolution of Top Incomes in the United States (Updated with 2012 Preliminary Estimates)," September 3, 2013, eml.berkeley.edu/~saez/saez-UStopincomes-2012.pdf.

10. Emmanuel Saez, "Striking It Richer: The Evolution of Top Incomes in the United States (Updated with 2018 Preliminary Estimates), February 2020, eml.berkeley.edu/~saez/saez-UStopincomes-2018.pdf.

11. Chad Stone, Danilo Trisi, Arloc Sherman, and Emily Horton, *A Guide to Statistics on Historical Trends in Income Inequality*, December 11, 2018 (Washington, DC: Center on Budget and Policy Priorities), cbpp.org/research/poverty-and-inequality/a-guide-to-statistics-on-historical-trends-in-income-inequality.

12. Michael, Batty, Jesse Bricker, Joseph Briggs, Elizabeth Holmquist, Susan McIntosh, Kevin Moore, Eric Nielsen, Sarah Reber, Molly Shatto, Kamila Sommer, Tom Sweeney, and Alice Henriques Volz (2019), "Introducing the Distributional Financial Accounts of the United States," Finance and Economics Discussion Series 2019-017. Washington: Board of Governors of the Federal Reserve System, https://doi.org/10.17016/FEDS.2019.017.

13. Ida Tarbell, *The History of the Standard Oil Company* (New York: McClure, Phillips, 1904).

14. Herbert Hoover, *The Memoirs of Herbert Hoover* 3 (New York: Macmillan Company, 1952), ecommcode.com/hoover/ebooks/pdf/FULL/B1V3_Full.pdf.

15. Nancy J. Altman, *The Battle for Social Security: From FDR's Vision to Bush's Gamble* (Hoboken, NJ: John Wiley & Sons, 2005), 14–20.

16. Tax Policy Center, "1913–2018 Historical Highest Marginal Income Tax Rates" (January 18, 2019), taxpolicycenter.org/statistics/historical-highest-marginal-income-tax-rates.

17. Dwight D. Eisenhower to Edgar Newton Eisenhower, "Document #1147," *The Papers of Dwight David Eisenhower* 15, *The Presidency: The Middle Way*, ed. Louis Galambos (Baltimore: Johns Hopkins University Press, 1996).

18. Ronald Reagan, "Inaugural Address," January 20, 1981, The American Presidency Project, presidency.ucsb.edu/documents/inaugural-address-11.

19. Bruce Bartlett, "'Starve the Beast,' Origins and Development of a Budgetary Metaphor," *Independent Review* 12, no. 1 (Summer 2007), independent.org/publications/tir/article.asp?id=641.

20. "Mondale's Acceptance Speech, 1984," All Politics, CNN/Time (July 19, 1984), cnn.com/ALLPOLITICS/1996/conventions/chicago/facts/famous.speeches/mondale.84.shtml.

21. George H.W. Bush, "Address Accepting the Presidential Nomination at the Republican National Convention in New Orleans," August 18, 1988, The American Presidency Project, presidency.ucsb.edu/documents/address-accepting-the-presidential-nomination-the-republican-national-convention-new.

22. Congressional Budget Office, *The Budget and Economic Outlook: Fiscal Years 2002–2011*, January 1, 2001, summary table 1, cbo.gov/sites/default/files/cbofiles/ftpdocs/27xx/doc2727/entire-report.pdf.

23. Tax Policy Center Briefing Book, 2018, taxpolicycenter.org/sites/default/files/briefing-book/bb_full_2018_1.pdf.

24. Ylan Mui, "White House to unveil Trump's election-year budget calling for extending individual tax cuts," CNBC, February 9, 2020, cnbc.com/2020/02/09/trump-admin-to-unveil-fiscal-2021-budget-calling-for-extending-tax-cuts.html; Kate Davidson and Andrew Restuccia, "Trump to Propose $4.8 Trillion Budget With Big Safety-Net Cuts," February 9, 2020, *Wall Street Journal*, wsj.com/articles/trump-to-propose-4-8-trillion-budget-with-big-safety-net-cuts-11581274525.

25. Andrew Fieldhouse and Ethan Pollack, "Tenth Anniversary of the Bush-era Tax Cuts," Economic Policy Institute, June 1, 2011, epi.org/publication/tenth_anniversary_of_the_bush-era_tax_cuts.

26. Institute on Taxation and Economic Policy, "TCJA by the Numbers, 2020," August 29, 2019, itep.org/tcja-2020/.

27. TPC Staff, "Distributional Analysis of the Conference Agreement for the Tax Cuts and Jobs Act," Tax Policy Center, December 18, 2017, 5, taxpolicycenter.org/sites/default/files/publication/150816/2001641_distributional_analysis_of_the_conference_agreement_for_the_tax_cuts_and_jobs_act_0.pdf.

28. Josh Levin, "The Welfare Queen," *Slate*, December 19, 2013, slate.com/articles/news_and_politics/history/2013/12/linda_taylor_welfare_queen_ronald_reagan_made_her_a_notorious_american_villain.html.

29. Jeff Stein and Aaron Gregg, "U.S. Military Spending Set to Increase for Fifth Consecutive Year, Nearing Levels During Height of Iraq War," *Washington Post* (April 18, 2019), washingtonpost.com/us-policy/2019/04/18/us-military-spending-set-increase-fifth-consecutive-year-nearing-levels-during-height-iraq-war/.

30. Ellen Dannin, "Federal Privatization and the Expensive Philosophy of the Circular A-76 Process," *Truthout*, March 14, 2014, truth-out.org/news/item/22440-federal-privatization-and-the-expensive-philosophy-of-the-circular-a-76-process.

31. Full Transcript: Trump's 2020 State of the Union Address (February 5, 2020), *New York Times*, https://www.nytimes.com/2020/02/05/us/politics/state-of-union-transcript.html

32. The acclaimed 2006 documentary film *Iraq for Sale: The War Profiteers* exposes how these contractors endangered the lives of Americans and Iraqis, while costing the government more and doing the work less well than would likely have been done by the government itself.

33. See, for example, Monique Morrissey, "Third Way's Surprising Retirement Proposal," epi.org/blog/ways-retirement-proposal.

34. For a discussion of how the one-step approach and two-step approach are essentially the same, see Altman, "The Striking Superiority of Social Security in the Provision of Wage Insurance," *Harvard Journal on Legislation* 50 (2013): 133–42; Health Policy Alternatives, Inc., "Prescription Drug Coverage for Medicare Beneficiaries: A Summary of the Medicare Prescription Drug Improvement and Modernization Act of 2003," Kaiser Family Foundation, December 10, 2003.

35. Health Policy Alternatives, Inc., "Prescription Drug Coverage for Medicare Beneficiaries: A Summary of the Medicare Prescription Drug Improvement and Modernization Act of 2003," Kaiser Family Foundation, December 10, 2003.

36. Kaiser Family Foundation, "Medicare Advantage Fact Sheet," May 1, 2014, kff.org/medicare/fact-sheet/medicare-advantage-fact-sheet.

37. Brad Plumer, "Study: Privatizing Government Doesn't Actually Save Money," *Washington Post* (September 15, 2011), washingtonpost.com/ blogs/wonkblog/post/study-privatizing-governmentdoesnt-actually-save-money/2011/09/15/gIQA2rpZUK_blog.html; "Privatization Myths Debunked," In the Public Interest, 2014, inthepublicinterest.org/node/457.

38. American Federation of State, County & Municipal Employees, *How to Prevent Privatization*, 2014, afscme.org/news/publications/privatization/pdf/How-To-Prevent-Privatization.pdf.

39. Dick Meister, "Ronald Reagan's War on Labor," 2014, dickmeister.com/id89.html; Harold Meyerson, "Class Warrior," *Washington Post* (June 9, 2004), https://www.washingtonpost.com/archive/opinions/2004/06/09/class-warrior/5fcf246d-f571-43d8-b236-064bbac8e407.

40. U.S. Bureau of Labor Statistics, Union Membership (Annual), January 22, 2020, bls.gov/news.release/pdf/union2.htm.

41. Paul Waldman, "The Republicans Are Winning Their War on Unions," *Washington Post* (January 27, 2018), washingtonpost.com/blogs/plum-line/wp/2018/06/27/the-republicans-are-winning-their-war-on-unions/.

42. Saharra Griffin and Malkie Wall, "President Trump's Anti-Worker Agenda," Center for American Progress Action Fund, August 28, 2019, americanprogressaction.org/issues/economy/reports/2019/08/28/174893/president-trumps-anti-worker-agenda/; Celine McNicholas, Margaret Poydock, and Lynn Rhinehart, "Unprecedented: The Trump NLRB's attack on workers' rights," Economic Policy Institute, October 16, 2019, epi.org/publication/unprecedented-the-trump-nlrbs-attack-on-workers-rights/; Mark Gruenberg, "Federal workers protest Trump anti-union edicts," United Steelworkers, October 6, 2019, m.usw.org/blog/2019/federal-workers-protest-trump-anti-union-edicts.

43. Craig K. Elwell, "Inflation and the Real Minimum Wage: A Fact Sheet," January 8, 2014, fas.org/sgp/crs/misc/R42973.pdf.

44. "The US minimum wage throughout the years," CNN Business (April 9, 2019), cnn.com/interactive/2019/business/us-minimum-wage-by-year/index.html.

45. Social Security Works, "Restoring Minimum Wage Would Strengthen Social Security Protections for Low-Wage Workers and Improve System Finances," February 21, 2014, https://socialsecurityworks.org/wp-content/uploads/2020/08 /Restoring-the-Minimum-Wage-Would-Strengthen-Social-Security-Protections -for-Low-Wage-Workers-and-Strengthen-System-Finances-1.pdfs.

46. Paul Krugman, "Reagan Did It," *New York Times* (May 31, 2009), nytimes .com/2009/06/01/opinion/01krugman.html?_r= 0.

47. Marin Clarkberg, "The Time-Squeeze in American Families: From Causes to Solutions," in *Balancing Acts: Easing the Burdens and Improving the Options for Working Families*, ed. Eileen Applebaum (Washington, DC: EPI Book, April 2000).

48. Doug Lederman, "A Historical Look at Student Debt," *Inside Higher Ed*, July 6, 2006, insidehighered.com/news/2006/07/06/historical-look-student-debt.

49. Zack Friedman, "Is There Really a Student Debt Crisis?" *Forbes* (December 19, 2019), forbes.com/sites/zackfriedman/2019/12/19/is-there-really-a-student -loan-crisis/#9f9c75f40250.

50. Andrew G. Berg and Jonathan D. Ostry (International Monetary Fund), "Equality and Efficiency," *Finance and Development* 48, no. 3 (September 2011), imf .org/external/pubs/ft/fandd/2011/09/berg.htm.

51. Dean Baker, "The Impact of the Upward Redistribution of Wage Income on Social Security Solvency," *CEPR Blog*, February 3, 2013, cepr.net/the-impact-of-the -upward-redistribution-of-wage-income-on-social-security-solvency/; Monique Morrissey, "Wages and Social Security," *Working Economics*, Economic Policy Institute Blog, July 16, 2012, epi.org/blog/wages-social-security.

52. Andrew Fieldhouse, "Rising Income Inequality and the Role of Shifting Market-Income Distribution, Tax Burdens, and Tax Rates," Economic Policy Institute, June 14, 2013, epi.org/publication/rising-income-inequality-role-shifting -market.

## Chapter 8

1. "Table 7-1: Summary details for regions and selected countries, 2019," in Anthony Shorrock, Jim Davies, and Rodrigo Lluberas, "Global Wealth Databook 2019," Credit Suisse Research Institute (October 2019), credit-suisse.com/about-us /en/reports-research/global-wealth-report.html.

2. There are many ways to design this increase. As chapter 2 explains, Social Security's benefit formula is progressive. Lower-income workers who work the same number of years as higher-income workers receive higher percentages of their wages replaced. An across the board increase can be designed to be proportionate, so that all get the same percentage increase. It can also be designed to be progressive, so that beneficiaries get the same dollar increase, but that is a higher percentage of low-earners' benefits. If, as the All Generations Plan does, it increases benefits so they are fully adequate for most workers at retirement, middle-income workers will get larger increases because, given Social Security's progressive benefit formula, they need more to have fully adequate benefits from Social Security.

3. The idea that Social Security was supposed to be merely a foundation upon which to build emerged in the 1940s and 1950s, when Social Security benefits were not increased, unions began to aggressively bargain for pensions, and conservatives argued against increasing Social Security's modest benefits. See Nancy Altman, *The Truth About Social Security: The Founders' Words Refute Revisionist History, Zombie Lies, and Common Misunderstandings* (Washington, DC: Strong Arm Press, 2018): 156–70.

4. The Social Security Amendments of 1956 gave women the option of claiming benefits starting as early as age sixty-two. The 1956 legislation specified that, for every month before age sixty-five that women claimed their workers' benefits, those benefits would be reduced by 5/9ths of 1 percent. Congress retained that same percentage when the Social Security Amendments of 1961 gave men the same right to retire early. When the Social Security Amendments of 1983 increased by two years, to age sixty-seven, the age below which the early retirement reductions begin, Congress retained the same 5/9ths of 1 percent for the thirty-six months between ages sixty-four and sixty-seven, but limited the monthly reduction to 5/12ths of 1 percent for the earliest twenty-four months (ages sixty-two and sixty-three), in order that the maximum early retirement reduction, at age sixty-two, would be no greater than 30 percent.

5. Government Accountability Office, "Raising the Retirement Ages Would Have Implications for Older Workers and SSA Disability Rolls," November 2010, 17–18, gao.gov/new.items/d11125.pdf.

6. Jacqueline Sergeant, "Majority of Americans Forced to Retire Early, Allianz Finds," *Financial Advisor*, April 14, 2020, fa-mag.com/news/your-retirement-start-date-might-not-be-when-you-want-it--study-says-55167.html; also see Allianz Life, "Reality Check: Most Americans Are Unprepared for When and How Retirement Will Happen," *Allianz Life Press Release*, April 13, 2020. Note: These data are from the 2020 Retirement Risk Readiness Study based on a nationally representative online sample of 1,000 persons, twenty-five and over, with annual household incomes of $50,000 or more for individuals, $75,000 for couples, or $150,000 in assets that are or can be invested.

7. Barry Bosworth, Gary Burtless, and Kan Zhang, "Later Retirement, Inequality in Old Age, and the Growing Gap in Longevity Between Rich and Poor," Brookings Economic Studies, Brookings Institution, Washington, DC, brookings.edu/wp-content/uploads/2016/02/BosworthBurtlessZhang_retirementinequality longevity_012815.pdf.

8. More technically, COLA adjustments start in December but are first received in the next month's, January's, benefit. According to the Social Security Administration, "A COLA effective for December of the current year is equal to the percentage increase (if any) in the CPI-W from the average for the third quarter of the current year to the average for the third quarter of the last year in which a COLA became effective. If there is an increase, it must be rounded to the nearest tenth of one percent. If there is no increase, or if the rounded increase is zero, there is no COLA for the year," ssa.gov/oact/cola/latestCOLA.html.

9. Gary Koenig and Mikki Waid, "Proposed Changes to Social Security's Cost-of-Living Adjustment: What Would They Mean for Beneficiaries?" *Insight on the Issues* 71, AARP Public Policy Institute (October 2012), aarp.org/content/dam/aarp/research/public_policy_institute/econ_sec/2012/proposed-changes-cola-insight-AARP-ppi-econ-sec.pdf.

10. U.S. Congress, House, Older Americans Act Amendments of 1987, HR 1451, 100th Congress, govtrack.us/congress/bills/100/hr1451/text.

11. The Center for Community Change and Older Women's Economic Security Task Force, "Expanding Social Security Benefits for Financially Vulnerable Populations," October 2013, iwpr.org/publications/pubs/expanding-social-security-benefits-for-financially-vulnerable-populations.

12. American Academy of Actuaries, "Women and Social Security," Issue Brief, June 2007, actuary.org/pdf/socialsecurity/women_07.pdf.

13. Social Security Administration, "Special Minimum Benefit," May 2014, ssa .gov/policy/docs/program-explainers/special-minimum.html.

14. Stephen C. Goss, memorandum to then-Senator Robert Bennett, February 12, 2009, 3–4, ssa.gov/oact/solvency/RBennett_20090212.pdf; Stephen C. Goss, memorandum to Fiscal Commission co-chairs, December 1, 2010, table B1, ssa .gov/OACT/solvency/FiscalCommission_20101201.pdf.

15. Justice in Aging, "Supplemental Security Income Restoration Act of 2019," justiceinaging.org/our-work/economic-security/ssi-restoration-act/.

16. SSI has a federal and a state component. Federal SSI payments ensure a uniform income floor, and states may provide additional payments to supplement this floor. When the SSI program was introduced in 1972, the Social Security Administration was chosen to administer the program because the basic system for paying monthly benefits to a large number of individuals was already in place; Social Security Administration, "SSI Annual Statistical Report, 2018," September 2019, ssa.gov /policy/docs/statcomps/ssi_asr/index.html.

17. Center on Budget and Policy Priorities, "Introduction to the Supplemental Security Income (SSI) Program," revised February 27, 2014, cbpp.org/cms /?fa=view&id=3367; note, too, that if Social Security is increased without changes to SSI, the result could ironically be that those that policymakers are seeking to help could be no better off, or may even be worse off, if they lose Medicaid.

18. Congressional Research Service, "Paid Family Leave in the United States," updated May 29, 2019, https://fas.org/sgp/crs/misc/R44835.pdf.

19. U.S. Congress, House, *FAMILY Act*, H.R.1185, congress.gov/bill/116th -congress/house-bill/1185/cosponsors?searchResultViewType=expanded&KWIC View=false.

20. U.S. Congress, Senate, *FAMILY Act*, S.463, congress.gov/bill/116th-congress /senate-bill/463/cosponsors?searchResultViewType=expanded&KWICView=false.

21. The germinal work, which inspired these various proposals, was done by Heather Boushey of the Center for American Progress. See Heather Boushey, Ann O'Leary, and Alexandra Mitukiewicz, "The Economic Benefits of Family and Medical Leave Insurance," Center for American Progress, December 12, 2013, american- progress.org/issues/economy/report/2013/12/12/81036/the-economic-benefits-of -family-and-medical-leave-insurance.

22. Naomi Jagoda, "Rubio rolls out paid parental leave bill," *The Hill* (August 2, 2018), thehill.com/policy/finance/400147-rubio-rolls-out-paid-parental-leave-bill.

23. Organisation for Economic Co-operation and Development, "OECD Family Database," July 2019, oecd.org/els/soc/PF1_3_Family_Cash_Benefits.pdf.

24. Mary "Molly" W. Dewson, "This Social Security—What Is It?," February 17, 1938, on Social Security Administration History website, ssa.gov/history /dewsonspeech.html; see also Arthur Altmeyer, "Temporary Disability Insurance Coordinated With State Unemployment Insurance Programs," March 1947, *Social Security Bulletin* 10, no. 3 (March 1947), ssa.gov/policy/docs/ssb/v10n3/v10n3p3.pdf; in particular note the description of Arthur Altmeyer's role in the Committee on Economic Security and early years of Social Security.

25. Benefits are also provided to the minor children of retired workers.

26. Social Security Administration, "Research Note #11: The History of Social Security 'Student' Benefits," January 2001, socialsecurity.gov/history/studentbenefit .html.

27. Stephen C. Goss, Letter to the Honorable Gwen Moore, December 11, 2019, ssa.gov/oact/solvency/GMoore_20191211.pdf.

28. Disabled Adult Child (DAC) benefits are sometimes called Childhood Disability (CDB) benefits.

29. In addition to receiving benefits on the death of an insured parent, the child can also receive benefits if the parent—or, under some circumstances, the grandparent—is retired or disabled. For a more detailed discussion, see appendix A.

30. The Arc (2020). Public Policy Agenda for the 116th Congress, thearc.org/wp-content/uploads/2019/08/18-122-Public-Policy-Agenda-booklet_DIGITAL-002-1.pdf.

31. "Table 7-1: Summary details for regions and selected countries, 2019," in Anthony Shorrock, Jim Davies, and Rodrigo Lluberas, "Global Wealth Databook 2019," Credit Suisse Research Institute (October 2019), credit-suisse.com/about-us/en/reports-research/global-wealth-report.html.

32. Social Security Administration, "1972 Social Security Amendments," ssa.gov/history/1972amend.html.

## Chapter 9

1. The United States' GDP was worth $21.2 billion in 2019, another number none of us will ever experience personally; Trading Economics, tradingeconomics.com/united-states/gdp.

2. Television History–The First 75 Years, "What Things Cost in 1935," last viewed February, 21, 2014, tvhistory.tv/1935%20QF.htm.

3. Grant McArther, "The World 70 Years from Now," News.com.au, August 19, 2013, news.com.au/finance/real-estate/the-world-70-years-from-now/story-fncq3gat-1226699742008.

4. Social Security Trustees, *2020 Annual Report of the Board of Trustees of the Federal Old-Age and Survivors Insurance and Federal Disability Insurance Trust Funds*, April 22, 2019; see ssa.gov/oact/solvency/provisions_tr2019/charts/chart_run155.html and ssa.gov/oact/solvency/provisions_tr2019/charts/chart_run135.html.

5. Organisation for Economic Co-operation and Development, "Pension Spending: Public, % of GDP, 2017 or latest available," *OECD Data*, data.oecd.org/socialexp/pension-spending.htm.

6. 2009 is the most recent year of comparative data at the time of this writing. In 2009, Social Security cost 4.9 percent of GDP. Social Security Trustees, *2013 Annual Report of the Board of Trustees of the Federal Old-Age and Survivors Insurance and Federal Disability Insurance Trust Funds*, table 2.D4, May 31, 2013, ssa.gov/oact/TR/2013/tr2013.pdf; plot points to table 2.D4 available at socialsecurity.gov/OACT/TR/2013/LD_figIID4.html; calculations of these countries' public spending on those components of their old-age, survivors, and disability benefits that are comparable to the U.S. Social Security system are conservatively and roughly estimated based on data from the Social Expenditure Database of the Organisation for Economic Co-operation and Development (OECD), Social Expenditure Database, 2012, oecd.org/social/expenditure.htm#socx_data.

7. Social Security Trustees, *2014 Annual Report of the Board of Trustees of the Federal Old-Age and Survivors Insurance and Federal Disability Insurance Trust Funds*, July 28, 2014, table 6.G4, ssa.gov/OACT/tr/2014/VI_G2_OASDHI_GDP.html and Social Security Trustees, 2020, table 6.G4.

8. Social Security spending as a share of the economy has increased from 4.03 percent of GDP in 2000 (Social Security Trustees 2014) to an estimated 4.98 percent in 2020 (Social Security Trustees 2020).

9. Dean Baker, "The Economic Impact of the Iraq War and Higher Military Spending," Center for Economic and Policy Research, May 2007, cepr.net /documents/publications/military_spending_2007_05.pdf.

10. Virginia P. Reno and Joni Lavery, "Can We Afford Social Security When Baby Boomers Retire?" *Social Security Brief* no. 22, National Academy of Social Insurance (May 2006), nasi.org/sites/default/files/research/SS_Brief_022.pdf.

11. Committee on Economic Security, *Economic Security Act*, January 1935, table 13, ssa.gov/history/reports/ces16.html.

12. U.S. Census Bureau, The 65 Years and Over Population: 2000 (October 2001), https://www.census.gov/prod/2001pubs/c2kbr01-10.pdf.

13. Jonathan Vespa, Lauren Medina, and David M. Armstrong, *Demographic Turning Points for the United States: Population Projections for 2020 to 2060, Current Population Reports*, P25-1144, U.S. Census Bureau, Washington, DC, 2020.

14. Vespa, Medina, and Armstrong, *Demographic Turning Points for the United States.*

15. Because of the uncertainties inherent in such long-range forecasts, Social Security's actuaries make three forecasts based on different sets of assumptions—optimistic, intermediate, and pessimistic. In making these forecasts, they make assumptions about dozens of factors, including, for example, price changes, wage changes, unemployment, economic growth, labor force participation, birth rates, life expectancies, and immigration rates. Long-range projections are subject to error and, indeed, to greater error the further out in time they go. Nevertheless, the projections are intended to be useful to policymakers who want to chart a stable course for Social Security's financing and provide a reasonable basis for mid-course corrections that are necessary from time to time.

16. Social Security Trustees, *2020 Annual Report.*

17. Self-employed workers make contributions equal to those made by regular employees and their employers. One half of such contributions are deductible from gross income when determining adjusted gross income on the IRS 1040 income tax form.

18. Social Security Trustees, *2020 Annual Report.*

19. Virginia P. Reno and Joni Lavery, "Fixing Social Security," National Academy of Social Insurance, 2009, nasi.org/sites/default/files/research/Fixing _Social_Security.pdf; perhaps the first to propose this were Bruce Webb and Dale Coberly in their Northwest Plan. To be clear, as appendix B discusses in more detail, this is an average annual increase of about fifty cents every week in the first year, and slightly more each of the nineteen subsequent years.

20. Jasmine V. Tucker, Virginia P. Reno, and Thomas N. Bethell, "Strengthening Social Security: What Do Americans Want?" National Academy of Social Insurance, January 2013, nasi.org/sites/default/files/research/What_Do_Americans_Want .pdf. Also see Office of the Chief Actuary, "Summary Measures and Graphs: E1.9," Social Security Administration, ssa.gov/oact/solvency/provisions_tr2019/charts /chart_run164.html.

21. Social Security Administration, Office of Research, Statistics & Policy Analysis, "OASDI and SSI Program Rates & Limits 2020," October 30, 2019, ssa.gov /policy/docs/quickfacts/prog_highlights/RatesLimits2020.html.

22. Dean Baker, "The Impact of the Upward Redistribution of Wage Income on Social Security Solvency," Center for Economic and Policy Research, February 3, 2013, https://cepr.net/the-impact-of-the-upward-redistribution-of-wage-income -on-social-security-solvency/.

23. Social Security Administration, Office of Research and Statistics, "Population Profiles," ssa.gov/policy/docs/population-profiles/tax-max-earners.html.

24. Social Security Administration, "Contribution and Benefit Base," https://www.ssa.gov/oact/cola/cbb.html

25. Social Security Administration, Office of the Actuary, "Long Range Solvency Provisions—Summary Measures and Graphs," September 11, 2013, ssa.gov/oact/solvency/provisions/charts/chart_run116.html.

26. Yung-Ping Chen, "The growth of fringe benefits: implications for social security," *Monthly Labor Review* 104, no. 11 (November 1981): 3–10, bls.gov/opub/mlr/1981/11/art1full.pdf.

27. Bureau of Labor Statistics Employer Costs for Employee Compensation Historical Listing (Annual), 1986–2001, Table 1. Civilian workers, by broad occupational group: employer costs per hour worked for employee compensation and costs as a percent of total compensation, 1991–2001 (June 19, 2002), bls.gov/ncs/ect/sp/ecechist.txt.

28. Bureau of Labor Statistics, Databases, "Employer Costs for Employee Compensation—December 2019," News Release, March 19, 2020, bls.gov/news.release/pdf/ecec.pdf.

29. Internal Revenue Service, "Publication 15—Main Content: 5. Wages and Other Compensation," 2014, irs.gov/publications/p15/ar02.html#en_US_2014_publink1000202313.

30. Internal Revenue Service, "Topic 424—401(k) Plans," December 12, 2013, irs.gov/taxtopics/tc424.html.

31. Office of the Chief Actuary, Social Security Administration, "Frequently Asked Questions About the Social Security Trust Funds," 2020, ssa.gov/OACT/ProgData/fundFAQ.html.

32. DATA.GOV, "Social Security Income, Outgo, and Assets," November 2020, catalog.data.gov/dataset/social-securitys-income-outgo-and-assets.

33. Social Security Trustees, *2020 Annual Report*.

34. Social Security Trustees, *2020 Annual Report*, Table IV.A3.

35. Additionally, there is sound policy logic in dedicating these revenues to Social Security. First is to pay down the so-called legacy debt, costs incurred at the start-up of the program or when new benefits were added, primarily by providing benefits to those close to retirement age. Today's premiums pay not only current costs but also these legacy costs. There is good reason for these costs to be paid from a progressive tax.

36. Catherine Mulbrandon, "Top Marginal Tax Rates 1916–2011," *Visualizing Economics* (blog), January 23, 2012, visualizingeconomics.com/blog/2012/01/24/comparing-tax-rates.

37. Tax Policy Center, "Historical Highest Marginal Income Tax Rates 1913 to 2020," February 4, 2020, taxpolicycenter.org/statistics/historical-highest-marginal-income-tax-rates.

38. See David Wessel, "Who are the rich and how can we tax them more?" Brookings (October 15, 2019), brookings.edu/policy2020/votervital/who-are-the-rich-and-how-might-we-tax-them-more/.

39. See previous note; National Center for Health Statistics, Centers for Disease Control and Prevention, "Mortality in the United States—2018 (January, 2020)" cdc.gov/nchs/products/databriefs/db355.htm.

40. Social Security Administration, "Thomas Paine," 2014, socialsecurity.gov/history/tpaine3.html.

41. Thornton Matheson, "Taxing Financial Transactions: Issues and Evidence,"

working paper, International Monetary Fund, March 2011, imf.org/external/pubs/ft/wp/2011/wp1154.pdf.

42. "Table 7-1: Summary details for regions and selected countries, 2019," in Anthony Shorrock, Jim Davies, and Rodrigo Lluberas, "Global Wealth Databook 2019," Credit Suisse Research Institute (October 2019), credit-suisse.com/about-us/en/reports-research/global-wealth-report.html.

43. National Academy of Sciences, "New Report Assesses the Economic and Fiscal Consequences of Immigration," News Release, September 21, 2016, nationalacademies.org/news/2016/09/new-report-assesses-the-economic-and-fiscal-consequences-of-immigration. Recognition of immigration's overall positive impact on the U.S. economy transcends party lines, with George W. Bush's Republican White House (2001–2009) espousing pro-immigration policies. See Don Gonyea, "The GOP's Evolution on Immigration," NPR (January 25, 2018), npr.org/2018/01/25/580222116/the-gops-evolution-on-immigration.

44. The 2020 Old Age, Survivors, and Disability Insurance Trustees Report projects, as its intermediate assumption, that annual net immigration over the next seventy-five years will average 1,261,000 persons, and states, "Increasing average annual total net immigration by 100,000 persons improves the long-range actuarial balance by about 0.08 percent of taxable payroll." See the long-range sensitivity analysis of immigration in the appendix of the 2020 OASDI Trustees Report. Consequently, doubling immigration generates 1.00 percent of taxable payroll. The report projects the present value of taxable payroll over the next seventy-five years as $554.6 trillion. See Table VI.F1, Note 1, 2020 Trustees Report. Therefore, 1.0 percent of taxable payroll equals $5.55 trillion. The calculations assume that the same age distribution, workforce participation, and other factors underlying the Trustees report numbers remain the same and that the change is linear.

45. See Stephen C. Goss, Testimony to the Senate Committee on Homeland Security and Governmental Affairs (February 4, 2015), ssa.gov/oact/testimony/SenateHomeSec_20150204.pdf.

46. Stephen Goss, Alice Wade, J. Patrick Skirvin, Michael Morris, K. Mark Bye, and Danielle Huston, "Effects of Unauthorized Immigration on the Actuarial Status of the Social Security 3 Trust Funds," Social Security Administration, April 2013, ssa.gov/oact/NOTES/pdf_notes/note151.pdf.

47. National Priorities Project, "U.S Military Spending vs. the World," nationalpriorities.org/campaigns/us-military-spending-vs-world/.

48. Mandy Smithburger and William Hartung, "Making Sense of the $1.25 Trillion National Security State Budget," POGO (May 7, 2019), pogo.org/analysis/2019/05/making-sense-of-the-1-25-trillion-national-security-state-budget/.

49. Ann Markusen, "How We Lost the Peace Dividend," The American Prospect (December 19, 2001), prospect.org/culture/books/lost-peace-dividend/.

50. "Table 7-1: Summary details for regions and selected countries, 2019," in Anthony Shorrock, Jim Davies, and Rodrigo Lluberas, "Global Wealth Databook 2019," Credit Suisse Research Institute (October 2019), credit-suisse.com/about-us/en/reports-research/global-wealth-report.html.

## Chapter 10

1. Frances Langum, "Lindsey Graham Says Social Security, Medicare Are 'Promises We Can't Keep,'" Politics, Crooks and Liars, August 23, 2019, crooksandliars.com/2019/07/lindsey-graham-says-social-security.

2. Joe Scarborough, Twitter, July 12, 2019, 2:16 p.m., twitter.com/joenbc/status /1149759558849634305.

3. Paul Krugman frequently uses the moniker "Very Serious People" against Washington insiders who parrot the same conventional thinking, which is, in fact, wrong. See, e.g., Joe Wiesenthal. "PAUL KRUGMAN: Alan Simpson Is 'All Wrong' and Conventional Wisdom on Economic Policy Is 'Stark Raving Mad'" *Business Insider* (July 14, 2012), https://www.businessinsider.com/paul -krugman-on-the-very-serious-people-2012-7. See, also, Paul Krugman, thread of tweets on Twitter (January 20, 2020), https://twitter.com/paulkrugman/status /1219269310390185985?lang=en.

4. Social Security Works, "PEW: Majorities across demographic groups say no cuts should be made to Social Security benefits in the future," March 2019, socialse-curityworks.org/2019/03/26/social-security-polling/.

5. Felicia Sonmez, "Sen. Ernst says lawmakers should discuss fixing Social Security 'behind closed doors,'" *Washington Post* (September 5, 2019), washington post.com/politics/sen-ernst-says-lawmakers-should-discuss-fixing-social-security -behind-closed-doors/2019/09/05/b678c428-cfec-11e9-b29b-a528dc82154a_story .html.

6. U.S. Senator Mitt Romney (R-UT), Sen. Joe Manchin, III (D-WV) Sen. Todd Young, (R-IN), Sen. Doug Jones, (D-AL), Sen. Kyrsten Sinema (D-AZ), Sen. Shelley Moore Capito (R-WV), Sen. Lamar Alexander (R-TN), Sen. Mike Rounds (R-SD), Sen. Angus S. King, Jr. (I-ME), Sen. Mark R. Warner (D-VA), and Sen. Rob Portman (R-OH) sponsored the Time to Rescue United States' Trusts (TRUST) Act. (U.S. Congress, congress.gov/bill/116th-congress/senate-bill/2733). In addition to Social Security, the commission would deal with Medicare and the Highway Trust Fund—a thinly veiled effort to push through cuts the American people over-whelmingly oppose. See Alex Lawson, "The TRUST Act is a plot to gut Social Security behind closed doors," *The Hill* (January 18, 2020), thehill.com/blogs/congress -blog/politics/478929-the-trust-act-is-a-plot-to-gut-social-security-behind-closed.

7. Trudy Lieberman, "How the Media Has Shaped the Social Security Debate," *Columbia Journalism Review* (April 18, 2012), cjr.org/campaign_desk /how_the_media_has_shaped_the_s.php?page=all.

8. Lieberman, "How the Media Has Shaped the Social Security Debate."

9. See Eric R. Kingson, "A Tale of Three Commissions: The Good, the Bad, and the Ugly," *Poverty & Public Policy* 2, no. 3 (August 2010); Eric R. Kingson, "The Deficit and the Debt," *Congressional Digest* 89, no. 2 (February 2010): 47–58; and "Two Commissions: Lessons for the Proposed Debt Commission," published back-ground paper written for congressional briefing, "Demystifying the Deficit, Social Security Finances, and Commissions," organized by the National Academy of Social Insurance.

10. Robert M. Ball, *The Greenspan Commission: What Really Happened* (New York: Century Foundation Press, 2010).

11. Social Security Administration, "Social Security Amendments of 1977: Leg-islative History and Summary of Provisions," March 1978, ssa.gov/policy/docs/ssb /v41n3/v41n3p3.pdf.

12. Social Security Trustees, *1978 Annual Report of the Federal Old-Age and Sur-vivors Insurance and Disability Insurance Trust Funds*, May 15, 1978, 2, ssa.gov/history /reports/trust/1978/1978.pdf; see also E.R. Kingson, "Financing Social Security: Agenda-Setting and the Enactment of 1983 Amendments to the Social Security Act," *Policy Studies Journal* (September 1984).

13. Social Security Trustees, *1979 Annual Report of the Federal Old-Age and Survivors Insurance and Disability Insurance Trust Funds*, April 13, 1979, 48, https://www.ssa.gov/oact/TR/historical/1979TR.pdf .

14. Social Security Trustees, *1981 Annual Report of the Federal Old-Age and Survivors Insurance and Disability Insurance Trust Funds*, July 2, 1981, 2, ssa.gov/history/reports/trust/1981/1981.pdf.

15. David Stockman, *The Triumph of Politics* (New York: Harper and Row, 1986), 228.

16. William Greider, "The Education of David Stockman," *The Atlantic* (December 1, 1981), theatlantic.com/magazine/archive/1981/12/the-education-of-david-stockman/305760.

17. Steven Greene Livingston, *U.S. Social Security: A Reference Handbook* (Santa Barbara, CA: ABC-CLIO, 2008): 24.

18. Nancy J. Altman, *The Battle for Social Security*, 231.

19. William Safire, "Language: Tracking the Source of the 'Third Rail' Warning," *New York Times* (February 18, 2007).

20. Nancy J. Altman, *The Battle for Social Security*, 234.

21. Matthew Skomarovsky, "Obama Packs Debt Commission with Social Security Looters," *Alternet* (March 28, 2010), alternet.org/2010/03/obama_packs_debt_commission_with_social_security_looters/.

22. Social Security Administration, "Executive Order 12335," December 6, 1981, ssa.gov/history/reports/gspan8.html.

23. "Executive Order 13531—National Commission on Fiscal Responsibility and Reform, February 18, 2010," The American Presidency Project, presidency.ucsb.edu/documents/executive-order-13531-national-commission-fiscal-responsibility-and-reform.

24. Social Security Administration, "Appendix C of the 1983 Greenspan Commission on Social Security Reform," January 1983, ssa.gov/history/reports/gspan5.html.

25. Social Security Administration, "Greenspan Commission: Report of the National Commission on Social Security Reform," January 1983, ssa.gov/history/reports/gspan.html.

26. See Eric R. Kingson, 2010; Eric R. Kingson, "The Deficit and the Debt," *Congressional Digest* 89, no. 2 (February 2010): 47–58. Published background paper, "Two Commissions: Lessons for the Proposed Debt Commission," written for congressional briefing, "Demystifying the Deficit, Social Security Finances, and Commissions" organized by the National Academy of Social Insurance.

27. Kingson, "The Deficit and the Debt."

28. Although Clinton's executive order established his commission as the "Bipartisan Commission on Entitlement Reform," the entitlements commission later came to be known as the "Bipartisan Commission on Entitlement *and Tax* Reform" (emphasis added)—the name used in the commission's final report.

29. Social Security Administration, "Report of the Bipartisan Commission on Entitlement and Tax Reform," December 1994, ssa.gov/history/reports/KerreyDanforth/KerreyDanforth.htm.

30. Remarks by Celinda Lake of Lake Research Partners based on focus groups conducted March 2010 in Richmond, Virginia, and Chicago, Illinois, and on behalf of the National Committee to Preserve Social Security and Medicare (NCPSSM), May 17, 2010.

31. Edward Schumacher-Matos, "Is 'Entitlements' a Dirty Word?" NPR (August 11, 2011), npr.org/blogs/ombudsman/2011/08/11/139557647/is-entitlements-a-dirty-word.

32. Bipartisan Commission on Entitlement and Tax Reform, Interim Report to the President (Washington, DC: Superintendent of Documents, April 1995). Summary available at Rita L. DiSimone, *Social Security Bulletin* 58, no. 2 (Summer 1995), ssa.gov/policy/docs/ssb/v58n2/index.html.

33. Robert A. Rosenblatt, "Entitlements Seen Taking Up Nearly All Taxes by 2012," *Los Angeles Times* (August 9, 1994), articles.latimes.com/1994-08-09/news /mn-25181_1_entitlement-programs; Eric Laursen, *The People's Pension: The Struggle to Defend Social Security Since Reagan* (Oakland, CA: AK Press, 2012): 206.

34. Social Security Administration, "Report of the Bipartisan Commission."

35. Government Printing Office, "Appointment of Deputy Chief of Staff for White House Operations," September 23, 1994, gpo.gov/fdsys/pkg/WCPD-1994 -09-26/html/WCPD-1994-09-26-Pg1830-2.htm.

36. Kim Geiger, "Alan Simpson Pens Scathing Letter to 'Greedy Geezers' Retiree Group," *Los Angeles Times* (May 23, 2012), articles.latimes.com/2012/may/23 /news/la-pn-alan-simpson-pens-scathing-letter-to-greedy-geezers-retiree-group -20120523.

37. Stephanie Condon, "Alan Simpson: Social Security Is Like a 'Milk Cow with 310 Million Tits!'" CBS News (August 25, 2010), cbsnews.com/news/alan-simpson -social-security-is-like-a-milk-cow-with-310-million-tits.

38. "The 400 Richest Americans: #147 Peter Peterson," *Forbes* (September 17, 2008), no longer online.

39. John Harwood, "Spending $1 Billion to Restore Fiscal Sanity," *New York Times* (July 14, 2008), nytimes.com/2008/07/14/us/politics/14caucus .html?ref=petergpeterson; in the 2013 *Forbes* ranking, his net worth was listed as $1.5 billion: "Peter Peterson," *Forbes* (September 2013), forbes.com/profile/peter -peterson.

40. Peter G. Peterson, "Social Security: The Coming Crash," *New York Review of Books* (December 2, 1982), nybooks.com/articles/archives/1982/dec/02/social -security-the-coming-crash.

41. Peter G. Peterson, "The Salvation of Social Security," *New York Review of Books* (December 16, 1982), nybooks.com/articles/archives/1982/dec/16/the -salvation-of-social-security.

42. The Concord Coalition, *The Zero Deficit Plan* (Washington, DC:1993); Neil Howe and Phillip Longman, "The Next New Deal," *Atlantic Monthly* (April 1992), theatlantic.com/past/politics/budget/newdeal.htm; Peter G. Peterson, "Entitlement Reform: The Way to Eliminate the Deficit," *New York Review of Books* (April 7, 1994), nybooks.com/articles/archives/1994/apr/07/entitlement-reform-the -way-to-eliminate-the-defici/; in the 1990s, he and others warned that without means-testing, "Social Security will be unable to meet its commitments to baby boomers and those who follow them into old age." Eric R. Kingson and J.H. Schulz, "Should Social Security be Means-Tested?" in *Social Security in the 21st Century*, eds. E.R. Kingson and J.H. Schulz (New York: Oxford University Press, 1997), 49.

43. Peter G. Peterson, *The Education of an American Dreamer: How a Son of Greek Immigrants Learned His Way from a Nebraska Diner to Washington, Wall Street, and Beyond* (New York: Hachette Book Group, Twelve, 2009).

44. Peter G. Peterson et al., "The Future of Social Security: An Exchange," *New York Review of Books* (March 17, 1983), nybooks.com/articles/archives/1983/mar/17 /the-future-of-social-security-an-exchange.

45. Social Security Trustees, *1983 Annual Report of the Federal Old-Age and Survivors Insurance and Disability Insurance Trust Funds*, June 27, 1983, 2, ssa.gov/history /reports/trust/1983/1983.pdf.

46. The Concord Coalition, "A Quarter Century of Policy Leadership," 2020, concordcoalition.org/.

47. Social Security Trustees, *1983 Annual Report*, 2.

48. Columbia Teachers College, "Teaching Kids About the National Debt," *Inside: The source for news, events and people at Teachers College, Columbia University*, February, 2010, tc.columbia.edu/i/media/251_022010Inside.pdf.

49. Director Patrick Creadon, *I.O.U.S.A.* (2008), watchdocumentaries.com/i -o-u-s-a/.

50. Thomas White, "I.O.U.S.A. Makes TV Debut on CNN," International Documentary Association, January 9, 2009, documentary.org/content/iousa-makes-tv -debut-cnn.

51. Creadon, *I.O.U.S.A.*

52. Laursen, *The People's Pension*, 606.

53. Peter G. Peterson Foundation, "Comeback America Initiative," December 16, 2010, pgpf.org/grants/comeback-america-initiative.

54. Bill Gaston, "The Demise of the Comeback America Initiative," *Stamford Advocate*, October 9, 2013, stamfordadvocate.com/opinion/article/The-demise-of -the-Comeback-America-Initiative-4882316.php.

55. Tom Curry, "Bill Clinton, Paul Ryan Headline Fiscal Summit Talks," MSNBC (May 15, 2012), nbcpolitics.nbcnews.com/_news/2012/05/15/11713917 -billclinton-paul-ryan-headline-fiscal-summit-talks?lite; see also fiscalsummit.com.

56. Louis Proyect, "Bipartisan Threats Against Social Security," *The Un-repentant Marxist* (blog) (September 7, 2008), louisproyect.org/2008/09/07/bipartisan-threats -against-social-security.

57. Peter G. Peterson Foundation, "Michael A. Peterson," May 1, 2020, pgpf.org /about; January 26, 2011, pgpf.org/board/michael-peterson.

58. Nicholas Confessore, "Public Goals, Private Interests in Debt Campaign," *New York Times* (January 9, 2013), nytimes.com/2013/01/10/us/politics/behind -debt-campaign-ties-to-corporate-interests.html.

59. Allen McDuffee, "Koch Brothers vs. Cato: Charles Koch Releases Full Statement," *Washington Post* (March 8, 2012), washingtonpost.com/blogs/think-tanked /post/koch-brothers-vs-cato-charles-koch-releases-full-statement/2012/03/08 /gIQAcWz0zR_blog.html.

60. Peter J. Ferrara, *Social Security: The Inherent Contradiction* (Washington, DC: Cato Institute, 1980).

61. Peter Ferrara, "Sorry Global Warming Alarmists, The Earth Is Cooling," *Forbes* (May 31, 2012), forbes.com/sites/peterferrara/2012/05/31/sorry-global-warming -alarmists-the-earth-is-cooling/#2836c6433de0.

62. The Heartland Institute, "Who We Are: Peter Ferrara," heartland.org/about -us/who-we-are/peter-ferrara.

63. Edwin Feulner, "Coors, R.I.P.," *National Review* (March 18, 2003), national-review.com/2003/03/coors-rip-edwin-j-feulner/.

64. James A. Dorn, "Social Security: Continuing Crisis or Real Reform?" *Cato Journal* 3, no. 2 (Fall 1983), object.cato.org/sites/cato.org/files/serials/files/cato -journal/1983/11/cj3n2-1.pdf.

65. Stuart Butler and Peter Germanis, "Achieving Social Security Reform: A 'Leninist' Strategy," *Cato Journal* 3, no. 2 (Fall 1983): 547, cato.org/sites/cato.org /files/serials/files/cato-journal/1983/11/cj3n2-11.pdf.

66. Butler and Germanis, "Achieving Social Security Reform," 556.

67. Laurence Kotlikoff, "Social Security: Time for Reform," June 1978, econ .ucla.edu/workingpapers/wp121.pdf.

68. See Alexander W. Blocker, Laurence J Kotlikoff, and Stephen A. Ross, "The True Cost of Social Security," NBER Working Paper No. w14427, October 2008, ssrn.com/abstract=1288426; and Laurence J. Kotlikoff and Scott Burns, *The Clash of Generations: Saving Ourselves, Our Kids, and Our Economy* (Boston: The MIT Press, 2014).

69. Stephen Marche, "The War Against Youth," March 26, 2012, *Esquire*, esquire .com/news-politics/a13226/young-people-in-the-recession-0412/.

70. Trudy Lieberman, "How the Media Has Shaped the Social Security Debate."

71. NPR, Transcript and Audio: First Obama-Romney Debate, October 3, 2012, npr.org/2012/10/03/162258551/transcript-first-obama-romney-presidential -debate.

72. Nancy Altman, "Trump and Ryan Agree: Let's Dismantle Social Security," *Huffington Post* (updated May 17, 2017), huffpost.com/entry/trump-and-ryan-agree -lets_b_9992656.

73. U.S. Congress, Strengthening Social Security Act of 2013, S. 567, 113th Congress, congress.gov/bill/113th-congress/senate-bill/567/all-info.

74. Mark Miller, "Can expanding Social Security solve the retirement crisis?" RetirementRevised.com (October 31, 2013), retirementrevised.com/can-expanding -social-security-solve-the-retirement-crisis/.

75. Bernie Sanders, Twitter, February 5, 2016, 5:31 pm, twitter.com /berniesanders/status/695751703598129152.

76. Hillary Clinton, Twitter, February 5, 2016, 7:21 pm, twitter.com /hillaryclinton/status/695764254855733248.

77. "2008 Democratic Party Platform," The American Presidency Project, presidency.ucsb.edu/documents/2008-democratic-party-platform; and "2008 Republican Party Platform," The American Presidency Project, presidency.ucsb.edu /documents/2008-republican-party-platform.

78. "2008 Democratic Party Platform."

79. "2008 Democratic Party Platform."

80. "2008 Republican Party Platform."

81. "2008 Democratic Party Platform."

82. "2008 Republican Party Platform."

83. "2008 Republican Party Platform."

84. "2008 Democratic Party Platform."

85. "2008 Democratic Party Platform."

86. "2016 Republican Party Platform."

## Chapter 11

1. Michael Hiltzik, "Abby Huntsman Wants to Lead Her Own Generation into Poverty," *Los Angeles Times* (March 14, 2014), latimes.com/business/hiltzik/la-fi -mh-abby-huntsman-20140314-story.html.

2. David C. John, "Misleading the Public: How the Social Security Trust Fund Really Works," Heritage Foundation, September 2, 2004, heritage.org/research /reports/2004/09/misleading-the-public-how-the-social-security-trust-fund-really -works.

3. Lance Roberts, "The Insecurity of Social Security," *Real Investment Advice* (August 10, 2017), realinvestmentadvice.com/the-insecurity-of-social-security/; The Concord Coalition, "Retirement: Social Security Is on an Unsustainable Path," undated, concordcoalition.org/retirement-social-security-unsustainable-path.

4. David C. John, "Time to Raise Social Security's Retirement Age," Heritage Foundation, November 22, 2010, heritage.org/research/reports/2010/11/time-to -raise-social-securitys-retirement-age.

5. Michael Tanner, "Still a Better Deal: Private Investment vs. Social Security," *Policy Analysis*, no. 692, Cato Institute (February 13, 2012), object.cato.org/sites/cato .org/files/pubs/pdf/PA692.pdf.

6. "White House explores $5,000 coronavirus stimulus check in exchange for delayed Social Security benefits," FOX 5, Washington, DC (May 13, 2020), fox5dc .com/news/white-house-explores-5000-coronavirus-stimulus-check-in-exchange -for-delayed-social-security-benefits.

7. Yuval Levin, "Old and Rich? Less Help for You," *New York Times* (February 19, 2013), nytimes.com/2013/02/20/opinion/old-and-rich-less-help-for-you .html.

8. Gary Galles, "Social Security: The Most Successful Ponzi Scheme in History," Ludwig von Mises Institute, November 22, 2013, mises.org/daily/6594 /SocialSecurity-TheMostSuccessfulPonzi-Scheme-in-History.

9. Robert Rector, "Amnesty Will Cost U.S. Taxpayers at Least $2.6 Trillion," Heritage Foundation, June 6, 2007, heritage.org/research/reports/2007/06/amnesty -will-cost-us-taxpayers-at-least-26-trillion.

10. Social Security Trustees, *2020 Annual Report of the Board of Trustees of the Federal Old-Age and Survivors Insurance and Federal Disability Insurance Trust Funds*, April 22, 2020, ssa.gov/OACT/TR/2020/tr2020.pdf.

11. "I Will Not Promise the Moon," Alf Landon Opposes the Social Security Act, History Matters, The U.S. Survey Course on the Web, http://historymatters.gmu .edu/d/8128/; See generally Nancy J. Altman, *The Battle for Social Security*, 101–103.

12. "Table 7-1: Summary details for regions and selected countries, 2019," in Anthony Shorrock, Jim Davies, and Rodrigo Lluberas, "Global Wealth Databook 2019," Credit Suisse Research Institute (October 2019), credit-suisse.com/about-us /en/reports-research/global-wealth-report.html.

13. Social Security Trustees, *2020 Annual Report*, Table IV.B.3.

14. Jennifer Schramm, "An Aging Labor Force and the Challenges of 65+ Jobseekers," *Insight on the Issues* 139, AARP Public Policy Institute (September 2018), aarp.org/content/dam/aarp/ppi/2018/09/an-aging-labor-force-and-the-challenges -of-sixty-five-plus-jobseekers.pdf.

15. Russell Heimlich, "Baby Boomers Retire," Pew Research Center, December 10, 2010, pewresearch.org/daily-number/baby-boomers-retire.

16. Robert J. Samuelson, "Let's Get Rid of (the Term) Entitlements," *Washington Post* (October 20, 2013), washingtonpost.com/opinions/robert-j-samuelson -lets-get-rid-of-the-term-entitlements/2013/10/20/e3bd464c-3809-11e3-8a0e -4e2cf80831fc_story.html.

17. Indeed, to keep Social Security's books completely separate from the books of the general fund of the United States, Congress, in 1990, enacted Pub. L. 101-508, title XIII, Sec. 13301(a), Nov. 5, 1990, 104 Stat. 1388-623, which unambiguously states that Social Security "shall not be counted . . . for purposes of (1) the budget of the United States Government as submitted by the President, [or] (2) the congressional budget." Social Security Administration, "P.L. 101-508, Approved November 5, 1990 (104 Stat.143)," 2014, ssa.gov/OP_Home/comp2/F101-508.html.

18. Tax Notes Staff, "The CARES Act: The Tax Provisions and What's Next," *Forbes* (April 6, 2020), forbes.com/sites/taxnotes/2020/04/06/the-cares-act-the-tax -provisions-and-whats-next/.

19. Robin Rudowitz, Kendal Orgera, and Elizabeth Hinton, "Medicare Financing: The Basics," Kaiser Family Foundation, March 21, 2019, kff.org/report-section/medicaid-financing-the-basics-issue-brief/.

20. Paul Krugman, "Administrative Costs," *New York Times* (July 6, 2009), krugman.blogs.nytimes.com/2009/07/06/administrative-costs/.

21. Robin Rudowitz, Kendal Orgera, and Elizabeth Hinton, "Medicaid Financing: The Basics," Kaiser Family Foundation, March 21, 2019, https://www.kff.org/report-section/medicaid-financing-the-basics-issue-brief/

22. David Rosnick, "Health Care Budget Deficit Calculator," Center for Economic and Policy Research, accessed July 30, 2014, cepr.net/calculators/hc/hc-calculator.html.

23. Robert D. Grove and Alice Hetzel, "Vital Statistics Rates in the United States, 1940–1960," U.S. Department of Health, Education, and Welfare, Public Health Service, 1968, table 38, cdc.gov/nchs/data/vsus/vsrates1940_60.pdf.

24. National Center for Health Statistics, "Infant Mortality Dashboard," National Vital Statistics System, Vital Statistics Rapid Release, Quarterly Provisional Estimates, cdc.gov/nchs/nvss/vsrr/infant-mortality-dashboard.htm.

25. See Social Security Trustees, *2020 Annual Report*, table 5.A.4, "Period Life Expectancy."

26. Isaac Sasson and Mark D. Hayward, "Association Between Educational Attainment and Causes of Death Among White and Black US Adults, 2010–2017," *JAMA.* 2019; 322(8): 756–63.

27. Laurence Kotlikoff, "America's Ponzi Scheme: Why Social Security Needs to Retire," PBS, April 7, 2014, pbs.org/newshour/making-sense/americas-ponzi-scheme-why-social-security-needs-to-retire/.

28. James H. Schulz and Robert Binstock, *Aging Nation: The Economics and Policies of Growing Older in America* (Baltimore: Johns Hopkins University Press, 2006); Eric R. Kingson, Barbara Hirshorn, and John Comman, *Ties That Bind: The Interdependence of Generations* (Cabin John, MD: Seven Locks Press, 1986).

29. "Table 7-1: Summary details for regions and selected countries, 2019," in Anthony Shorrock, Jim Davies, and Rodrigo Lluberas, "Global Wealth Databook 2019," Credit Suisse Research Institute (October 2019), credit-suisse.com/about-us/en/reports-research/global-wealth-report.html.

30. Paul Krugman, "Little Black Lies," *New York Times* (January 28, 2005), nytimes.com/2005/01/28/opinion/28krugman.html.

31. Stanford School of Medicine, "Life Expectancy: The Crossover Phenomenon," 2014, geriatrics.stanford.edu/ethnomed/african_american/health_risk_patterns.

32. Lauren Medina, Shannon Sabo, and Jonathan Vespa, "Living Longer: Historical and Projected Life Expectancy in the United States, 1960 to 2060, United States Bureau of the Census," *Current Population Reports,* P25-1145, February 2020, census.gov/content/dam/Census/library/publications/2020/demo/p25-1145.pdf.

33. Romig, "Social Security Lifts More Americans Above Poverty."

34. Center on Budget and Policy Priorities, "Policy Basics: Top Ten Facts About Social Security," August 14, 2019, cbpp.org/research/social-security/policy-basics-top-ten-facts-about-social-security?fa=view&id=3261#_edn25.

35. Social Security Administration, "Fact Sheet: Social Security Is Important to African Americans," April 2019, ssa.gov/news/press/factsheets/africanamer-alt.pdf.

36. Romig, "Social Security Lifts More Americans Above Poverty."

37. Paoloa Scommenga, "Exploring the Paradox of U.S. Hispanics' Longer Life Expectancy," Population Research Center, July 12, 2013, prb.org/us-hispanics-life-expectancy/.

38. The Senior Citizens League, "Ask the Advisor: Do Members of Congress Pay into Social Security?" October 4, 2011, seniorsleague.org/2011/ask-the-advisor-do-members-of-congress-pay-into-social-security.

39. Social Security Administration, "Frequently Asked Questions: Q5: Is it True That Members of Congress Do Not Have to Pay into Social Security?" accessed July 30, 2014, ssa.gov/history/hfaq.html.

40. Stephen Goss et al. "Effects of Unauthorized Immigration on the Actuarial Status of the Social Security Trust Funds," Social Security Administration, April 2013, socialsecurity.gov/OACT/NOTES/pdf_notes/note151.pdf.

41. Franklin Delano Roosevelt, "Speech at Madison Square Garden," The Miller Center, October 31, 1936, millercenter.org/president/speeches/detail/3307.

## Chapter 12

1. Sun Tzu, *The Art of War*, translated by Thomas Cleary (Boston: Shambhala Publications, 1988).

2. "Table 7-1: Summary details for regions and selected countries, 2019," in Anthony Shorrock, Jim Davies, and Rodrigo Lluberas, "Global Wealth Databook 2019," Credit Suisse Research Institute (October 2019), credit-suisse.com/about-us/en/reports-research/global-wealth-report.html.

3. Dwight D. Eisenhower to Edgar Newton Eisenhower, "Document #1147," *The Papers of Dwight David Eisenhower 15, The Presidency: The Middle Way*, ed. Louis Galambos (Baltimore: Johns Hopkins University Press, 1996).

4. E.J. Dionne Jr., "Audacity Without Ideology," *Washington Post* (January 15, 2009), washingtonpost.com/wp-dyn/content/article/2009/01/14/AR2009011403128.html?referrer=emailarticle; Obama used the phrase "grand bargain" even before he was inaugurated in 2009.

5. National Commission on Fiscal Responsibility and Reform, *Moment of Truth: Report of the National Commission on Fiscal Responsibility and Reform*, National Commission on Fiscal Responsibility and Reform, December 1, 2010. For a detailed explanation of why and how the proposal would lead over time to the radical transformation of Social Security, see Nancy J. Altman, "The Striking Superiority of Social Security in the Provision of Wage Insurance," *Harvard Journal on Legislation* 50 (2013): 109–168.

6. Alex M. Parker, "On the 'Super Committee's' Menu: Social Security Cuts and Tax Hikes," *U.S. News & World Report* (November 7, 2011), usnews.com/news/articles/2011/11/07/on-the-super-committees-menu-social-security-cuts-and-tax-hikes.

7. The Editorial Board, "The Supercommittee Collapses," *New York Times* (November 21, 2011), nytimes.com/2011/11/22/opinion/the-deficit-supercommittee-collapses.html.

8. Nancy J. Altman. and Eric R. Kingson, *Social Security Works! Why Social Security Isn't Going Broke and How Expanding It Will Help Us All* (New York: The New Press, 2015).

9. Chana Joffe-Walt, "Unfit for Work: The Startling Rise of Disability in America," NPR (March 2013), apps.npr.org/unfit-for-work.

10. Joffe-Walt, "Unfit for Work."

11. Edward Glaeser, "2013 Is the Year to Go to Work, Not Go on Disability," *Bloomberg* (December 26, 2012), bloomberg.com/news/2012.

12. David Pattison and Hilary Waldron, "Growth in New Disabled Worker Entitlements, 1970–2008," *Social Security Bulletin* 73, no. 4 (November 2013), ssa.gov/policy/docs/ssb/v73n4/v73n4p25.html.

13. Stephen C. Goss, "Statement Before the House Committee on Ways and Means, Subcommittee on Social Security," March 14, 2013, ssa.gov/legislation/testimony_031413a.html.

14. Social Security Administration, "Follow-up Report on Anti-Fraud Efforts Requested at the January 16, 2014 Hearing on Disability Fraud," Report submitted to Subcommittee on Social Security Hearing of United States House of Representatives, Ways and Means Committee, January 16, 2014, ssa.gov/legislation/SSA_Report_to_Chairman_Johnson_2_14_2014.pdf; Coalition Against Insurance Fraud, "Fraud in life and disability insurance: Final report of the Life & Disability Fraud Task Force," April 2017, insurancefraud.org/downloads/Coalition_life_disability_report_04-17.pdf.

15. Dimitris Karapiperis, "Insurance Fraud," Center for Insurance and Policy Research, March 2014, naic.org/cipr_newsletter_archive/vol13_insurance_fraud.pdf.

16. Office of the Inspector General, *Management Challenge Report: Fiscal Year 2018 Inspector General's Statement on the Social Security Administration's Major Management and Performance Challenges* (Baltimore: Social Security Administration, November 2018), 7, oig.ssa.gov/sites/default/files/audit/full/pdf/A-02-18-50307.pdf.

17. Xavier Becerra, "Becerra Opening Statement at Social Security Subcommittee Hearing on Preventing Disability Scams, Ways and Means Committee Democrats," February 26, 2014, https://waysandmeans.house.gov/media-center/press-releases/becerra-opening-statement-social-security-subcommittee-hearing

18. Jonathan M. Stein, "Another Disability Disaster in the Making," *New York Times* (January 15, 2020), nytimes.com/2020/01/16/opinion/trump-disability.html.

19. Stein, "Another Disability Disaster in the Making"; see also Katherine P. Collins and Anne Erfle, "Social Security Disability Reform Act of 1984: Legislative History and Summary of Provisions," *Social Security Bulletin* 48, no. 4 (April 1985); and Robert Pear, "Reagan Suspends Benefits Cutoff," *New York Times* (April 14, 1984), nytimes.com/1984/04/14/us/reagan-suspends-benefits-cutoff.html.

20. Social Security Administration, "Disability Insurance Trust Fund," November 2009, ssa.gov/oact/progdata/describedi.html.

21. Social Security Administration, "OASDI and SSI Program Rates and Limits, 2020," October 2019, ssa.gov/policy/docs/quickfacts/prog_highlights/RatesLimits2020.html.

22. Deirdre Shesgreen, "Speaker John Boehner has tried to get pope to Capitol for 20 years," *USA Today* (September 22, 2015), ncronline.org/news/politics/speaker-john-boehner-has-tried-get-pope-capitol-20-years.

23. Material drawn from authors' contribution to Strengthen Social Security Coalition, Transition Report for the New Commissioner of Social Security: How to Ensure the World-Class Service the American People Deserve (March 2013).

24. Arthur J. Altmeyer, *The Formative Years of Social Security* (Madison: University of Wisconsin Press, 1966): 55.

25. United States Senate Special Committee on Aging, "Reductions in Face-to-Face Services at the Social Security Administration, Summary of Committee Staff Investigation," March 2014, https://www.aging.senate.gov/imo/media/doc/SSA%20Hearing%20Staff%20Memo1.pdf.

26. Social Security Administration, Annual Performance Plan for Fiscal Year 2015 and Revised Final Performance Plan for Fiscal Year 2014 and Annual Performance Report for Fiscal Year 2013, 13.

27. Social Security Administration, "Social Security Begins Issuing Annual State-ments to 125 Million Workers," September 30, 1999, ssa.gov/pressoffice/statement .html.

28. Marc Fisher, "Social Security, Treasury target taxpayers for their parents' decades-old debts," *Washington Post* (April 10, 2014), https://www.washingtonpost .com/politics/social-security-treasury-target-hundreds-of-thousands-of-taxpayers -for-parents-old-debts/2014/04/10/74ac8eae-bf4d-11e3-bcec-b71ee10e9bc3_story .html.

29. Despite funding administration from its own dedicated resources, and despite an accumulated reserve of $2.9 trillion, the Social Security program's administrative funds are subject to the annual appropriations process, essentially treated like expenditures that lack dedicated revenue. In addition to administering the Social Security program, SSA also administers the Supplemental Security Income (SSI) program. SSI is funded from general revenue, and accordingly SSA receives annual appropriations from general revenue for the administration of SSI.

30. Andrew Kaczynski, "Trump on Social Security in his 2000 Book: A Ponzi Scheme We Must Privatize," *BuzzFeed News* (September 29, 2015), buzzfeed-news.com/article/andrewkaczynski/trump-on-social-security-in-his-2000-book -a-ponzi-scheme-we.

31. Lily Batchelder, "Trump Is a Bad Businessman. Is He a Tax Cheat, Too?" *New York Times* (May 9, 2019), nytimes.com/2019/05/09/opinion/trump-tax-returns .html.

32. Sean Hannity, Exclusive: "Donald Trump Talks 2012, Calls Obama the 'Worst President Ever,'" Fox News (April 14, 2011), foxnews.com/transcript /exclusive-donald-trump-talks-2012-calls-obama-the-worst-president-ever.

33. Sam Stein, "Boehner, Pence: Raising Social Security Retirement Age an Option," *Huffington Post* (December 6, 2017), huffpost.com/entry/boehner-pence -social-security-retirement-age_n_674793.

34. *Face the Nation* transcript (March 19, 2017), cbsnews.com/news/face-the -nation-transcript-march-19-2017-cruz-pelosi-mulvaney/.

35. See, for example, Tara Golshan, "Trump said he wouldn't cut Medicaid, Social Security, and Medicare. His 2020 budget cuts all 3," *Vox* (March 12, 2019), vox .com/policy-and-politics/2019/3/12/18260271/trump-medicaid-social-security -medicare-budget-cuts.

36. Nicole Goodkind, "Mitch McConnell Calls for Social Security, Medicare, Medicaid Cuts After Passing Tax Cuts, Massive Defense Spending," *Newsweek* (October 16, 2018), newsweek.com/deficit-budget-tax-plan-social-security-medi caid-medicare-entitlement-1172941.

37. David Dayen, "Unsanitized: The Essential Imbalance of the 2020 Bailout," *The American Prospect* (March 26, 2020), prospect.org/coronavirus/unsanitized -essential-imbalance-2020-bailout/.

38. Jeff Stein, Josh Dawsey, and John Hudson, "Top White House Advisers, Unlike Their Boss, Increasingly Worry Stimulus Is Costing Too Much," *Washington Post* (May 10, 2020), washingtonpost.com/business/2020/05/10/top-white-house -advisers-unlike-their-boss-increasingly-worry-stimulus-spending-is-costing-too -much/.

39. Joaquin Castro and John Larson, Letter to the Honorable Keith Krach, Under-secretary of State for Economic Growth, Energy, and the Environment, Department of State, May 13, 2020, castro.house.gov/imo/media/doc/Castro%20Larson%20 State%20Department%20Social%20Security.pdf.

40. Castro and Larson, Letter to the Honorable Keith Krach.

41. Carrie Lukas, "Why Running Parent Leave Through Social Security Is the Smartest Live Option," *The Federalist* (February 2, 2018), thefederalist.com/2018/02/02/running-parent-leave-social-security-smartest-live-option/.

42. Michael Hiltzik, "Trump's proposal to eliminate the Social Security payroll tax may be his worst idea yet," *Chicago Tribune* (April 11, 2020), chicagotribune.com/business/ct-hiltzik-trump-social-security-payroll-tax-20170411-story.html.

43. Nancy Altman, "Trump's Plan for 'Permanent' Reduction in Payroll Contributions Would Undermine Social Security," Social Security Works, April 8, 2020, socialsecurityworks.org/2020/04/08/trump-payroll-undermine-social-security/.

44. Video of the 1984 presidential debate, "Ronald Reagan: Social Security has nothing to do with the deficit," WeAreSocialSecurity, youtube.com/watch?v=ihUoRD4pYzI.

45. The National Archives, "Congress and the New Deal: Social Security," archives.gov/exhibits/treasures_of_congress/text/page19_text.html.

46. Andrew Saul, "Expanding Social Security Field Office Hours," Social Security Matters, Social Security Administration, December 2, 2019, blog.ssa.gov/expanding-social-security-field-office-hours/.

47. Erich Wagner, "Arbitrator Finds Social Security Violated Federal Labor Law in Negotiations with Administrative Law Judges," *Government Executive Daily* (May 14, 2020), govexec.com/management/2020/05/arbitrator-finds-social-security-violated-federal-labor-law-negotiations-administrative-law-judges/165410/.

48. Mike Causey, "Ticking telework timebomb," *Federal News Network* (November 26, 2019), federalnewsnetwork.com/ntmike-causey-federal-report/2019/11/ticking-telework-timebomb/.

49. See Ian Haney Lopez, *Dog Whistle Politics: How Coded Racial Appeals Have Reinvented Racism and Wrecked the Middle Class* (New York, Oxford University Press, 2014): 69.

50. Arthur Delaney, "New Trump Disability Rule Targets Non-English Speakers," *Huffington post* (February 2, 2020), huffpost.com/entry/trump-disability-english_n_5e4de3a4c5b6db25902219c3.

## Chapter 13

1. Franklin D. Roosevelt, "Message to Congress Reviewing the Broad Objectives and Accomplishments of the Administration," June 8, 1934, ssa.gov/history/fdrcon34.html.

2. Committee for a Responsible Federal Budget, "Pre-COVID, Social Security and Medicare Faced Insolvency," April 22, 2020, crfb.org/blogs/pre-covid-social-security-and-medicare-faced-insolvency.

3. David E. Rosenbaum, "Reagan's 'Safety Net' Proposal: Who Will Land, Who Will Fall; News Analysis," *New York Times* (March 17, 1981), nytimes.com/1981/03/17/us/reagan-s-safety-net-proposal-who-will-land-who-will-fall-news-analysis.html.

4. Ronald Reagan, "A Time for Choosing," October 27, 1964, https://www.reaganlibrary.gov/sreference/a-time-for-choosing-speech.

5. "Transcript: GOP Response from Rep. Paul Ryan," NPR (January 25, 2011), npr.org/2011/01/26/133227396/transcript-gop-response-from-rep-paul-ryan.

6. Taylor Telford, "Income Inequality Is Highest Since Census Started Tracking It, Report Shows," *Washington Post* (September 27, 2019).

7. Chad Stone, Danilo Trisi, Arloc Shermon, and Jennifer Beltran, "A Guide to

Statistics on Trends in Income Inequality," Center for Budget and Policy Priorities, January 13, 2020. Note: as per data presented in report, wealth inequality in 2018 is greater than at any time since the late 1920s.

## Appendix A

1. Social Security Administration, "OASDI and SSI Program Rates and Limits, 2020," October 2019, ssa.gov/policy/docs/quickfacts/prog_highlights/RatesLimits2020.html.

2. Social Security Administration, "OASDI and SSI Program Rates and Limits."

3. See Social Security Financing Amendments of 1977, U.S. House of Representatives, Report of the Committee on Ways and Means to Accompany H.R. 9346, House Report No. 702, Part 1 (Washington, DC: U.S. Government Printing Office, October 12, 1977), 18. Because the wages covered by the maximum taxable wage base represented only 85 percent of total wages in 1977, Congress also enacted several ad hoc increases to the wage base, over and above the automatic adjustments, so that the base would be restored to covering 90 percent of all wages. The 90 percent level was reached in 1982.

4. Social Security Administration, *Annual Statistical Supplement*, November 2019, ssa.gov/policy/docs/statcomps/supplement/2019/supplement19.pdf. See table 4.B1 for ratio of taxable payroll to total covered earnings in 2018, which is 83.1 percent.

5. Social Security Administration, *Annual Statistical Supplement*, November 2019.

6. Social Security Administration, "Benefits Planner: Retirement," 2020, ssa.gov/planners/retire/retirechart.html.

7. Social Security Administration, "Benefits Planner: Credits," 2020, ssa.gov/planners/retire/retirechart.html.

8. Social Security Administration, "Benefits Planner: Retirement," 2020 ssa.gov/planners/retire/retirechart.html.

9. Social Security Administration, "Primary Insurance Amount," 2020, ssa.gov/OACT/cola/piaformula.html.

10. Michael Clingman, Kyle Burkhalter, and Chris Chaplain, "Replacement Rates for Hypothetical Retired Workers," *Actuarial Note Number 2019.9*, Social Security Administration Number, Office of the Chief Actuary, Baltimore, Maryland, Table A, April 2019, ssa.gov/OACT/NOTES/ran9/an2019-9.pdf.

11. Geoffrey Kollmann, "Social Security: Summary of Major Changes in the Cash Benefits Program," CRS Legislative Histories 2, May 18, 2000.

12. Social Security Act, Title II, section 216(l); 42 U.S.C § 416. ssa.gov/OP_Home/ssact/title02/0216.htm.

13. Social Security Administration, "Retirement Benefits," April 2013. ssa.gov/pubs/EN-05-10035.pdf.

14. Social Security Administration, "Effect of Early or Delayed Retirement on Retirement Benefits," August 2010, ssa.gov/oact/ProgData/ar_drc.html.

15. Social Security Administration, "Effect of Early or Delayed Retirement."

16. Social Security Administration, "OASDI and SSI Program Rates and Limits, 2020."

17. Social Security Administration, *Annual Statistical Report on the Social Security Disability Insurance Program, 2018*, October 2019, ssa.gov/policy/docs/statcomps/di_asr/2018/di_asr18.pdf.

18. Social Security Administration, "Monthly Statistical Snapshot," February 2020, ssa.gov/policy/docs/quickfacts/stat_snapshot/.

19. Social Security Administration, "What's New in 2020," ssa.gov/redbook/newfor2020.htm.

20. Social Security Administration, *Annual Statistical Report, 2019.*

21. Social Security Administration, *Annual Statistical Report, 2019.*

22. Social Security Administration, "Monthly Statistical Snapshot, February 2020," March 2020, ssa.gov/policy/docs/quickfacts/stat_snapshot/.

23. Social Security Administration, *Annual Statistical Supplement, 2019.*

24. Social Security Administration, "Monthly Statistical Snapshot, February 2020."

25. Social Security Administration, "Monthly Statistical Snapshot, February 2020."

26. Social Security Administration, "Retirement Benefits," April 2013, ssa.gov/pubs/EN-05-10035.pdf.

27. Social Security Administration, "Survivors Benefits," July 2013, ssa.gov/pubs/EN-05-10084.pdf.

28. Social Security Administration, "Research Note #11: The History of Social Security 'Student' Benefits," January 2001, socialsecurity.gov/history/studentbenefit.html.

29. Social Security Administration, *Annual Statistical Supplement, 2019*, Table 5A.6, ssa.gov/policy/docs/statcomps/supplement/2014/5a.html.

30. Social Security Administration, "Benefits for Children with Disabilities," 2020, ssa.gov/pubs/EN-05-10026.pdf.

31. Kathryn Anne Edwards, Anna Turner, and Alexander Hertel-Fernandez, *A Young Person's Guide to Social Security*, Economic Policy Institute and National Academy of Social Insurance, July 2012, nasi.org/research/2012/young-persons-guide-social-security#:~:text=A%20Young%20Person's%20Guide%20to%20Social%20Security%2C%20released%20by%20the,debates%20about%20Social%20Security's%20future.

## Appendix B

1. Social Security Trustees, *2020 Annual Report of the Board of Trustees of the Federal Old-Age and Survivors Insurance and Federal Disability Insurance Trust Funds*, April 22, 2020, ssa.gov/OACT/TR/2020/tr2020.pdf.

2. Social Security Administration, "Primary Insurance Amount," https://www.ssa.gov/oact/cola/piaformula.html.

3. Michael Clingman, Kyle Burkhalter, and Chris Chaplain, "Replacement Rate for Hypothetical Retired Workers," Actuarial Note Number 2020.9, Social Security Administration, 2020, ssa.gov/oact/NOTES/ran9/an2020-9.pdf.

4. All estimates of costs or savings, unless otherwise noted, are for the traditional seventy-five-year valuation period and were derived by the Social Security Administration's Office of the Chief Actuary. Most of the numbers can be found on that office's website at ssa.gov/oact/.

5. Section 201 of the Social Security Act (42 U.S.C. 401).

6. United States Senate Committee on Finance, "Wyden Unveils Proposal to Fix Broken Tax Code, Equalize Treatment of Wages and Wealth, Protect Social Security," finance.senate.gov/ranking-members-news/wyden-unveils-proposal-to-fix-broken-tax-code-equalize-treatment-of-wages-and-wealth-protect-social-security-.

# INDEX

# PUBLISHING IN THE PUBLIC INTEREST

Thank you for reading this book published by The New Press. The New Press is a nonprofit, public interest publisher. New Press books and authors play a crucial role in sparking conversations about the key political and social issues of our day.

We hope you enjoyed this book and that you will stay in touch with The New Press. Here are a few ways to stay up to date with our books, events, and the issues we cover:

- Sign up at www.thenewpress.com/subscribe to receive updates on New Press authors and issues and to be notified about local events
- Like us on Facebook: www.facebook.com/newpressbooks
- Follow us on Twitter: www.twitter.com/thenewpress

Please consider buying New Press books for yourself; for friends and family; or to donate to schools, libraries, community centers, prison libraries, and other organizations involved with the issues our authors write about.

The New Press is a 501(c)(3) nonprofit organization. You can also support our work with a tax-deductible gift by visiting www.thenewpress.com/donate.